Law, Darwinism,
& Public Education

Law, Darwinism, & Public Education

The Establishment Clause and the Challenge of Intelligent Design

Francis J. Beckwith

ROWMAN & LITTLEFIELD PUBLISHERS, INC.
Lanham • Boulder • New York • Oxford

ROWMAN & LITTLEFIELD PUBLISHERS, INC.

Published in the United States of America
by Rowman & Littlefield Publishers, Inc.
A Member of the Rowman & Littlefield Publishing Group
4720 Boston Way, Lanham, Maryland 20706
www.rowmanlittlefield.com

12 Hid's Copse Road
Cumnor Hill, Oxford OX2 9JJ, England

British Library Cataloguing in Publication Information Available

Library of Congress Cataloging-in-Publication Data

Beckwith, Francis.
  Law, Darwinsim & public education : the establishment clause and the
challenge of intelligent design / Francis J. Beckwith.
       p. cm.
Includes bibliographical references and index.
  ISBN 0-7425-1430-7 (hardcover : alk. paper) — ISBN 0-7425-1431-5
(pbk. : alk. paper)
  1. Religion in the public schools—Law and legislation—United States
2. Evolution—Study and teaching—Law and legislation—United States
3. Creationism—Study and teaching—Law and legislation—United States
4. Science and law—United States. 5. Religion and science—United
States. I. Title: Law, Darwinsim, and public education. II. Title.
  KF4162 .B43 2002
  344.73'0796—dc21
                                    2002009416

Printed in the United States of America

⊗™ The paper used in this publication meets the minimum requirements of American
National Standard for Information Sciences—Permanence of Paper for Printed Library
Materials, ANSI/NISO Z39.48-1992.

This work is dedicated to my wife, Frankie. It is because of her support and sacrifice that I was able to spend the 2000–2001 school year at the Washington University School of Law in St. Louis in order to work on this book.

Contents

Acknowledgments

I would like to thank the Board of Regents of Trinity International University (TIU), and especially the university's provost Barry Beitzel, for graciously providing me with a sabbatical and leave of absence so that I could work on this book free of my ordinary responsibilities as a faculty member. Although I have since left Trinity, I am grateful for the many colleagues and students on both the Santa Ana (California) and Deerfield (Illinois) campuses who were, and some of whom continue to be, a source of encouragement and support. During my last year at Trinity, Kevin Holsclaw (Interim Dean, Trinity Law School), stood out as a model of professionalism, collegiality, and friendship. Aristotle (and Professor Praetorius) would have been proud. Because of the backing of both Dean Holsclaw and Joe Wyse (Assistant Dean of Administration), in fall 2001 I was able to teach a course on the topic of this book ("Law, Religion, and Science") during the time in which I was revising the manuscript. The student contributions to that course, in classroom and extracurricular discussions as well as on their final exams, helped me to think more clearly and rigorously about some of the issues in jurisprudence and philosophy of science over which contrary positions on this topic rest.

This book had its genesis (pardon the pun) in a dissertation I completed as part of the Master of Juridical Studies (J.S.M.) degree I earned at the Washington University School of Law in St. Louis, "Rethinking *Edwards v. Aguillard*?: The Establishment Clause of the First Amendment and the Challenge of Intelligent Design" (2001). Certain members of the law school's academic community deserve special recognition. A warm thank you to my advisor, Stanley F. Paulson (William Gardiner Hammond Professor of Law, School of Law, and Professor of Philosophy, Department of Philosophy), for his guidance and insights. My three constitutional law professors—F. Bruce LaPierre (Constitutional Law II), Theodore Ruger (Constitutional Law I), and Susan F.

Appleton (Reproductive Control Seminar)—were terrific teachers who nurtured and enhanced in me the love for constitutional law and jurisprudence that I had had for many years. Four of my other professors—Dorsey Ellis (Torts), John Haley (Contracts), John Drobak (Norms and the Law), and Barbara Flagg (Nontraditional Perspectives on the Law)—each in his or her own way taught me about the substance of the law and its importance to the fabric of civil society. Michele Shoresman (Director of Graduate Studies) always made me feel welcome, taking the time to talk with me even when she was busy with other more pressing matters, as if I were an old friend rather than merely one of many law school grad students with whom she had to deal. Her charitable spirit, academic excellence, and first-class professionalism did not go unnoticed. Washington University is lucky to have her.

Eddie Colanter, a former student of mine who is now a Ph.D. candidate at Claremont Graduate University, suggested in 1999 that I pursue just the sort of degree I earned at Washington University. I am grateful for his wisdom. During my time in St. Louis, three other Trinity students were particularly supportive of my work: Michael Holmes (Trinity Law School), James Nowotny (Trinity Law School), and Michael Peterson (Trinity Graduate School). They helped melt the frost of that final winter.

In addition to Professor Paulsen, J. P. Moreland (Distinguished Professor of Philosophy, Biola University), William A. Dembski (Associate Research Professor in the Conceptual Foundations of Science, Baylor University), David DeWolf (Professor of Law, Gonzaga University School of Law), John Calvert, Esq. (Lathrop & Gage, L. C.), and Stephen C. Meyer (Associate Professor of Philosophy, Whitworth College) graciously read portions of earlier versions of this book and allowed me to employ the benefit of their insights in the final version.

A thank you to David DeWitt, a practicing attorney and one of my M.A. students at Trinity, who, on his own initiative, found for me on the Internet a copy of the illusive 1981 California Superior Court case *Segraves v. California*.

My former colleague at Trinity Law School, Myron Steeves, who is now president of the Newport Institute for Ethics, Law, & Public Policy, deserves a special acknowledgment and thanks. During my nine months in St. Louis he graciously talked with me numerous times about this book and its contents, sharing with me his learned understanding of religion and the law. Myron also read the revised manuscript and provided valuable suggestions.

In addition to my wife, Frankie, to whom this book is dedicated, my parents (Harold and Elizabeth Beckwith), my grandmother (Frances Guido, who passed away on May 19, 2002), and my siblings (James, Patrick, and Elizabeth Ann) were a constant source of inspiration and encouragement during my time in St. Louis, as they have always been during my career.

Finally, if not for the personal generosity of W. Howard Hoffman, M.D., and a fellowship from the Center for Science and Culture, the Discovery Institute (Seattle), this book would not have been possible.

Although the above persons and institutions, in greater and lesser degrees, were influential, supportive, and/or instrumental in the formation of this work, I take full responsibility for its contents. Many of them agree with the views I espouse and the positions I defend in this book, but some of them do not. Hence, my acknowledgment of any person or institution should not imply total or even partial agreement with my views. All the shortcomings of this book are entirely mine.

Introduction

In 1987, in *Edwards v. Aguillard,* the United States Supreme Court declared as unconstitutional a Louisiana statute that required the state's public schools to teach creationism if evolution is taught and to teach evolution if creationism is taught.[1] The Court ruled that the statute violated the Establishment Clause of the First Amendment of the U.S. Constitution. That decision was the culmination of a series of court battles and cultural conflicts that can be traced back to the famous Scopes Trial of 1925 in Dayton, Tennessee.[2] Although many thought, and continue to think, that creationism was dealt a fatal blow in *Edwards,* a new movement, made up of largely well-educated and well-credentialed scholars, has given new life to the debate.

A. THE RISE OF INTELLIGENT DESIGN

The main thrust of this new movement, known as Intelligent Design (ID),[3] is that intelligent agency, as an aspect of scientific theory making, has more explanatory power in accounting for the specified, and sometimes irreducible, complexity of some physical systems, including biological entities, and/or the existence of the universe as a whole, than the blind forces of unguided and everlasting matter. ID proponents also argue that the rejection of intelligent agency by mainstream science is the result of presupposing the philosophical doctrine of methodological naturalism,[4] an epistemological position that ID proponents maintain is a necessary presupposition for the veracity of the evolutionary edifice and entails ontological materialism as a worldview,[5] but is arguably not necessary for the practice of science qua science.[6] Other proponents argue that the exclusive teaching of naturalistic evolution in public schools may violate political liberalism's call to state neutrality.[7] And yet others maintain that certain philosophical arguments—e.g., arguments for a substance view of persons, the existence of an immaterial first cause, and the existence of non-material entities and moral properties[8]—reveal the weaknesses of both methodological naturalism and ontological materialism. These and other arguments are discussed in chapter 3 of this book.

Among the scholars affiliated with ID are Phillip E. Johnson,[9] William Dembski,[10] Alvin Plantinga,[11] J. P. Moreland,[12] Michael Behe,[13] Dean Kenyon,[14] Dallas Willard,[15] Stephen C. Meyer,[16] Walter Bradley,[17] Hugh Ross,[18] David Berklinski,[19] Paul Nelson,[20] Henry F. Schaefer III,[21] Jonathan Wells,[22] William Lane Craig,[23] and Robert Kaita.[24] The intellectual epicenter of ID is the Center for Science and Culture (CSC), housed in the Seattle-based think tank the Discovery Institute. According to its Web site, CSC seeks "to challenge materialism on specifically scientific grounds. Yet Center Fellows do more than critique theories that have materialistic implications. They have also pioneered alternative scientific theories and research methods that recognize the reality of design and the need for intelligent agency to explain it."[25] The works of these and other ID scholars have been published by prestigious academic presses and respected academic journals. These works have also received attention by the wider academic and research community. The following is a brief sample of this activity.

Dembski's monograph on ID, *The Design Inference: Eliminating Chance through Small Probabilities,* was published in 1998 by Cambridge University Press in its prestigious monograph series in Probability, Induction, and Decision Theory.[26] It was assessed in a number of important journals, including *Philosophy of Science,*[27] in which it was reviewed by the renowned philosopher of science Elliot Sober and two of his colleagues at the University of Wisconsin. In 2002, a sequel to *The Design Inference, No Free Lunch: Why Specified Complexity Cannot Be Purchased without Intelligence* was published by Rowman & Littlefield, a widely respected academic press.[28] Among the scholars who have endorsed this book is Darwinian Michael Ruse, the Lucyle T. Werkmeister Professor of Philosophy at Florida State University and a leading philosopher of biology. Writes Ruse: "I strongly disagree with the position taken by . . . Dembski. But I do think that he argues strongly and those of us who do not accept his conclusions should read his book and form our own opinions and counterarguments. He should not be ignored."[29] Dembski's work has appeared in many journals across different disciplines.[30]

Paul Nelson's book, *On Common Descent,* a critique of neo-Darwinism and based on his University of Chicago Ph.D. dissertation (in philosophy of biology), will be published by the University of Chicago Press as a volume in its prestigious Evolutionary Monographs series. In 2001, State University of New York (SUNY) Press published a monograph by Del Ratzsch, a philosopher of science at Calvin College, *Nature, Design, and Science: The Status of Design in Natural Science.*[31] A volume in SUNY Press's Philosophy and Biology series, it is, according to its author, "not a piece of advocacy" against or for design, but rather, "a philosophical attempt to clarify some of the conceptual landscape which productive pursuit of broader design debates must negotiate." Ratzsch concludes that though design theorists still have much more work to do, "there is little to be said for the prohibitionism that forbids even the attempt to pursue whatever potential [for design theory] there might be."[32]

J. P. Moreland and William Lane Craig are editors of the book *Naturalism: A Critical Analysis,* published by Routledge in 2000.[33] Craig, an accomplished scholar in the philosophy of science and philosophy of religion, has published books with Oxford University Press and MacMillan as well as numerous articles in such journals as *British Journal for the Philosophy of Science* and the *Journal of Philosophy.*[34]

In addition to his published work critical of philosophical naturalism,[35] Alvin Plantinga presented a provocative paper at the 1998 Eastern Division Meeting of the American Philosophical Association in which he suggested, among other things, that naturalistic evolution should be taught in public schools *only if* students are informed that the theory's truth is contingent upon its controversial and disputed epistemological and metaphysical presuppositions.[36]

Phillip E. Johnson's 1991 book, *Darwin on Trial,* which provoked an acerbic review by the late Harvard paleontologist Stephen Jay Gould in *Scientific American,*[37] "has inspired academic symposia at Universities such as Stanford, Harvard, Chicago, Cornell, SMU [Southern Methodist University] and the University of Texas. In these settings, [Johnson] has exchanged views with such scientific and philosophic luminaries as Michael Ruse, Stephen Gould, William Provine and Steven Weinberg."[38] Ruse has said of Johnson and his books, "Johnson is a brilliant man and these are clever and skillfully written books. I hope you are not convinced by them but do not underestimate them."[39]

In 1996, Michael Behe, a biochemist who has published in peer-reviewed journals,[40] released his ground-breaking and best-selling book, *Darwin's Black Box: The Biochemical Challenge to Evolution.*[41] It was reviewed in many major periodicals including *Quarterly Review of Biology, Nature, American Scientist,* and the *Boston Review.*[42] Soon after its publication in December 1997, William F. Buckley's *Firing Line* program (PBS) hosted a special debate on the issue, "Resolved: Evolution Should Acknowledge Creation."[43] Participants included Buckley, Johnson, Behe, Berlinski, Ruse, Barry W. Lynn (Executive Director, Americans United for Separation of Church and State), Eugenie C. Scott, and Kenneth R. Miller. The participation of Scott and Miller in the debate is significant, for their presence shows the seriousness with which ID is taken by the scientific establishment. Scott, a Darwinian opponent of ID, is a biological anthropologist and former university professor who since 1987 has been executive director of the National Center for Science Education. Miller, another opponent of ID, is a Brown University biology professor and author of a book strongly critical of ID, *Finding Darwin's God: A Scientist's Search for Common Ground between God and Evolution*, which he published two years after the *Firing Line* debate.[44]

In 2000 both Baylor University and Yale University hosted major conferences on ID.[45] The American Museum of Natural History (New York City) in April 2002 presented as part of its lecture series a public discussion entitled "Evolution or Intelligent Design?: Examining the Intelligent Design Issue." According to the museum's Web site, this public discussion was "[c]opresented with *Natural History Magazine,* which will publish a series of articles by some of the panelists in the April [2002] issue."[46] Participating in the program were Behe, Dembski, Scott, Miller, and Robert T. Pennock, a philosophy of science professor at Michigan State University who in 1999 published with M.I.T. Press an important monograph critical of ID, *Tower of Babel: The Evidence against the New Creationism,*[47] that was nominated for a Pulitzer Prize, the National Book Award, and the PEN Award.[48]

In 2001, the *New York Times,* the *Los Angeles Times,* and the *Chronicle of Higher Education*[49] published major front-page pieces on the ID movement. In 1998, the journal *Rhetoric & Public Affairs,* published by Michigan State University Press and sponsored by the Department of Speech Communication and the Center for Presidential Studies of the George Bush School of Government of Texas A&M University, dedicated an entire issue to a symposium on the Intelligent Design Argument.[50] Contributors included supporters and critics of ID, though the former outnumbered the latter. A book based on that issue is set for release by Michigan State University Press in 2003.[51] Cambridge University Press is set to release in 2004 a collection of essays edited by Dembski and Ruse, *Debating Design: From Darwin to DNA,* which will include articles by both opponents and proponents of ID.[52] An 805-page anthology, *Intelligent Design Creationism and Its Critics: Philosophical, Theological, and Scientific Perspectives,* was released by M.I.T. Press in late 2001, which, according to *Washington Times* journalist Richard N. Ostling, "signaled ID's growing importance."[53] Although an uneven collection shrouded in controversy, this edited volume includes essays by leading ID supporters including Behe, Dembski, Johnson, and Plantinga as well as foes Ruse, Pennock, Richard Dawkins, and Philip Kitcher.[54]

It is clear that unlike their creationist predecessors, ID proponents have developed highly sophisticated arguments, have had their works published by prestigious presses and in academic journals, have aired their views among critics in the corridors of major universities and institutions, and have been recognized by leading periodicals, both academic and nonacademic. This is no small accomplishment. Given the negative image of "creationists,"[55] what the ID movement has accomplished in fewer than two decades is nothing short of astounding.

B. INTELLIGENT DESIGN IN THE PUBLIC SQUARE

In addition to its academic work, the ID movement has been able to exercise its considerable intellectual muscle and sophisticated level of argument in the public square, shaping the direction and nature of public debate on evolution in numerous venues. Several events since the late 1990s are noteworthy in this regard.

In 1998 the U.S. Civil Rights Commission conducted a hearing in Seattle in order to hear testimony on the question of whether public schools are engaged in viewpoint discrimination when they exclusively teach naturalistic evolution and its materialist ontology while not offering to students critiques of these perspectives such as ID.[56] Testifying in favor of evolutionary exclusivity was Eugenie Scott. Opposing Scott's point of view were Stephen C. Meyer and Richard Sybrandy. Meyer is a senior fellow at the Discovery Institute with a Ph.D. in the history and philosophy of science from Cambridge University (In 1998 he was a Whitworth College philosophy professor, a position from which he resigned in 2002). Sybrandy is an attorney whose client was public school teacher Roger DeHart, a Burlington, Washington, high school biology instructor who was forbidden by his superiors from raising in the classroom critical questions about evolution or offering intelligent design as a possible alternative. (We will briefly cover Mr. DeHart's case in chapter 4, section B, part 2.b.)

In 1999 the state board of education in Kansas revised its standards for the teaching of evolution in public schools.[57] The revisions included the modest, and defensible, claims that natural selection adds no new genetic information and that science is defined as the "human activity of seeking *logical explanations* for what we observe in the world around us."[58] The standards also implied that microevolution does not entail macroevolution.[59] The board did not require the teaching of creationism or Intelligent Design. It merely *suggested* that science teachers present the deliverances of their disciplines, on the matter of evolution, with tentativeness and modesty. It did not, for example, mandate that the state's teachers instruct their students that microevolution entails macroevolution, though teachers were free to do so if they wanted to. Moreover, these standards were "explicitly not binding on local school boards as an official curriculum,"

but were "designed to assist in the development of local curriculum by presenting the 'benchmarks' by which students will ultimately be evaluated on mandatory standardized tests."[60] But the board's suggestion did not sit well with many
who saw the revisions as the first step in a slippery slope back to the spectacle
of the Scopes Trial. Consequently, a number of writers and scholars, including
Stephen Jay Gould, publicly and forcefully voiced their displeasure with, and
contempt for, the board's nonbinding admission that it may be legitimate to allow criticisms of the evolutionary paradigm in the state's science classrooms.[61]
The Kansas school board's controversial revisions were removed in February
2001 as a result of a new election in which voters replaced members of the board
that had supported the revisions.[62]

In early 2002, President George W. Bush signed the No Child Left Behind
Act of 2001, which included an amendment sponsored by Senator Rick Santorum (R-PA). Adopted by a 91-8 vote of the U.S. Senate, the amendment
reads:

> The Conferees recognize that a quality science education should prepare stu-
> dents to distinguish the data and testable theories of science from religious or
> philosophical claims that are made in the name of science. Where topics are
> taught that may generate controversy (such as biological evolution), the cur-
> riculum should help students to understand the full range of scientific views that
> exist, why such topics may generate controversy, and how scientific discoveries
> can profoundly affect society.[63]

In a statement published in the *Congressional Record,* Senator Santorum
defends this amendment on the grounds that there are important philosophical and religious "questions implied by much of what science does," and
therefore, "it is entirely appropriate that the scientific evidence behind them
is examined in science classrooms." "[T]he true purposes of education, science, and law," Santorum claims, are thwarted by "efforts to shut down scientific debates." Pointing out that this raises a question of academic freedom
for both teachers and students, he cites "the debate over origins" as "an excellent example" of what he means. The senator singles out those who espouse ID as among "a number of scholars" who "are now raising scientific
challenges to the usual Darwinian account of the origins of life."[64]

In 2002 the Ohio Board of Education began its periodic task of reviewing
the state's education curriculum and revising it if necessary. Although the
board's curriculum advisory panel strongly endorsed that Ohio's schools
teach evolution exclusively, the state decided to entertain some changes. So,
at the invitation of the Department of Education, John Calvert, a Kansas attorney and Intelligent Design partisan, testified on January 13, 2002, to the
Science Standards Committee of the State Board. Calvert suggested to the

committee that Ohio remove methodological naturalism from its science curriculum and incorporate the modifications that were submitted by Robert Lattimer, a physical chemist and a member of the Ohio Science Standards Writing Team.[65] The Web site of one public interest group that supports these modifications, Science Excellence for All Ohioans (SEAO), explains them in the following way:

> The draft standards in the area of origins science, as they now stand, exclusively support the teaching of biological evolution. We are not opposed to the teaching of Darwinian evolution; we just want it portrayed as a theory with widespread support, but not without uncertainties. For the standards to be fair, reasonable, and objective, we believe language should be added in the following areas:
>
> 1. A distinction should be made between the well-accepted *microevolution* (minor genetic variation) and the much more controversial *macroevolution* (descent with modification from a single common ancestry).
> 2. The standards should state that biological evolution and chemical evolution are *naturalistic* theories that specifically exclude *design* from consideration. Naturalism is the principle—espoused by some scientists—that all phenomena in nature must have a *natural* (materialistic or physical) explanation.
> 3. The *historical* nature of origins science should be explained. Theories of biological origins attempt to explain events that have already taken place. Such theories, including Darwinian evolution and intelligent design, are *tentative;* they cannot be proven to be either true or false.
> 4. A *teach the controversy* approach should be used with respect to biological origins. The scientific evidence for and against biological evolution (Darwinism) should be presented, and the disagreement over traditional vs. naturalistic definitions of science should be covered.[66]

Further hearings were conducted on the question of whether alternatives to the evolutionary paradigm ought to be offered in Ohio public schools. On February 4, 2002, David Haury, an Associate Professor of Science Education at Ohio State University, met with the board. Haury suggested that the state retain its evolution-only curriculum. Although he maintained that methodological naturalism is a necessary precondition of science, he seemed to imply that it would be wrong for Ohio to promote philosophical naturalism (or ontological materialism).[67]

The board invited a panel of experts to testify on March 11, 2002.[68] Testifying in favor of the modifications were Meyer and Jonathan Wells, a senior fellow at the Discovery Institute with Ph.D.s in both molecular and cell biology (University of California, Berkeley) and religious studies (Yale). Wells is the author of *Icons of Evolution: Science or Myth? Why Much of What We Teach about Evolution Is Wrong,*[69] a book in which its author maintains that

many of the leading textbooks that cover evolution present false and mis-
leading information about the facts and arguments supporting the Darwinian
paradigm. It has, as one would guess, come under sharp criticism by the scientific community.[70]

Testifying against the modifications, and their allowing the possibility of
teaching ID, were Lawrence Krauss, chair of the physics department at Case
Western Reserve University, and Brown University biologist Kenneth Miller,
the coauthor of a biology textbook that is a target of Wells's book.[71] Krauss
objected to the board allowing equal numbers from each side to testify, for he
"estimated, given the criticisms of professional organizations, that scientists
would break down more like 10,000 to 1 against the idea" of intelligent design. Miller complained that the "scientific controversy" over origins voiced
by ID proponents, such as Wells and Meyer, is "nonexistent among the vast
majority of scientists," and that the so-called controversy comes from outside
the scientific community "in a move to pressure legislators and school officials to overrule the scientific mainstream."[72] Nevertheless, fifty-two Ohio
scientists, including professors from Ohio State University, Case Western Reserve University, and the University of Cincinnati, released a public statement
supporting the modifications.[73]

In early 2002, coinciding with the Board of Education debate, the House of
Representatives of the Ohio legislature considered a bill that incorporates the
spirit of Dr. Lattimer's modifications as well as the substance of the Santorum Amendment. The proposed legislation, House Bill 481, reads:

> It is the intent of the general assembly that to enhance the effectiveness of sci-
> ence education and to promote academic freedom and the neutrality of state
> government with respect to teachings that touch religious and nonreligious be-
> liefs, it is necessary and desirable that "origins science," which seeks to explain
> the origins of life and its diversity, be conducted and taught objectively and
> without religious, naturalistic, or philosophic bias or assumption. To further this
> intent, the instructional program provided by any school district or educational
> service center shall do all of the following:
>
> (A) Encourage the presentation of scientific evidence regarding the origins of
> life and its diversity objectively and without religious, naturalistic, or philo-
> sophic bias or assumption;
> (B) Require that whenever explanations regarding the origins of life are pre-
> sented, appropriate explanation and disclosure shall be provided regarding the
> historical nature of origins science and the use of any material assumption which
> may have provided a basis for the explanation being presented;
> (C) Encourage the development of curriculum that will help students think
> critically, understand the full range of scientific views that exist regarding the
> origins of life, and understand why origins science may generate controversy.[74]

In March 2002, Senator Santorum and two Ohio congressmen, Representatives John A. Boehner (Chair, House Education and Workforce Committee) and Steve Chabot (Chairman, House Constitution Subcommittee), inserted themselves into the Ohio controversy. Senator Santorum published an op-ed piece in the *Washington Times* in which he called upon the Ohio Board of Education to include the modifications to its science standards, for "students should be taught a variety of viewpoints in the classroom. Dissenting theories should not be repressed, but discussed openly. To do otherwise is to violate intellectual freedom. Such efforts at censorship abrogate critical thinking and will ultimately thwart scientific progress."[75] He cites in support of this argument his amendment to the No Child Left Behind Act of 2001. However, opponents of both the modifications as well as HB 481 maintain that the Santorum Amendment does not have the force of law because it was removed from the final version of the act and appears only in the Joint Explanatory Statement of the Committee of Conference.[76] In reply, representatives Boehner and Chabot, in a letter to Board of Education members Jennifer L. Sheets and Cyrus B. Richardson, argue that the Santorum Amendment is part of the law and that opponents to the modifications and the House legislation are simply mistaken.[77] The pro-ID Discovery Institute admits that "while the Santorum statement may not have the 'force of law,' it is a powerful statement of federal education policy, and it provides authoritative guidance on how the statutory provisions of the No Child Left Behind Act (such as state-wide science assessments) are to be carried out."[78] Although the Conference Report is not technically part of the act, conference report language is relevant, and sometimes crucial, to assessing the purpose of legislation, interpreting a law as well as implementing it appropriately,[79] for the report is the result of a committee instituted to fulfill the U.S. Constitution's requirement that "in order for a bill to be presented to the President for signature, it must pass both the House and Senate in the exact same form."[80] Thus, contrary to what ID opponents have claimed,[81] the Santorum Amendment is a significant victory for opponents of the Darwinian paradigm.

C. CONCLUSION

ID, of course, has its critics,[82] some of whom accuse it of being merely "stealth creationism,"[83] an intellectually respectable cover for furthering the political and/or cultural ends of Christian fundamentalism.[84] This accusation, even if true, does not amount to a critique of the actual arguments for ID as a scientific research program. Nor is it a constitutional argument against the teaching of ID in public schools. Rather, it is merely an intellectually respectable cover for an informal logical fallacy, *argumentum ad hominem*.[85] On other hand, there have been serious philosophical and scientific arguments raised against ID,[86] to which ID proponents have replied.[87]

However, my primary concern in this book is not with the soundness or persuasive power of the scientific and philosophical arguments of ID proponents, even though we touch on those arguments and their strengths. Rather, my chief focus is on answering a question of constitutional jurisprudence and political philosophy: Given the Supreme Court's holding in *Edwards,* would a statute or government policy requiring or permitting the teaching of ID in public schools violate the Establishment Clause of the First Amendment? In order to answer this question (in chapter 4), I first answer two others, each of which is covered in chapters 2 and 3 respectively: (1) What was the Court's holding in *Edwards?* and (2) What is Intelligent Design? However, prior to answering these questions, in chapter 1 I define terms and review some of the most important court cases that led up to *Edwards.*

NOTES

1. *Edwards v. Aguillard,* 482 U.S. 578 (1987).
2. Ray Ginger, *Six Days or Forever?: Tennessee v. John Thomas Scopes* (Boston: Beacon Press, 1958); Edward J. Larson, *Summer of the Gods: The Scopes Trial and America's Continuing Debate over Science and Religion* (New York: Basic Books, 1997); Edward J. Larson, *Trial and Error: The American Controversy over Creation and Evolution* (New York: Oxford University Press, 1985); Ronald L. Numbers, *Darwinism Comes to America* (Cambridge, MA: Harvard University Press, 1998), 76–91; Stephen Goldberg, *Culture Clash: Law and Science in America* (New York: New York University Press, 1994), 69–83; R. M. Cornelius, "Their Stage Drew All the World: A New Look at the Scopes Evolution Trial," *Tennessee Historical Quarterly,* 15, 2 (Summer 1981); *The World's Most Famous Court Trial: State of Tennessee v. John Thomas Scopes* (Complete stenographic report of trial, July 10–21, 1925, including speeches and arguments of attorneys) (New York: Da Capo Press, 1971); *Scopes v. State,* 289 S.W. 363 (1927); *Epperson v. Arkansas,* 393 U.S. 97 (1968); *McLean v. Arkansas Board of Education,* 529 F. Supp. 1255 (1982).
3. For a diversity of perspectives on ID's history and publications, *see* John Angus Campbell, "Intelligent Design, Darwinism, and the Philosophy of Public Education," *Rhetoric & Public Affairs,* 1, 4 (1998); Thomas M. Lessel, "Intelligent Design: A Look at Some of the Relevant Literature," *Rhetoric & Public Affairs,* 1, 4 (1998); William A. Dembski, "The Intelligent Design Movement," *Cosmic Pursuit* (Spring 1998), *available at* http://www.arn.org/docs/dembski/wd_idmovement.htm (March 25, 2002); Numbers, *Darwinism Comes to America,* 15–21; and Barbara Forrest, "In-

telligent Design Creationism's 'Wedge Strategy'," in *Intelligent Design Creationism and Its Critics: Philosophical, Theological, and Scientific Perspectives,* ed. Robert T. Pennock (Cambridge, MA: M.I.T. Press, 2001).

4. *Methodological naturalism,* which is assessed in chapter 3, is, according to Dembski, "the view that science must be restricted solely to undirected natural processes" (William A. Dembski, *Intelligent Design: The Bridge between Science and Theology* [Downers Grove, IL: InterVarsity Press, 1999], 119). According to Phillip Johnson, "[a] methodological naturalist defines science as the search for the best naturalistic theories. A theory would not be naturalistic if it left something out (such as the existence of genetic information or consciousness) to be explained by a supernatural cause." Therefore, "all events in evolution (before the evolution of intelligence) are assumed attributable to unintelligent causes. The question is not *whether* life (genetic information) arose by some combination of chance and chemical laws, to pick one example, but merely *how* it did so" (Phillip E. Johnson, *Reason in the Balance: The Case against Naturalism in Science, Law, and Education* [Downers Grove, IL: InterVarsity Press, 1996], 208).

5. *Ontological materialism,* which I employ interchangeably with the terms *naturalism, philosophical naturalism, scientific materialism,* and *materialism,* is the view that the natural universe is all that exists and all the entities in it can be accounted for by strictly material processes without resorting to any designer, Creator, or nonmaterial entity as an explanation or cause for either any aspect of the natural universe or the universe as a whole. Thus, if science is the paradigm of knowledge (as is widely held in our culture), and it necessarily presupposes *methodological naturalism,* then ontological materialism is the only worldview for which one can have "knowledge."

Although for the purposes of this book, the terms *naturalism* and *materialism* are employed interchangeably, they are not necessarily synonymous. As Moreland points out, "[O]ne could be a naturalist without being a physicalist [or materialist], say be embracing Platonic forms, possibilia or abstract objects like sets, and one can be a physicalist [or materialist] and not a naturalist (e.g., if one held that God is a physical object)" (J. P. Moreland, "Theistic Science and Methodological Naturalism," in *The Creation Hypothesis: Scientific Evidence for an Intelligent Designer,* ed. J. P. Moreland [Downers Grove, IL: InterVarsity Press, 1994], 50). However, in the context of this book, materialism and naturalism (or philosophical naturalism) are treated as synonymous terms.

6. *See,* for example, J. P. Moreland, "Theistic Science and Methodological Naturalism," in *The Creation Hypothesis: Scientific Evidence for an Intelligent Designer,* ed. J. P. Moreland (Downers Grove, IL: InterVarsity Press, 1994); Johnson, *Reason in the Balance,* 205–18; Phillip E. Johnson, "Dogmatic Materialism," *The Boston Review* (February/March 1997), *available at* http://www.polisci.mit.edu/bostonreview/ br22.1/ johnson.html (January 14, 2001); Dembski, *Intelligent Design,* 97–183; Alvin Plantinga, "Methodological Naturalism?" *Origins & Design,* 18, 1 (1997), *available at* http://www.arn.org/docs/odesign/od181/methnat181.htm (February 16, 2001), Alvin Plantinga, "Methodological Naturalism? Part 2," *Origins & Design,* 18, 2 (1997), *available at* http://www.arn.org/docs/odesign/od182/methnat182.htm (February 16,

2001); Jonathan Wells, "Unseating Naturalism: Recent Insights from Developmental Biology," in *Mere Creation: Science, Faith and Intelligent Design,* ed. William A. Dembski (Downers Grove, IL: InterVarsity Press, 1998).

7. Alvin Plantinga, "Creation and Evolution: A Modest Proposal," Paper delivered at the Eastern Division meeting of the American Philosophical Association, Washington, DC (December 27–30, 1998) (no pagination). This paper was published in late 2001 under the same title in *Intelligent Design Creationism and Its Critics*.

8. *See,* for example, Moreland, "Theistic Science and Methodological Naturalism"; J. P. Moreland, "Creation Science and Methodological Naturalism," in *Man and Creation: Perspectives on Science and Theology,* ed. Michael Bauman (Hillsdale, MI: Hillsdale College Press, 1993); William Lane Craig and J. P. Moreland, eds., *Naturalism: A Critical Analysis* (New York: Routledge, 2000).

9. Jefferson E. Peyser Professor of Law (retired spring 2001), Boalt Hall School of Law, University of California; J.D., University of Chicago.

10. Associate Research Professor in the Conceptual Foundations of Science, Baylor University; Ph.D. in mathematics, University of Chicago; Ph.D. in philosophy, University of Illinois, Chicago. He has also done postdoctoral work in mathematics at Cornell University and the Massachusetts Institute of Technology, in physics at the University of Chicago, and in computer science at Princeton University.

11. John A. O'Brien Professor of Philosophy, University of Notre Dame; Ph.D. in philosophy, Yale University.

12. Distinguished Professor of Philosophy, Biola University; Ph.D. in philosophy, University of Southern California.

13. Professor of Biological Sciences at Lehigh University in Pennsylvania; Ph.D. in biochemistry from the University of Pennsylvania.

14. Professor of Biology, San Francisco State University; Ph.D. in biophysics, Stanford University. He has been a National Science Foundation postdoctoral fellow at the University of California (Berkeley), a visiting scholar to Trinity College, Oxford University, and a postdoctoral fellow at NASA-Ames Research Center.

15. Professor of Philosophy, University of Southern California; Ph.D. in philosophy, University of Wisconsin.

16. Ph.D. in history and philosophy of science, Cambridge University.

17. Professor of Mechanical Engineering, Texas A & M University; Ph.D. in materials science, University of Texas, Austin.

18. Ph.D. in astronomy, University of Toronto. He was a postdoctoral fellow at the California Institute of Technology for five years.

19. Ph.D. in math, Princeton University. He has been a postdoctoral fellow in mathematics and molecular biology at Columbia University.

20. Ph.D. in philosophy of biology, University of Chicago.

21. Graham Perdue Professor of Chemistry, and Director of the Center for Computational Quantum Chemistry, University of Georgia; Ph.D. in chemical physics, Stanford University. He has been nominated for the Nobel Prize several times.

22. Ph.D. in molecular and cell biology, University of California (Berkeley); Ph.D. in religious studies, Yale University. He has done postdoctoral research at the Uni-

versity of California at Berkeley, and has taught biology at California State University, Hayward.

23. Research Professor of Philosophy, Biola University; Ph.D. in philosophy, University of Birmingham (U.K.); D.Theol., University of Munich.

24. Principal Research Physicist, Plasma Physics Laboratory, Princeton University; Ph.D. in physics, Rutgers University. He teaches in Princeton University's department of astrophysical sciences.

25. http://www.discovery.org/crsc/ (May 10, 2002). The Web site goes on to say, "This new research program—called 'design theory'—is based upon recent developments in the information sciences and many new evidences of design. Design theory promises to revitalize many long-stagnant disciplines by recognizing mind, as well as matter, as a causal influence in the world. It also promises, by implication, to promote a more holistic view of reality and humanity, thus helping to reverse some of materialism's destructive cultural consequences."

26. William A. Dembski, *The Design Inference: Eliminating Chance through Small Probabilities,* Cambridge Studies in Probability, Induction, and Decision Theory (New York: Cambridge University Press, 1998).

27. Brian Fitelson, Christopher Stephens, and Eilliot Sober, "How Not to Detect Design," *Philosophy of Science,* 66, 3 (1999).

28. William A. Dembski, *No Free Lunch: Why Specified Complexity Cannot Be Purchased without Intelligence* (Lanham, MD: Rowman & Littlefield, 2002).

29. From a 2002 Science & Religion brochure distributed by Rowman & Littlefield as well as the back of the dust jacket of the first printing of the hardcover edition of *No Free Lunch.*

30. *See,* for example, William A. Dembski, "Uniform Probability," *Journal of Theoretical Probability,* 3 (1990); William A. Dembski, "Reverse Diffusion-Limited Aggregation," *Journal of Statistical Computation and Simulation,* 37 (1990); William A. Dembski, "Randomness by Design," *Nous,* 25 (1991); William A. Dembski and Stephen C. Meyer, "Fruitful Interchange or Polite Chitchat?: The Dialogue between Theology and Design," *Zygon,* 33 (1998).

31. Paul A. Nelson, *On Common Descent,* Evolutionary Monograph Series (Chicago: University of Chicago Press, forthcoming); Del Ratzsch, *Nature, Science, and Design: The Status of Design in Natural Science,* Philosophy and Biology Series (Albany: State University of New York Press, 2001).

32. Ratzsch, *Nature, Science, and Design,* vii, 151.

33. Craig and Moreland, eds., *Naturalism.*

34. William Lane Craig and Quentin Smith, *Theism, Atheism, and Big Bang Cosmology* (New York: Oxford University Press, 1993); William Lane Craig, *The Cosmological Argument from Plato to Leibniz* (New York: Macmillan, 1980) and *The Kalam Cosmological Argument* (New York: Macmillan, 1979); William Lane Craig, "God, Creation, and Mr. Davies," *British Journal for the Philosophy of Science,* 37 (1986) and "Barrow and Tipler on the Anthropic Principle vs. Divine Design," *British Journal for the Philosophy of Science,* 38 (1988); and William Lane Craig, "Tachyons, Time Travel, and Divine Omniscience," *Journal of Philosophy,* 85 (1988).

35. *See,* for example, Alvin Plantinga, "An Evolutionary Argument against Naturalism," *Faith in Theory and Practice: Essays on Justifying Religious Beliefs,* ed. Carol White and Elizabeth Radcliffe (Chicago: Open Court, 1993); Alvin Plantinga, *Warrant and Proper Function* (New York: Oxford University Press, 1993), 216–237; and Plantinga, "Methodological Naturalism?" "Methodological Naturalism?: Part 2."

36. Plantinga, "Creation and Evolution," in *Intelligent Design Creationism.* Plantinga opens his paper with the following comments: "The topic of our meeting is the question: should Creationism be taught in the (public) schools? That is an excellent question, and Professor Pennock has interesting things to say about it. I want to begin, however, by asking a complementary question, after which I shall return to this one: should evolution be taught in the public schools?" (779); *see* chapter 3, part C of this present volume.

37. Phillip E. Johnson, *Darwin on Trial* (Chicago: Regnery Gateway, 1991); Stephen Jay Gould, "Impeaching a Self-Appointed Judge," *Scientific American* (July 1992).

38. http://www.discovery.org/crsc/ (May 10, 2002).

39. Michael Ruse, *The Evolution Wars: A Guide to the Debates* (Santa Barbara, CA: ABC-CLIO, 2000), 285. The two books of Johnson's to which Ruse is referring are *Darwin on Trial* and *Reason in the Balance.*

40. *See,* for example, M. J. Behe, "Tracts of Separated, Alternating, and Mixed Adenosine and Cytidine Residues in the Genomes of Prokaryotes and Eukaryotes," *DNA Sequence,* 8 (1998); H. L. Puhl and M. J. Behe, "Poly[dA] Poly [dT] Forms Very Stable Nucleosomes at Higher Temperatures," *Journal of Molecular Biology,* 245 (1995); M. J. Behe, "An Overabundance of Long Oligopurine Tracts Occurs in the Genome of Simple and Complex Eukaryotes," *Nucleic Acids Research,* 23 (1995); M. J. Behe, E. E. Lattman, and G. D. Rose, "The Protein-Folding Problem: The Native Fold Determines Packing, but Does Packing Determine the Native Fold?" *Proceedings of the National Academy of Sciences,* 88 (1991); R. C. Getts and M. J. Behe, "Eukaryotic DNA Does Not Form Nucleosomes as Readily as Some Prokaryotic," *Nucleic Acids Research,* 19 (1991); and K. Luthman and M. J. Behe, "Sequence Dependence of DNA Structure: The B, Z, and A Conformations of Polydeoxynucleotides Containing Repeating Units of 6 to 16 Base Pairs," *Journal of Biological Chemistry,* 263 (1988).

41. Michael Behe, *Darwin's Black Box: The Biochemical Challenge to Evolution* (New York: The Free Press, 1996).

42. Neil W. Blackstone, "Argumentum Ad Ignorantam," *Quarterly Review of Biology,* 72 (1997); J. A. Coyne, "God in the Details," *Nature,* 383 (1996); Robert Dorit, review of *Darwin's Black Box* by Michael Behe, *American Scientist,* 85, 5 (1997), *available at* http://www.sigmaxi.org/amsci/amsci/bookshelf/leads97/darwin97%2D09.html (March 25, 2002); H. Allen Orr, "Darwin v. Intelligent Design (Again)," *Boston Review* (December 1996/January 1997), *available* at http://bostonreview.mit.edu/br21.6/orr.html (March 25, 2002). This review (as well as another in the same issue) provoked a number of replies. These were published in "Is Darwin in the Details?" *Boston Review* (February/March 1997), *available* at http://bostonreview.mit.edu/br22.1/ (March 25, 2002). The respondents were Michael Behe, Phillip E. Johnson, David Berlinski, Russell

F. Doolitle, Douglas J. Futuyama, Robert S. DiSilverstro, Michael Ruse, James A. Shapiro, Richard Dawkins, and Daniel Dennett.

43. "PBS *Firing Line* Debate on Creation/Evolution, December 19, 1997," at http://www.arn.org/fline1297.htm (April 23, 2002). See Walter Goodman, "Once Again, of God, Man and Everything in Between," *New York Times* (December 19, 1997), *available at* http://www.arn.org/docs/fline1297/fl_goodman.htm (April 23, 2002); and Laurie Goodstein, "Christians and Scientists: New Light for Creationism," *New York Times* (December 21, 1997), *available at* http://www.arn.org/docs/fline1297/fl_goodstein.htm (April 23, 2002).

44. Kenneth R. Miller, *Finding Darwin's God: A Scientist's Search for Common Ground between God and Evolution* (New York: Cliff Street Books, 1999).

45. The Nature of Nature: An Interdisciplinary Conference on the Role of Naturalism in Science, Baylor University, April 12–15, 2000; Science and the Evidence for Design in the Universe, Yale University, November 2–4, 2000. *See* "Yale Symposium Will Explore New Evidence Supporting the Theory of Intelligent Design," *M2 Presswire* (November 1, 2000), *available at* 2000 Westlaw 28278632.

46. http://www.amnh.org/programs/lectures/index.html?src=p_h# (April 23, 2002).

47. Robert T. Pennock, *Tower of Babel: The Evidence against the New Creationism* (Cambridge, MA: M.I.T. Press, 1999).

48. http://www.msu.edu/unit/lbs/news/research_pub.html (April 23, 2002).

49. James Glanz, "Biologists Face a New Theory of Life's Origins," *New York Times* (April 8, 2001), 1, 18; Teresa Watanabe, "Enlisting Science to Find the Fingerprints of a Creator," *Los Angeles Times* (March 25, 2001), *available at* http://www.arn.org/docs/news/fingerprints032501.htm (June 30, 2002); Beth McMurtrie, "Darwinism under Attack," *Chronicle of Higher Education* (December 21, 2001), *available at* http://chronicle.com/free/v48/i17/17a00801.htm (March 15, 2002).

50. Symposium, "The Intelligent Design Argument," *Rhetoric & Public Affairs,* 1, 4 (1998).

51. John A. Campbell and Stephen C. Meyer, eds., *Darwinism, Design, and Public Education* (East Lansing, MI: Michigan State University Press, forthcoming 2003).

52. William A. Dembski and Michael Ruse, eds., *Debating Design: From Darwin to DNA* (New York: Cambridge University Press, forthcoming 2004).

53. Pennock, ed., *Intelligent Design Creationism*; Richard N. Ostling, "Ohio School Board Debates Teaching 'Intelligent Design'," *Washington Times* (March 14, 2002), *available at* http://www.discovery.org/news/ohioSchoolBoardDebates.html (March 24, 2002).

54. According to a public statement released by Dembski, he did not give permission for M.I.T. Press and the book's editor, Pennock, to republish the essays of his that appeared in this volume. Although M.I.T. Press and Pennock did not technically violate the law since Dembski does not own the copyright to these articles, it seems at least bad academic practice for them to republish these pieces without at least inviting Dembski to revise and update them in order to make the strongest case for his position as possible, since, after all, Pennock did solicit from *opponents* of ID new essays "to provide direct replies to challenges that intelligent design creationists made

in some specific reprinted article" (Pennock, preface, in *Intelligent Design Creationism,* xi). Dembski writes:

> In my case, Pennock chose a popular 2,000-word essay of mine titled "Who's Got the Magic?" and followed it with a 9,000-word rebuttal by him titled "The Wizards of ID." For the other essay of mine, Pennock chose "Intelligent Design as a Theory of Information," which was a popular piece on information theory that's now five years old. I've written much on that topic since then, and the essay itself is now outdated. Moreover, Pennock followed that essay with three critical responses. One of those responses, by Elliott Sober, was a lengthy technical review (from the journal *Philosophy of Science*) of my technical monograph *The Design Inference* (Cambridge University Press, 1998). No portion of that monograph or anything comparable from my work was included in Pennock's book. Finally, I was given no chance to respond to my critics. . . . Pennock chose popular and outdated work of mine, positioned various critiques of my work with it, gave me no opportunity to reply to my critics, and packaged it all in a volume titled *Intelligent Design Creationists and Their Critics* [sic], thus casting me as a creationist, which in contemporary academic culture is equivalent to being cast as a flat earther, astrologer, or holocaust denier. There's no way I would have allowed my work to appear under such conditions if I had any say in the matter. Pennock saw to it that I had no say in the matter. (William A. Dembski, "How Not to Debate Intelligent Design" [January 8, 2002], *available at* http://www.arn.org/docs2/news/dembskiattackspennock010702.htm [March 25, 2002].)

55. For example, in a footnote in *Epperson,* Justice Abe Fortas writes in his majority opinion, "Clarence Darrow, who was counsel for the defense in the Scopes trial, in his biography published in 1932, somewhat sardonically pointed out that States with anti-evolution laws did not insist upon the fundamentalist theory in all respects. He said: 'I understand that the States of Tennessee and Mississippi both continue to teach that the earth is round and that the revolution on its axis brings the day and night, in spite of all the opposition'" (*Epperson,* 393 U.S., 102 n. 9).

56. *See* U.S. Civil Rights Commission, *Hearing: On Curriculum Controversies in Biology* (unedited transcript) (August 21, 1998), at http://www.discovery.org/viewDB/index.php3?/program=CRSC&command=view&id=92 (June 30, 2002).

57. *See* Johnson's sympathetic analysis of the school board's revisions: Phillip E. Johnson, *The Wedge of Truth: Splitting the Foundations of Naturalism* (Downers Grove, IL: InterVarsity Press, 2000), 63–83. For an analysis more critical and less polemical than Johnson's, *see* Marjorie George, "And Then God Created Kansas?: The Evolution/Creationism Debate in America's Public Schools," *University of Pennsylvania Law Review,* 149 (January 2001).

58. Kansas State Board of Education, *Kansas Curricular Standards for Science Education* (adopted December 7, 1999), 38 (*Kansas I*); *Kansas I,* 71. This latter suggestion was intended to teach the lesson that science is fundamentally about arguments and evidence and not about excluding non-naturalistic points of view a priori. In other words, the board intended to exclude methodological naturalism as a necessary precondition of science and ontological materialism as an entailment. *See* John H. Calvert and Wiliam S. Harris, *Teaching Origins Science in Public Schools* (Shawnee Mission, KS: Intelligent Design Network, 2001), *available at* http://www.intelligentdesign network.org/legalopinion.htm (May 11, 2002).

59. *Kansas I,* 37, 69. *Macroevolution* is the view that the complex diversity of living things in our world, through small, incremental, and beneficial mutations over long eons of time, are all the result of one bacterial cell. That is, all living beings share a common ancestor, giving the appearance of being designed though in reality engineered by the unintelligent forces of natural selection. (More on natural selection in chapter 1, part A, section 2.) *Microevolution* is the view that biological species adapt over time to changing environments and pass on those adaptations genetically to their offspring; evolution in this sense simply refers to "limited variation within fixed boundaries" (Dembski, *Intelligent Design,* 113), which differs from macroevolution, "the unlimited capacity of organisms to transform beyond all boundaries" (Dembski, *Intelligent Design,* 250).

60. Lisa D. Kirkpatrick, "Forgetting the Lessons of History: The Evolution of Creationism and Current Trends to Restrict the Teaching of Evolution in Public Schools," *Drake Law Review,* 49 (2000), 126.

61. *See,* for example, Gene Weingarten, "And So God Says to Charles Darwin: Let There Be Light in Kansas," *Journal and Courier* (August 17, 1999), *available at* http://www.geocities.com/Paris/Cathedral/6070/evolve.html (March 31, 2001); A. N. Wilson, "Land of the Born Again Bone Heads," *Evening Standard* (August 13, 1999), *available at* 1999 Westlaw 23722898; and Stephen Jay Gould, "Dorothy, It's Really Oz: A Pro-Creationist Decision in Kansas Is More Than a Blow against Darwin," *Time* (August 23, 1999), *available at* http://www.arn.org/docs/kansas/gouldks823.htm (April 20, 2002).

62. *See* Kansas State Board of Education, *Kansas Science Education Standards* (Adopted February 14, 2001), *available at* http://www.ksde.org/outcomes/science_stds2001.pdf (April 24, 2002) (*Kansas II*). For example, the board changed the word "logical" to "natural" in its definition of science: "Science is the human activity of seeking natural explanations for what we observe in the world around us" (*Kansas II,* 4).

63. No Child Left Behind Act of 2001 (H.R. 1), *available at* http://www.ed.gov/offices/OESE/esea/ (April 22, 2002). There is also a U.S. government Web site dedicated exclusively to this act, http://www.NoChildLeft Behind.gov/ (April 22, 2002); No Child Left Behind Act of 2001, Conference Report, to accompany H.R. 1, *available at* ftp://ftp.loc.gov/ pub/thomas/cp107/hr334.txt (April 22, 2002). For critical analyses for the Santorum Amendment, see the links to essays and op-ed pieces on the Web site of the American Association for the Advancement of Science: http://www.aaas.org/spp/dser/news.htm#santorum (April 24, 2002).

64. *Congressional Record* (December 18, 2001), *available at* http://thomas.loc.gov/cgi-bin/query/D?r107:2:./temp/ ~r107Om6HoU:e99900: (April 22, 2002).

65. Lattimer's suggested modifications are at http://www.arn.org/docs/ohio/ohioreport020402.htm#Modifications (May 10, 2002).

66. http://www.sciohio.org/start.htm. The Web site of the opposition, Ohio Citizens for Science, is http://ecology. cwru.edu/ohioscience/ (April 22, 2002).

67. According to one account of the meeting:

Dr. Haury explained the scientific meaning of certain terms used in the science standards (science, theory, hypothesis, scientific law, proof, evolution, etc.), and discussed some of the misconceptions regarding the theory of evolution. For example, Dr. Haury explained that beliefs about the origin of life are not included in evolution, which is concerned about how species adapt to their environments over time. Also, science is concerned with finding ways to explain the material world, and does not try to explain the metaphysical world. The current draft of the standards includes evolution but not "intelligent design," which is a belief that life was created by a higher intelligence. (Joan Platz, "LWV Ohio's Education Update," in *Voter: League of Women Voters of the Greater Dayton Area,* 80, .3 [March 2002], 7, *available at* http://lwvdayton.org/VtrArch/Vtr3-02.pdf [May 10, 2002].)

For a response to Haury's testimony, *see* Letter of John Calvert to the Co-Chairmen of the Standards Committee of the State Board of Education of Ohio (February 27, 2002), *available at* http://www.intelligentdesignnetwork.org/letterreHauryremarks. htm (May 10, 2002).

68. *See* Francis X. Clines, "Ohio Board Hears Debate on Alternative to Darwinism," *New York Times* (March 12, 2002), *available at* http://www.discovery.org/news/ohioBoard/HearsAlternative.html (April 22, 2002), and Kate Beem, "Ohio Emerges As Next Battleground for Schools' Evolution Debate," *Kansas City Star* (April 2, 2002), *available at* http://www.kansascity.com/m1d/kansascitystar/2979815.htm? template=content/Modules/printstory.jsp (April 24, 2002).

69. Jonathan Wells, *Icons of Evolution: Science or Myth? Why Much of What We Teach about Evolution Is Wrong* (Chicago: Regnery/Gateway, 2000). See http://www. iconsofevolution.net (Web site supporting Wells's work) and http://www.nmsr.org/ iconanti.htm (Web site critical of Wells's work) (April 22, 2002).

70. *See* Kevin Padian and Alan D. Gishlick, "The Talented Mr. Wells," review of *Icons of Evolution: Science or Myth?* by Jonathan Wells, *Quarterly Review of Biology,* 77, 1 (March 2002), *available at* http://www.journals.uchicago.edu/QRB/journal/ issues/v77n1/770103/770103.web.pdf (April 22, 2002); Eugenie C. Scott, "Evolution: Fatally Flawed Iconclasm," review of *Icons of Evolution: Science or Myth?* by Jonathan Wells, *Science* (June 2001), *available at* http://www.scienceormyth.org/ icons%20of%20evolution.html (April 22, 2002); Jerry A. Coyne, "Creationism by Stealth," review of *Icons of Evolution: Science or Myth?* by Jonathan Wells, *Nature,* 410 (2001), *available at* http://wwwhumanist.com/Messages/004_12apr01.htm (April 22, 2002); and Larry D. Martin, "An Iconoclast for Evolution?" review of *Icons of Evolution: Science or Myth?* by Jonathan Wells, *The World and I* (February 1, 2001), *available at* http://www.arn.org/docs/wells/jw_iconoclast0201.htm (April 22, 2002). See also the following Web sites that contain numerous critical reviews of Wells's work: "Reviews: *Icons of Evolution* by Jonathan Wells," at http://www.don-lindsayarchive.org/creation/ icons_of_evolution.html (April 22, 2002); and "Icons of Evolution: Legitimate Questions of Evolution, or Stealth Creationism?" at http://www.cbs.dtu.dk/dave/IconsReview.html (April 22, 2002). Wells has replied to his critics at http://www.discovery.org/ crsc/and http://iconsofevolution.org/ (April 22, 2002).

71. Kenneth R. Miller and Joseph Levine, *Biology,* 5th ed. (Upper Saddle River, NJ: Prentice-Hall, 2000).

72. Clines, "Ohio Board Hears Debate."

73. *Fifty-Two Ohio Scientists Call for Academic Freedom on Darwin's Theory,* Press Release (March 20, 2002), *available at* http://www.discovery.org/news/52Sci-

entistsCallForAcadem.html (April 22, 2002). Given this press release, if Professor Krauss's statistics are correct—that the opposition to teaching ID is 10,000 to 1 among scientists—that means that there are 520,000 scientists who are residents of Ohio. Since Ohio's population is roughly 11 million (11,186,000 as of 1997; see http://www.census.gov/Press-Release/state01.prn [April 22, 2002]), and since 1 out of every 4 residents (2,250,000) is under the age of 18 (see http://www.census.gov/Press-Release/state03.prn [April 22, 2002]), and assuming that there are no scientists younger than 18 in Ohio, that means that roughly 1 out of every 15 residents of Ohio over the age of 18 is a scientist.

74. The text of the bill can found at http://www.arn.org/docs/ohio/hb481 explanation.htm#HB%20No.%20481 (April 22, 2002).

75. Rick Santorum, "Illiberal Education in Ohio," *Washington Times* (March 14, 2002), *available at* http://www.arn.org/docs/ohio/washtimes_santorum031402.htm (April 22, 2002).

76. Ohio Citizens for Science Web page, at http://ecology.cwru.edu/ohioscience/santorum.asp (April 22, 2002). The Conference Report is *available at* ftp://ftp.loc.gov/pub/thomas/cp107/hr334.txt (April 20, 2002).

77. March 15, 2002, letter to Jennifer L. Sheets and Cyrus B. Richardson from Representatives John A. Boehner and Steve Chabot. It is *available at* http://www.sciohio.org/boehner-chabot2.pdf (April 20, 2002).

78. The Discovery Institute, "Biologist Ken Miller Flunks Political Science on Santorum," at http://www.discovery.org/viewDB/index.php3?command=view&id=1149&program=CRSC (April 22, 2002).

79. *See* Stephen C. Meyer, "Teach the Controversy," *Cincinnati Enquirer* (March 30, 2002), *available at* http://www.discovery.org/viewDB/index.php3?command=view&id=1134&program=CRSC (April 22, 2002); and Discovery, "Biologist Ken Miller Flunks."

80. U.S. House of Representatives Committee on Rules, Majority Office, "Committees of Conference and Consideration of Conference Reports" (Parliamentary Outreach Program), at http://www.house.gov/rules/ conf_rept_cons.htm (April 22, 2002).

81. *See*, for example, Kenneth R. Miller, "The Truth about the 'Santorum Amendment' Language on Evolution," at http://www.millerandlevine.com/km/evol/santorum.html (April 22, 2002); and National Center for Science Education, "Santorum Amendment Stripped from Education Bill," at http://www.ncseweb.org/resources/news/2001/US/866_santorum_amendment_stripped_fr_12_21_2001.asp (April 22, 2002).

82. See, for example, Pennock, *Tower of Babel*; Eugenie C. Scott, "Not (Just) in Kansas Anymore," *Science,* 288 (1999); and Miller, *Finding Darwin's God.*

83. Victor J. Stenger, "Intelligent Design: The New Stealth Creationism," at http://spot.colorado.edu/~vstenger/ (January 14, 2001).

84. Eugenia C. Scott distinguishes between Catholics and mainline Protestants, both of whom accommodated some form of evolution, and "fundamentalist Protestants," those whose opposition to evolution is motivated by "religious ideology, and only one narrow portion of religious ideology" (Eugenie C. Scott, "Just When You Thought It Was Safe to Teach Evolution," *Freethought Today* [January/February 2000], *available at* http://www.ffrt.org/fttoday /jan_feb00/scott.html [Jan. 14, 2001]).

See also, Eugenie C. Scott, "Creationism Evolves," review of *Tower of Babel* by Robert T. Pennock, *Scientific American* (August 1999), *available* at http://www. sciam.com/1999/0899issue/0899reviews1.html (Jan. 14, 2001). In this review, Scott argues that because creationists lost in *Edwards* they are now "calling not for creation science but for . . . 'intelligent-design theory'."

85. According to Ronald L. Numbers, "one annoyed critic no doubt captured the feelings of many when he described [ID] as 'the same old creationist bullshit dressed up in new clothes'" (Numbers, *Darwinism Comes to America,* 20, quoting from David K. Webb, Letter to the Editor, *Origins & Design,* 5 [Spring 1996], 17). Numbers cites a few more examples: "When the Jewish magazine *Commentary* in 1996 published a version of ID theory by the mathematician and novelist David Berlinski, letters of protest poured onto the editor's desk. [Daniel] Dennett ridiculed Berlinski's stylish essay as 'another hilarious demonstration that you can publish bull[shi]t at will—just as long as you say what an editorial board wants to hear in a style it favors.' Another reader characterized Berlinski's 'intuitions about the Design of the World as neither more nor less reliable than those of flat-earthers, goat entrail-readers, or believers in the Oedipus complex'" (Numbers, *Darwinism Comes to America,* 20, quoting from Daniel Dennett and Karl F. Wessel in "Denying Darwin: David Berlinski and Critics," *Commentary* [September 1996], 6, 11).

86. *See,* for example, Pennock, *Tower of Babel*; Miller, *Finding Darwin's God;* Bruce H. Weber, "Irreducible Complexity and the Problem of Biochemical Emergence," *Biology & Philosophy,* 14 (1999); Niall Shanks and Karl H. Joplin, "Redundant Complexity: A Critical Analysis of Intelligent Design in Biochemistry," *Philosophy of Science,* 66, 2 (1999); Fitelson, Stephens, and Sober, "How Not to Detect Design"; and Howard J. Van Till, "Does 'Intelligent Design' Have a Chance? An Essay Review," *Zygon,* 34, 4 (1999).

87. *See,* for example, Michael J. Behe, "Self-Organization and Irreducibly Complex Systems: A Reply to Shanks and Joplin," *Philosophy of Science,* 67, 1 (2000); Michael J. Behe, "Answering Scientific Criticisms of Intelligent Design," in *Science and Evidence for Design in the Universe,* ed. Michael J. Behe, William A. Dembski, and Stephen C. Meyer, The Proceedings of the Wethersfield Institute, vol. 9 (San Francisco: Ignatius Press, 2000); Phillip E. Johnson, review of *Tower of Babel* by Robert T. Pennock, *Books & Culture,* 5, 5 (September/October 1999); *Responses to CSC Critics,* at http://www.discovery.org/crsc/ (this Web page is continually updated); Johnson, *The Wedge,* 39–62, 105–142; Paul A. Nelson, "Is 'Intelligent Design' Unavoidable—Even by Howard Van Till?: A Response," *Zygon,* 34, 4 (1999); and in many places throughout Dembski, *No Free Lunch.*

Chapter One

Creator in the Courtroom

The question that this book attempts to address is made more difficult to fairly and sensibly answer because of the cultural baggage with which it has been associated in both the academic world and the popular press. One's opinion concerning evolution, creation, and intelligent design, and how one views the relationship between science, religion, and public education, are shaped by the cultural, philosophical, and jurisprudential assumptions that one brings to the discussion. This is no less true for philosophers and scientists than it is for journalists, soccer moms, federal and state judges, and Supreme Court justices. Consequently, prior to specifically answering (in chapter 4) the question of whether requiring or permitting the teaching of Intelligent Design in public schools would violate the Establishment Clause in light of the Supreme Court's most important decision on the matter of teaching origins, *Edwards v. Aguillard*, it is essential that we clarify and clearly define important terms—*creationism, evolution,* and *intelligent design*—as well as review prior court cases whose historical impact and reasoning influenced the Court's majority opinion in *Edwards*.

A. IMPORTANT TERMS

1. Creationism

Creationism is minimally the belief that nature, indeed the entire universe, could not have come into being without a Supreme Being as its ultimate cause. In other words, an exhaustive materialist (or naturalist) description and explanation of the events and entities in the universe is not a real possibility, for there are causes, agents, and entities, including God, that are nonmaterial (or non-natural) and are thus nondetectable under the strictures of a material-ist paradigm. Under this definition of creationism, young-earth creationism, old-earth creationism, and even Aristotle's cosmological views are "creation-ist,"[1] for each posits a Supreme Being as the ultimate cause of the universe and maintains that there are nonmaterial entities, such as agents, that can be causes for physical events and other entities. Because the differences between each type of creationism are often not appreciated, we will briefly define young-earth and old-earth creationism.

Young-earth creationism, according to Phillip E. Johnson (who himself is *not* a young-earth creationist), is associated with the "term 'creation-science,' as used in the Louisiana law [in the *Edwards* case], [and] is commonly un-derstood to refer to a movement of Christian fundamentalists based upon an extremely literal interpretation of the Bible." "Creation-scientists," writes Johnson, "do not merely insist that life was *created;* they insist that the job was completed in six days no more than ten thousand years ago, and that all evolution since that time has involved trivial modifications rather than basic changes. . . . [Young-earth creationism] attributes the existence of fossils to Noah's flood."[2]

Old-earth creationism is the view "that the earth and the universe were cre-ated far more than just a few thousand years ago as has been the traditional belief among Christians. . . . Rather [it is the belief that] . . . the earth is some four or five billion years old and the universe some ten to twenty billion years old. . . . [Old earth creationism also maintains] that unguided evolution is not capable of producing the features we see in our universe—not the universe it-self, life, its actual variety, not humankind."[3] Another old-earth creationist writes that according to this perspective

> living systems need to be robust to be able to adapt to the constantly changing environment. I believe that God incorporated this capacity for robustness in liv-ing systems to match the continuously changing environment by including ge-netic diversity in living systems and by allowing further modification of this di-versity through mutations. Thus, I believe that *microevolution,* which I mean to include both changes in genetic population distributions within species as well as mutations that modify existing characteristics (as distinct from the more du-bious claim of mutations that create entirely new characteristics), are part of God's systemic design.[4]

One may even include theistic evolution as a form of creationism.[5] Theis-tic evolution (or "the fully gifted creation") is the view that a complete and exhaustive description of origins and nature in wholly material terms is in principle compatible with the existence of God and other apparently nonma-terial philosophical and theological entities (e.g., souls, minds, moral properties, etc.). Some issues raised by theistic evolution could, however, exclude it as a version of creationism.[6] For example, it is not clear what theoretical role God or other nonmaterial entities and agents play for the theistic evolutionist. In other words, if the theoretical components, empirical predictions, and materialist presuppositions of evolution are adequate to account for the order and nature of things without either a Creator or other nonmaterial entities, then per Ockham's Razor, they are superfluous.

In popular culture, "creationism" is synonymous with creation science, a view whose proponents embrace young-earth creationism. As we shall see, the statutes in Arkansas, struck down as unconstitutional in *Epperson* and *McLean,* seemed to have had this type of creationism in mind. The Louisiana statute rejected in *Edwards* was thought by the Court to be in the same tradition as those rejected in *Epperson* and *McLean,* though the language of the statute was more circumspect than its predecessors.[7]

However, when I use the term *creationism* in this book I am referring exclusively to "creation science" or young-earth creationism, which was repudiated by the courts in the two Arkansas cases as well as in *Edwards*.

2. Evolution

Like creationism, *evolution* can mean different things. Sometimes it is used as a synonym for "Darwinism,"[8] both the theory defended by Charles Darwin (1809–1882) in his *Origin of Species*[9] as well as the subsequent refinements of Darwin's theory. Arguing from what he observed occurs when domestic breeders engage in selection, Darwin offered *natural selection* as the engine by which species adapt, survive, acquire new characteristics, and pass them on to their offspring:[10]

> Owing to this struggle, variations, however slight and from whatever cause proceeding, if they be in any degree profitable to an individual of any species, in its infinitely complex relations to other organic beings and to external nature, will tend to the preservation of that individual, and will generally be inherited by the offspring. The offspring, also, will thus have a better chance of surviving, for, of the many individuals of any species which are periodically born, but a small number can survive. I have called this principle, by which each slight variation, if useful, is preserved by the term of Natural Selection, in order to mark its relation to man's power of selection. We have seen that man by selection can certainly produce great results, and can adapt organic beings to his own uses, through the accumulation of slight but useful variations, given to him by the hand of Nature. But Natural Selection, as we shall hereafter see, is a power incessantly ready for action, and is as immeasurably superior to man's feeble efforts, as the works of Nature are to those of Art.[11]

In one sense, no one, not even hard-line creationists, deny this sort of evolution, if all that is meant by evolution is that biological species adapt over time to changing environments and pass on those adaptations genetically to their offspring. This is typically called *microevolution*. This should be distinguished from *macroevolution,* the view that the complex diversity of living things in our world, through small, incremental, and beneficial mutations over long eons of time, are all the result of one bacterial cell. That is, all living beings share a common ancestor, giving the appearance of being designed though in reality engineered by the unintelligent forces of natural selection. In the words of Richard Dawkins:

> Natural selection is the blind watchmaker, blind because it does not see ahead, does not plan consequences, has no purpose in view. Yet the living results of natural selection overwhelmingly impress us with the appearance of design as if by a master watchmaker, impress us with the illusion of design and planning.[12]

The notion of common descent is fundamental to macroevolution even if Darwinian and neo-Darwinian accounts of this descent are replaced or supplemented by another theory (e.g., punctuated equilibrium, recombination, the founder effect, genetic drift). This is why Antony Flew correctly points out that "[i]t is wrong to identify either the Darwinism of *The Origin of Species* or Neo-Darwinism with biological evolution without prefix or suffix. That to which any account of the evolution of species is necessarily opposed is any doctrine of their immutability [i.e., some form of essentialism]; combined, presumably, with the claim that they were, whether simultaneously or successively, specially created by *ad hoc* supernatural agency."[13]

Consequently, if evolution were only a theory of biology, and its explanatory power merely ruled out special creation of complex biological entities, Dawkins, Flew, and their allies could reasonably entertain a Watchmaker responsible for the design of the universe as a whole and/or the initial biological entity from which life arose. Evolution, however, is more than a theory applicable to biology and biochemistry. It also asserts that the bacterial cell from which all life arose sprung from inorganic matter. According to Douglas J. Futuyama, "The implications [in arguing that life came from inorganic matter] are so daunting that Darwin himself was reluctant to commit his beliefs to paper. In *The Origin of Species* he limited himself to saying that 'probably all organic beings which have ever lived on earth, have descended from one primordial form, into which life was first breathed'—a phrase which is certainly open to theological interpretation." Futuyama, however, argues that "[w]e will almost certainly never have direct fossil evidence that living molecular structures evolved from nonliving precursors. Such molecules surely could not have been preserved without degradation. *But a combination of geochemical evidence and laboratory experiment shows that such evolution is not only plausible but almost undeniable.*"[14]

Moreover, inorganic matter, indeed the matter of the entire universe, is said to have resulted from an initial explosion called the Big Bang, an event that occurred over 15 billion years ago.[15] Thus, evolution is a grand materialist explanation for the diversity and apparent design of entities that make up what we call nature, including both organic and inorganic entities.[16] In the words of Futuyama, "order in nature is no evidence of design."[17] "Darwin's great contribution," writes philosopher James Rachels, "was the final demolition of the idea that nature is the product of intelligent design."[18]

Many scientists and philosophers have cashed out the implications of this view. For example, philosopher Paul Churchland explains why he embraces a materialist view of mind: "The important point about the standard evolutionary story is that the human species and all of its features are the wholly physical outcome of a purely physical process. . . . If this is the correct account of our origins, then there seems neither need, nor room, to fit any nonphysical substances or properties into our theoretical account of ourselves. We are creatures of matter. And we should learn to live with that fact."[19]

Ruse, who testified as an expert witness for the plaintiffs in *McLean*,[20] writes that morality, in order to work, must *seem* real, operating "as a collective illusion of the human race, fashioned and maintained by natural selection in order to promote individual reproduction."[21] That is, "we think that we have obligations to others because it is in our biological interests to have these thoughts."[22] Ruse writes elsewhere: "Considered as a rationally justifiable set of claims about an objective something, [morality] is illusory. I appreciate that when somebody says, 'Love thy neighbor as thyself,' they think they are referring above and beyond themselves. . . . Nevertheless, to a Darwinian evolutionist it can be seen that such reference is truly without foundation. Morality is just an aid to survival and reproduction, and has no being beyond or without this. . . . [A]ny deeper meaning is illusory."[23] George Gaylord Simpson explains the "meaning of evolution":

> Although many details remain to be worked out, it is already evident that all the objective phenomena of the history of life can be explained in purely naturalistic or, in a proper sense of the sometimes abused word, materialistic factors. . . . Man is the result of a purposeless and natural process that did not have him in mind.[24]

In his widely used textbook, *Evolution,* Monroe W. Strickberger writes that "[t]he variability on which selection depends may be random, but adaptions are not; they arise because selection chooses and perfects on what is adaptive. In this scheme a god of design and purpose is not necessary."[25]

Francis Crick, discoverer (with James D. Watson) of the molecular structure of deoxyribonucleic acid (DNA), presents with exceptional clarity the
materialism of the evolutionary paradigm and its implications:

> In addition to our knowledge of basic chemistry and physics, the earth sciences
> (such as geology) and cosmic science (astronomy and cosmology) have devel-
> oped pictures of our world and our universe that are quite different from those
> common when traditional religions were founded. The modern picture of the
> universe, and how it developed in time, forms the essential background to our
> present knowledge of biology. That knowledge has been completely trans-
> formed in the last 150 years. Until Charles Darwin and Alfred Wallace inde-
> pendently hit on the basic mechanism driving biological evolution—the
> process of natural selection—the "Argument from Design" appeared unan-
> swerable. . . . We now know that all living things, from bacteria to ourselves,
> are closely related at the biochemical level. . . . A modern neurobiologist sees
> no need for the religious concept of a soul to explain the behavior of humans
> and other animals. . . . Many educated people, especially in the Western world,
> . . . share the belief that the soul is a metaphor and that there is no personal life
> before conception or after death.[26]

Thus, what I mean by evolution, in this book, is *naturalistic* evolution, the
view that the entire universe and all the entities in it can be accounted for by
strictly material processes without resorting to any designer, Creator, or nonmaterial entity or agent as an explanation for either any aspect of the natural
universe or the universe as a whole. That is, an exhaustive materialist description of the universe is in principle possible. Therefore, to say that evolution is true—as understood by its leading proponents such as those cited
above—is to say that naturalism (or materialism) as a worldview is true, for
the former *entails* the latter, for the latter is a necessary condition of the former. Consequently, to challenge that necessary condition—by appealing to
something even as modest as Intelligent Design (to say nothing of full-blown
Creationism)—poses a threat to the materialist edifice. However, by attempt-
ing to rebut this threat—by taking on the arguments for ID—evolutionists implicitly accept the first, and most important premise, of the ID movement.
That is, naturalistic evolution provides an answer to the *very same* question ID
provides an answer: What is the origin of apparent design in biological organisms and/or other aspects of the natural universe and/or the universe as a
whole? Evolution answers the question by appealing to the forces of unguided
matter (and/or energy), the latter to intelligent agency. But if this is the case,
then the legal grounds for teaching ID in public schools, as we shall see (in
chapter 4), are strengthened, for it would mean that an origins curriculum that
excludes design and offers to students naturalism as the only approved metaphysical position of the state may itself run afoul of the Establishment Clause.

Because the evolutionary commitment to materialism has shaped the way in which we think of science,[27] and because science is considered to have a place of epistemological privilege in our culture, knowledge claims that challenge this paradigm either explicitly or implicitly (e.g., claims that immaterial entities such as souls, natures, substances, God, and so on have or may have ontological standing) are dismissed as metaphorical,[28] a God-of-the-gaps strategy,[29] problems to be resolvable by a future naturalistic explanation,[30] or a confusing of two mutually exclusive categories,[31] one of which ("science") has the proper role of evaluating the rationality of the other ("religion").

An example of the latter is instructive in understanding how the epistemological questions over the nature of science are depicted to the general public. Consider the following comments made by the National Association of Biology Teachers (NABT) as part of an official statement published on its Web site:

> This same examination, pondering and possible revision have firmly established evolution as an important natural process explained by valid scientific principles, and clearly differentiate and separate science from various kinds of nonscientific ways of knowing, including those with a supernatural basis such as creationism. Whether called "creation science," "scientific creationism," "intelligent-design theory," "young-earth theory" or some other synonym, creation beliefs have no place in the science classroom. Explanations employing nonnaturalistic or supernatural events, whether or not explicit reference is made to a supernatural being, are outside the realm of science and not part of a valid science curriculum. Evolutionary theory, indeed all of science, is necessarily silent on religion and neither refutes nor supports the existence of a deity or deities.[32]

This statement, of course, begs an important question: If there are other "ways of knowing" besides materialist science, what happens when they conflict? For example, many neuropsychologists tell us that human beings are merely physical systems, property things, and "thought" is entirely the result of the firing of neurons in the brain. The mind may be an "epiphenomenon," but it is not a nonmaterial thing that really exists. That is, there are no nonmaterial substances, like souls or minds, from which thought arises. Suppose, however, a philosophical theologian, armed with arguments defending the existence of the soul, arguments she believes are persuasive and rationally defensible apart from appeals to special revelation, rejects the neuropsychologist's materialist description of human nature? Who wins? I suspect that the NABT would say the neuropsychologist wins, for he is proposing a scientific theory (i.e., a materialist explanation) while the philosophical theologian is appealing to non-natural entities (i.e., immaterial substances) and thus is suggesting "another way of knowing." This is just a kind, though condescending, way of saying that the philosophical theologian is giving us her "beliefs" (or "religious opinion") and not providing us with any real knowledge. And thus, contrary to what the NABT is saying, evolutionary theory's presuppositional commitment (methodological naturalism) and metaphysical entailment (ontological materialism) have a lot to say about the plausibility and/or rationality of "religious beliefs."

3. Intelligent Design

Intelligent Design, or ID, is a research program embraced by a small, though growing, platoon of academics who maintain that intelligent agency, as an aspect of scientific theory making, has more explanatory power in accounting for the specified, and sometimes irreducible, complexity of some physical systems, including biological entities, and/or the existence of the universe as a whole, than the blind forces of unguided matter. Design theorists also argue that there are other deep philosophical problems with methodological naturalism and ontological materialism, and that it is perfectly appropriate for these problems to serve as conceptual checks against theories, including theories about the nature of "science" that presuppose and/or entail philosophical materialism. Although most design theorists are theists, there is a wide range of opinion within their camp.[33] And unlike their creationist predecessors, most are well-credentialed scholars with academic appointments and with publications in both academic journals and prestigious monograph series.[34]

Clearly, ID proponents (like theistic evolutionists) are creationists, if one defines that term broadly. However, because creationism is treated as synonymous with creation science (or young-earth creationism) in both the popular culture as well as the legal cases we cover in this book, it is best, for the sake of accuracy, to treat ID as a separate school of thought. In fact, as we shall see in chapter 4, there are important and real distinctions between creation science and ID that make a legal difference on whether the teaching of ID in public schools would pass constitutional muster. A more detailed presentation of ID is the focus of chapter 3.

B. THE CASES

Prior to the U.S. Supreme Court's *Edwards v. Aguillard* decision in 1987, there were three cases that shaped, and continue to shape, the popular and judicial understandings of the debate over teaching evolution in public schools: The Scopes Trial (1925), *Epperson v. Arkansas* (1968), and *McLean v. Arkansas* (1982).

1. The Scopes Trial

The first important court case concerning religion, science, and education was the 1925 Scopes Trial, immortalized in the fictionalized movie account *Inherit the Wind*. As the story goes, John T. Scopes, a young science teacher from Dayton, Tennessee, was prosecuted for teaching evolution in a public school, an act prohibited by a Tennessee statute.[35] Although in the film version the classroom of a wise and insightful teacher is invaded by a group of weapon-wielding narrow-minded fundamentalists, in the real life story the Scopes Trial was the result of collusion initiated by Dayton locals whose sole interest was to obtain free publicity for their small and obscure town.

The American Civil Liberties Union (ACLU) published an advertisement in the May 4, 1925, edition of a Chattanooga, Tennessee, paper soliciting a teacher-plaintiff: "We are looking for a Tennessee teacher who is willing to accept our services in testing this [anti-evolution] law in the courts. . . . Our lawyers think a friendly test can be arranged without costing a teacher his or her job. Distinguished counsel have volunteered their services. All we need now is a willing client." According to legal historian Edward J. Larson, "This announcement . . . was preceded by the assurance of the city school superintendent that the test case would not occur there. But the paper served a wider area. Out in the rising hill country forty miles north of Chattanooga, eager civic boosters in Dayton read into the announcement an opportunity to put their town on the map." George W. Rappelyea, manager of a Dayton-area coal company, "conceived the idea of staging an anti-evolution test case in Dayton" after reading the ad. "The next day, he shared his idea with other local businessmen, lawyers, and school officials, who agreed to the scheme to boost business." Scopes agreed to be the teacher who would stand trial. Although Scopes was not a biology teacher, "he had conducted a review for the biology final exam and the course textbook he used, Hunter's *A Civic Biology,* prominently featured evolution. On these grounds, Rappelyea swore out a warrant against Scopes and wired the ACLU to help while the school-board chairman called the Chattanooga newspaper." Ironically, Tennessee had just passed a declaratory judgment act, which meant that Scopes did not have "to be charged with violating the anti-evolution law." While "Dayton civic leaders apparently never considered this course, . . . the ACLU welcomed the drama of a criminal trial."[36]

Scopes was represented by Clarence Darrow, attorney for the ACLU. The ACLU, in its literature, had made the argument that antievolution statutes were unfair: "The attempts to maintain a uniform orthodox opinion among teachers should be opposed. . . . The attempts of education authorities to inject into public schools and colleges propaganda in the interest of any particular theory of society to the exclusion of others should be opposed."[37] At trial, Darrow raised a number of constitutional objections to the Tennessee statute, stressing its infringement on the teacher's academic freedom.[38] Ironically, an appeal to academic freedom was part of the case put forth by supporters of the Louisiana statute struck down in *Edwards*.[39] That statute required that public schools teach creation science if evolution is taught and vice versa.[40]

The prosecution, which included three-time Democratic presidential candidate William Jennings Bryan, maintained that the state of Tennessee had a right to shape its public school curricula and that the statute did not prevent an individual from exercising his freedom of speech. For the law applied only to individuals who sought and received employment in public education, and *only when* these individuals were teaching in a public school classroom. They could, without fear of legal reprisals, speak freely of evolution on their own time. Ultimately, this argument won the day. According to Larson, the trial judge, John T. Raulston, "sided with the state and upheld the statute on the basis of several recent federal and state supreme court decisions generally affirming legislative control over public education. To him, the statute seemed reasonable."[41]

Although the trial court ruled against Scopes, in 1927 the Supreme Court of Tennessee, on appeal, reversed Scopes's conviction because the $100 fine assessed to Scopes should have been assessed by the jury and not the judge.[42] Nevertheless, the court upheld Tennessee's antievolution statute as constitutional.

Like the 1995 O. J. Simpson criminal trial, the 1925 Scopes Trial was an international phenomenon. And like the Simpson trial, the court's judgment in Scopes was less important than its impact on the wider culture.[43] This is why "in the trial of public opinion and the press," as historian George Marsden points out, "it was clear that the twentieth century, the cities, and universities had won a resounding victory, and that the country, the South, and the fundamentalists were guilty as charged."[44] An article in *Current History Illustrated,* a magazine published by the *New York Times,* concluded that "although Scopes was found guilty of a misdemeanor for teaching evolution, and was fined $100, Bryan was beaten and beaten badly."[45]

It was not until the 1960s that a court ruled that an antievolution statute violated the federal Constitution. That case is *Epperson v. Arkansas.*

2. *Epperson v. Arkansas*

Epperson concerns a 1929 Arkansas statute that prohibited the teaching of evolution in all state-supported educational institutions, including universities, colleges, and public schools.[46] The statute states that "it shall be unlawful for any teacher or instructor . . . to teach the theory or doctrine that mankind ascended or descended from a lower order of animals and also it shall be unlawful for any teacher, textbook commission, or other authority exercising the power to select textbooks for above mentioned educational institutions to adopt or use in any such institution a textbook that teaches the doctrine or theory that mankind descended or ascended from a lower order of animals."[47] Those convicted under this statute would be guilty of a misdemeanor, forced to resign their posts, and may be fined up to $500.[48]

Epperson concerned a tenth-grade biology teacher in Little Rock, Susan Epperson. At the beginning of the 1965 school year she was provided with a new textbook from which she was to instruct her biology students. Adopted by the school administration on the recommendation of the system's biology teachers, this textbook, unlike the one Epperson had used the previous school year, "contained a chapter setting forth 'the theory about the origin . . . of man from a lower form of animal.'"[49] This put Epperson in a difficult dilemma: if she uses the textbook, she violates an Arkansas statute and subjects herself to criminal prosecution and dismissal;[50] on the other hand, if she does not use the textbook, she could be dismissed for insubordination. Joined by "H. H. Blanchard, a parent of children attending the public schools," Epperson instituted an "action in the Chancery Court of the State, seeking a declaration that the Arkansas statute is void and enjoining the State and the defendant officials of the Little Rock school system from dismissing her for violation of the statute's provisions."[51]

Holding that the antievolution statute violated the Fourteenth Amendment, the Chancery Court pointed out "that this Amendment encompasses the prohibitions upon state interference with freedom of speech and thought which are contained in the First Amendment."[52] Consequently, because this statute "tends to hinder the quest for knowledge, restrict freedom to learn, and restrain the freedom to teach,"[53] it violates the First Amendment and is thus unconstitutional.

The Arkansas Supreme Court reversed on appeal. In a two-sentence Per Curium opinion, the Court upheld the statute on the grounds that it "is a valid exercise of the state's power to specify the curriculum in its public schools."[54] The Court did acknowledge that the statute lacked clarity, for it was unclear to the Court whether the statute prohibited either teaching the theory of evolution, teaching the theory of evolution as true, or both. However, because the Court believed that resolving this vagueness was not necessary in order to make a decision, and because the issue was not raised at trial, it volunteered no opinion on the matter. Ironically, in their concurring opinions in *Epperson,* Justices Hugo Black and Potter Stewart[55] would have struck down the statute on the grounds of vagueness rather than on the grounds held by the U.S. Supreme Court's majority opinion.[56]

That opinion held that the Arkansas statute "must be stricken because of its conflict with the constitutional prohibition of state laws respecting an establishment of religion or prohibiting the free exercise thereof." The Court drew this conclusion on the basis of what it called "the overriding fact" that the statute "selects from the body of knowledge a particular segment which it proscribes for the sole reason that it is deemed in conflict with a particular religious doctrine; that is, with a particular interpretation of the Book of Genesis by a particular religious group."[57] Thus, the statute had *no secular purpose*. In order to establish the veracity of this "overriding fact" the Court cited two reasons: (1) "no suggestion has been made that Arkansas' law may be justified by considerations of state policy other than the religious view of some of its citizens," and (2) "fundamentalist sectarian conviction was and is the law's reason for existence."[58] The second reason was supported by citing the historical origin of the Arkansas statute and its connection to the Tennessee statute adjudicated in *Scopes*.[59] This line of argument—appealing to the apparent motives of the statute's supporters rather than to the stated purpose of the statute itself—plays a dominant place in subsequent creation science cases (i.e., *McLean, Edwards*), even though the Court has, in the words of Justice Black, "consistently held that it is not for us to invalidate a statute because of our views that the 'motives' behind its passage were improper; it is simply too difficult to determine what those motives were."[60]

Although the Court concedes that it is within the state's power to shape public school curricula, that right "does not carry with it the right to prohibit, on pain of criminal penalty, the teaching of a scientific theory or doctrine where that prohibition is based upon reasons that violate the First Amendment."[61] Thus, the Court is *not* saying that publicly supported criticism of Darwinism (or evolution) is unconstitutional, but rather, that *prohibiting* academic discussion of these issues in the classroom—discussions necessary for the advancement of human knowledge—is inconsistent with the First Amendment *if the prohibition* has the effect of advancing sectarian religious *or* antireligious beliefs. However, this does not mean that the state has an obligation to protect people from hearing or reading things that offend their religious or antireligious sensibilities. It just means that the state and its institutions may not purposely advance or inhibit religious and antireligious beliefs. As Justice Clark points out, "the state has no legitimate interest in protecting any or all religions from views distasteful to them."[62]

The Court did not base its holding, as the Chancery Court did, on the teacher's right to freedom of speech, even though it explores, and rejects, that option in the beginning of its opinion.[63] What is controlling in *Epperson*, according to the Court, is the principle that "government . . . must be neutral in matters of religious theory, doctrine, and practice. It may not be hostile to any religion or to the advocacy of nonreligion; and it may not aid, foster, or promote one religion or religious theory against another or even against the militant opposite. The First Amendment mandates governmental neutrality between religion and religion, and between religion and nonreligion."[64] Because "Arkansas did not seek to excise from the curricula of its schools and universities all discussion of the origin of man," its "law cannot be defended as an act of religious neutrality." For "[t]he law's effort was confined to an attempt to blot out a particular theory [i.e., evolution] because of its supposed conflict with the biblical account, literally read."[65]

As we shall see (in chapter 4), this call to neutrality, ironically, may turn out to be the strongest argument to allow (or perhaps require) Intelligent Design (ID) to be taught in public educational institutions, for ID proponents maintain that supporters of naturalistic evolution presuppose methodological naturalism in their epistemology that, not surprisingly, entails materialism as a worldview, a worldview that denies the existence of, or at least denies that one can know that there exists, nonmaterial entities such as God, souls, moral properties, or immaterial agents responsible for apparently natural phenomena. Justice Black's concurring comments in *Epperson* are instructive in this regard:

> A second question that arises for me is whether the Court's decision forbidding the State to exclude the subject of evolution from its schools infringes the religious freedom of those who consider evolution an anti-religious doctrine. If the theory is considered anti-religious, as the Court indicates, how can the State be bound by the Federal Constitution to permit its teachers to advocate such an "anti-religious" doctrine to schoolchildren? The very cases cited by the Court as supporting its conclusion that the State must be neutral, not favoring one religious or anti-religious view over another. . . . Since there is no indication that the literal Biblical doctrine of the origin of man is included in the curriculum of Arkansas schools, does not the removal of the subject of evolution leave the State in a neutral position toward these supposedly competing religious and anti-religious doctrines? Unless this Court is prepared simply to write off as pure nonsense the views of those who consider evolution an anti-religious doctrine, then this issue presents problems under the Establishment Clause far more troublesome than are discussed in the Court's opinion.[66]

It is interesting to note that a California Superior Court, in the case of *Segraves v. California Board of Education* (1981),[67] seems to have grasped the underlying principle of Justice Black's assessment, though it is not clear whether the judge in the case, Irving H. Perluss, actually consulted it. This case, though having no precedential authority in a federal court, may have within it tucked away a kernel of wisdom that could be extracted by a federal court, perhaps even the U. S. Supreme Court, or even an ingenious and creative school board.

Segraves concerned the children of Kelly Segraves, cofounder of the Creation Science Resource Center. Mr. Segraves, whose children attended public schools, "argued that the State of California had violated the religious freedom of his children by teaching evolution as fact."[68] According to the Court, the issue "is whether or not the free exercise of religion by Mr. Segraves and his children was thwarted by the instruction in science that his children had received in school, and if so, has there been sufficient accommodation of their views?"[69] The court held that the state's Antidogmatism Policy, adopted by the California Board of Education, if incorporated into the Science Framework and practiced by teachers in the science classroom, is an adequate compromise that protects the Segraveses' free exercise rights without violating the Establishment Clause. The state's guideline called for "(1) Dogmatism to be changed to conditional statements where speculation is offered as explanation for origins, and (2) Science should emphasize 'how' and not 'ultimate cause' for origins."[70] That is, the question of origins should be taught conditionally. Although it is not clear how this would be accomplished, at least one philosopher, Alvin Plantinga, has seen the wisdom of this holding and has employed its logic in his own proposal to resolve the debate over origins in public education.[71]

Plantinga argues that the key condition doing all the intellectual work is epistemological, that is, what one believes counts as "knowledge" will shape what one thinks about the origin and nature of the universe. For example, if one embraces a naturalist epistemology, believing that only natural, nonagent-directed and/or -caused explanations count as knowledge in the hard sciences, then naturalistic evolution is more likely true than not. However, if one embraces a different epistemology, one that allows for non-natural, agent-directed and/or -caused explanations in the hard sciences, then some form of creationism (or Intelligent Design) is more likely true than not.[72] We cover Plantinga's argument in greater detail in section C of chapter 3.

The *Segraves* court ordered that a copy of the policy "shall be disseminated to all the publishers, institutions, school districts, schools, and persons regularly receiving the science framework." According to the court, this order applies to those who have received the framework in the past as well as those who will receive it in the future.[73] In 1989, however, the California Board of Education adopted the State Board of Education Policy on the Teaching of Natural Sciences,[74] which does not explicitly mention evolution,[75] but nevertheless presents a framework that, according to some commentators, effectively removes the underlying principle of the Antidogmatism Policy and is thus contrary to the order of the *Segraves* court.[76] For even though the 1989 framework decries dogmatism it does not require that the science of origins be taught conditionally as did the 1972 policy. Rather, the 1989 framework asserts that only *natural* explanations, even ones that attempt to explain the order and nature of being itself, count as "science" as well as real knowledge:

> The domain of the natural sciences is the natural world. Science is limited by its tools—observable facts and testable hypotheses.
>
> Discussions of any scientific fact, hypothesis, or theory related to the origins of the universe, the earth, and life (the how) are appropriate to the science curriculum. . . . A scientific fact is an understanding based on confirmable observations and is subject to test and rejection. . . . Scientific theories are constantly subject to testing, modification, and refutation as new evidence and new ideas emerge.[77]

On the other hand, non-natural explanations, even ones that attempt to explain the order and nature of being itself, *precisely the same* phenomena the board states natural explanations are employed to account for, *do not* count as "science," and thus the board implies that they cannot count as real knowledge that could serve as a defeater to naturalistic explanations:

> Discussions of divine creation, ultimate purposes, or ultimate causes (the why) are appropriate to the history-social science and English-language arts curricula. . . . Philosophical and religious beliefs are based, at least in part, on faith and are not subject to scientific test and refutation. . . . If a student should raise a question in a natural science class that the teacher determines is outside the domain of science, the teacher should treat the question with respect. The teacher should explain why the question is outside the domain of natural science and encourage the student to discuss the question further with his or her family and clergy.[78]

It is difficult to take seriously such educational pronouncements from a document whose authors cannot even present their views without relying on self-refutation as their ground of principle: "Nothing in science or in any other field of knowledge shall be taught dogmatically. A dogma is a system of beliefs that is not subject to scientific test and refutation. Compelling belief is inconsistent with the goal of education; the goal is to encourage understanding." So, the California Board of Education, a government body, employs the coercive power of the state to compel its educators to adhere to a belief—"nothing in science or in any other field of knowledge shall be taught dogmatically"—that is itself not subject to scientific test and refutation and is thus affirmed dogmatically, in order to instruct its teachers to teach only "science" and not engage in compelling others to hold beliefs that are dogmatic and thus not subject to scientific test and refutation. Consequently, if school districts are to obey their state board's framework and incorporate it into their science curricula, each district must, ironically, *reject* the board's definition of what counts as science and/or knowledge, since it is a claim that is either self-refuting (i.e., it is a claim *of* science that is inconsistent with itself) or it is a philosophical claim (i.e., it is a claim *about* science and thus cannot be part of the science curriculum because it is not a claim *of* science), a "belief based, at least in part, on faith and" is "not subject to scientific test and refutation." Of course, each board member is free "to discuss the question further with his or her family and clergy."[79]

Although from the time of the *Epperson* ruling in 1968 until the next case we cover, *McLean v. Arkansas* (1982), there were several other court cases that dealt with the teaching of evolution in public schools,[80] none really added anything jurisprudentially interesting to the debate, except perhaps some insights into academic freedom that could be employed by a future court to uphold a teacher's right to teach Intelligent Design.[81]

Before covering *McLean,* we take a brief excursion into the Supreme Court's Establishment Clause jurisprudence and the formation of what has come to be called "the Lemon test." There are three reasons for this: (1) the test played a substantial role in the Court's holding in *Edwards,* (2) members of the current Court as well as legal scholars have expressed doubts about the test, and (3) the test was proposed as a standardization of prior Establishment Clause decisions.

3. The Lemon Test and Establishment Clause Jurisprudence[82]

Prior to the Lemon test, as we saw in *Epperson,* the Court employed a neutrality test, maintaining that the state must remain neutral between religions and between religion and irreligion, though what precisely the Court means by "neutrality" has been a topic of scholarly debate.[83] However, in *Lemon v. Kurtzman,*[84] the Court provided a three-part test that is used by many courts to determine whether or not a given public policy or law runs afoul of this neutrality and thus the Establishment Clause. The Court believed that this test is based on the history of the Court's decisions on the matter of church and state. Thus, if a challenged policy or law passes this test, it is constitutional. However, it need only fail one prong of the test in order to be declared unconstitutional:

> Every analysis in this area [church/state cases] must begin with consideration of the cumulative criteria developed by the Court over many years. Three such tests may be gleaned from our cases. First, the statute must have a secular legislative purpose; second, its principle or primary effect must be one that neither advances nor inhibits religion, Board of Education v. Allen, 392 U.S. 236, 243 (1968); finally, the statute must not foster "an excessive government entangle-

ment with religion" Walz [v. Tax Comm'n of New York City], 397 U.S. 664, 668 (1970).[85]

The operative terms in this test are *secular purpose, principle and primary effect,* and *excessive government entanglement,* all of which, as we will see, were applied in *McLean,* though the secular purpose prong is the only one employed by the Court in *Edwards.*

Because the First Amendment also has a Free Exercise Clause, and because apparently "neutral" laws may inhibit religion and/or its Free Exercise, the Court has ruled that the government may *accommodate* religion and that such an accommodation may pass the Lemon test:

> *Everson* and *Allen* put to rest any argument that the State may never act in such a way that has the *incidental effect of facilitating religious activity.* . . . If this were impermissible. . . . a church could not be protected by the police and fire department, or have its public sidewalk kept in repair. The Court has never held that religious activities must be discriminated against in this way.[86]

It should be noted that some scholars[87] as well as some post-Lemon opinions by Supreme Court justices[88] have criticized and questioned certain aspects of the Lemon test. For example, in *Lynch v. Donnelly,* Justice Sandra Day O'Connor proposed an alternative to the Lemon test, one that is commonly called the "endorsement test." According to this test, if a government action creates a *perception* that it is either endorsing or disfavoring a religion, the action is unconstitutional. The concern of this test is whether the disputed activity suggests "a message to nonadherents that they are outsiders, not full members of the political community, and an accompanying message to adherents that they are insiders, favored members of the political community."[89] However, who counts as a "nonadherent" has seemed to change. In *Lynch* Justice O'Connor suggests that nonadherents are "ordinary citizens," actual flesh and blood human beings, who are the recipients of the government's message. In a subsequent case, *Wallace v. Jaffre,* she proposes a type of "reasonable person standard," suggesting that the nonadherent is an objective observer fully informed of all the facts: "The relevant issue is whether an objective observer, acquainted with the text, legislative history, and implementation of the statute, would perceive it as a state endorsement of prayer in public schools."[90] Thus, a law may pass or fail the endorsement test depending on who (or what) counts as a nonadherent. It is interesting to note that in *Edwards* the Court quotes from O'Connor's *Lynch* concurrence as part of its application of the first prong of the Lemon test in rejecting Louisiana's balanced treatment statute (*see* chapter 2).[91]

In *Lee v. Weisman,* Justice Anthony Kennedy put forth a no coercion test in his majority opinion.[92] In that case, the Court found that a public middle school's invitation to a local clergyman to perform an invocation and benediction at a graduation ceremony is unconstitutional. According to Justice Kennedy, "[t]he Establishment Clause was inspired by the lesson that in the hands of government what might begin as a tolerant expression of religious views may end in a policy to indoctrinate and coerce. Prayer exercises in elementary and secondary schools carry a particular risk of indirect coercion."[93] Justice Kennedy does not seem to be suggesting that the coercion test is a summary of the Lemon test or that it ought to replace it. Rather, he seems to be putting forth a supplemental standard, another analytical device, by which to assess an alleged case of religious establishment,[94] and whose origin he finds in the inspiration that motivated the Framers of the First Amendment.[95] Thus, the no coercion test is more of a throwback than a new judicial innovation.[96] Although *Lee* dealt exclusively with the question of apparent school-sponsored prayer, it does not take much imagination to extend its no coercion principle to the question of the teaching of ID in public school, which I do in chapter 4.

In some recent cases the Court in its holdings seems to be moving toward some variation of the endorsement test as a proxy or substitute for the Lemon test (even when the holding does not explicitly mention the endorsement test).[97] These cases involve the providing of public funds to, and/or the use of public facilities by, individuals and/or institutions that propagate religious-oriented speech. The Court's holdings in these cases seem to be saying that if a state funds or provides public facilities or forums for citizens affirming differing points of view, and it cannot reasonably be inferred that the government would be endorsing a religion if these venues included expressions of religious points of view, the state cannot, and is not required to, exclude religious points of view from the benefits accorded to others in these venues simply because these views are religious. The Court, however, has applied the endorsement test to *limit* the communication of a viewpoint when the speaker (or inanimate proxy) is a representative or agent of the state, and/or whose religious views may be reasonably perceived as being endorsed by the state.[98] On the other hand, in the context of public education, the Court has acknowledged the academic freedom of teachers (agents of the state) and students as grounded in their First Amendment right of freedom of expression.[99] Perhaps this is why proponents of the Louisiana statute, struck down in *Edwards,* crafted their case by appealing to both "balanced treatment" and "academic freedom."[100]

It is difficult to know what establishment test the Court currently embraces. According to Gerald Gunther and Kathleen M. Sullivan, although the Court's use of the Lemon test has faced a variety of criticism, it "has not formally renounced" the test, "but has relied on it less and less in recent years. The Court's decisions over the last decade increasingly employ entirely different sets of analytical devices for distinguishing establishments."[101] These devices include the neutrality test, Lemon test, the endorsement test (in both its forms), and the no coercion test. Perhaps this is where the Court is heading: different tests for different sorts of establishment cases. However, because the *Edwards* Court applied the Lemon test, my analysis of *Edwards* focuses on the Court's application of that establishment test, though in chapter 4 I assess a possible ID statute by employing the resources of each of these tests.

4. McLean v. Arkansas

Although not a Supreme Court case, *McLean* is an important one, for it is the only case in federal court that dealt with some of the philosophical and scientific questions that simmer beneath the surface in the creation/evolution debate. In addition, it led to a number of books,[102] some of which were penned by expert witnesses who testified in the case. Moreover, *McLean* is sometimes referred to as "Scopes II" because of the massive media attention it received,[103] the colorful Federal District Court judge who presided over the case (William R. Overton), and the parade of well-known expert witnesses from a diversity of disciplines and religious points of view.[104]

McLean concerned an Arkansas statute, Act 590 of 1981, the "Balanced Treatment for Creation-Science and Evolution-Science Act."[105] It mandated that "[p]ublic schools within this State shall give balanced treatment to creation-science and to evolution-science."[106] Judge Overton applied the Lemon test in his analysis of this statute, pointing out that if the statute fails any one prong of the test, then it violates the Establishment Clause.[107] However, he concluded that the Act failed all three prongs. Although there are other issues brought up in the opinion,[108] we focus only on Judge Overton's application of the Lemon test.

Judge Overton's application of the first prong of the Lemon test—does the law have a secular purpose?—focused on two points: (1) the history and motivations of the statute's proponents (including the history of the creation-evolution controversy), and (2) the wording of the act.

Concerning the first point, the judge argued that the act's origin can be traced back to the time of the Scopes Trial, revealing a historical context that is important in interpreting the true purpose of the act.[109] In addition, both the act's author[110] as well as its legislative sponsor[111] "had publicly proclaimed the sectarian purpose of the proposal," the latter doing so "contemporaneously with the legislative process."[112] Moreover, the act's nonsecular purpose can be detected from "the lack of any legislative investigation,

debate or consultation with any educators or scientists" as well as "the unprecedented intrusion in school curriculum."[113] Although Judge Overton
conceded to the state that "the courts should look to legislative statements of
a statute's purpose in Establishment Clause cases and accord such pronouncements with great deference" and that "remarks by the sponsor or author of a bill are not considered controlling in analyzing legislative intent,"
"courts are not bound . . . by legislative statements of purpose or legislative
disclaimers."[114] In defense of this assertion, the judge cites case law that
shows that "in determining the legislative purpose of a statute, courts may
consider evidence of the historical context of the Act," "the specific sequence of events leading up to passage of the Act, departures from normal
procedural sequences, substantive departures from the normal," "and contemporaneous statements of the legislative sponsor."[115]

Concerning the second point, Judge Overton claimed that even if the state
were correct that "the Court is limited to an examination of the language of
the Act, the evidence is overwhelming that both the purpose and effect of Act
590 is the advancement of religion in the public schools."[116] In order to support this conclusion, the judge took a critical look at some of the act's language. The offending portion is from section 4 of the act:

Definitions. As used in this Act:

(a) "Creation-science" means the scientific evidences for creation and evidences for creation and inferences from these scientific evidences. Creation-
science includes the scientific evidences and related inferences that indicate:
(1) Sudden creation of the universe, energy, and life from nothing; (2) The insufficiency of mutation and natural selection in bringing about development of
all living things from a single organism; (3) Changes only within fixed limits
of originally created kinds of plants and animals; (4) Separate ancestry for man
and apes; (5) Explanation of the earth's geology by catastrophism, including
the occurrence of a worldwide flood; and (6) A relatively recent inception of
the earth and living things.

(b) "Evolution-science" means the scientific evidences for evolution and inferences from those scientific evidences. Evolution-science includes the scientific evidences and related inferences that indicate: (1) Emergence by naturalistic processes of the universe from disordered matter and emergence of life from
nonlife; (2) The sufficiency of mutation and natural selection in bringing about
development of present living kinds from simple earlier kinds; (3) Emergence
by mutation and natural selection of present living kinds from simple earlier
kinds; (4) Emergence of man from a common ancestor with apes; (5) Explanation of the earth's geology and the evolutionary sequence by uniformitarianism;
and (6) An inception several billion years ago of the earth and somewhat later
of life.

(c) "Public schools" mean public secondary and elementary schools.[117]

According to Judge Overton, "[t]he evidence establishes that the definition of 'creation science' contained in 4(a) has as its unmentioned reference the first 11 chapters of the Book of Genesis."[118] Citing the expert testimony of both plaintiff's and defendant's witnesses, the judge shows, in an informative footnote, that five of the six aspects of creation science in the act have a parallel in the Book of Genesis (literally interpreted).[119] Thus, the act has no secular purpose, and consequently fails the first prong of the Lemon test.

In his application of the second prong of the Lemon test—does the law advance or inhibit religion?—Judge Overton explores two issues: (1) Is Act 590 pedagogically sound? and (2) Is creation-science really science? In answer to the first question, he once again refers to the language of the act. He argues that section 4(b), "as a statement of the theory of evolution . . . is simply a hodgepodge of limited assertions, many of which are factually inaccurate." In addition, the act's two-model approach "is simply a contrived dualism," for there are not merely two options: creation science and godless evolution.[120] Thus, Act 590 is not pedagogically sound.

It is worth noting that Judge Overton, in claiming that the act is a contrived dualism, makes an odd statement in regard to this conclusion: "Although the subject of origins of life is within the province of biology, the scientific community does not consider origins of life a part of evolutionary theory. The theory of evolution assumes the existence of life and is directed to an explanation of how life evolved. Evolution does not presuppose the absence of a creator or God and the plain inference conveyed by Section 4 is erroneous."[121] This statement is odd because it is clearly inconsistent with what one finds in the literature.[122] Its oddness is likely the result of the judge equivocating on the term *evolution*. For if all that is meant by evolution is that biological species adapt over time to changing environments and pass on those adaptations genetically to their offspring, not even most creationists would disagree with that modest definition of evolution. Thus, Judge Overton is correct that the existence of God and evolution, if defined in this most unpretentious fashion, are not inconsistent.

However, as we have seen, the evolution Judge Overton defines is not what many citizens find objectionable, and it is not what is actually affirmed by proponents of evolutionary theory. What these citizens find objectionable, and what is actually affirmed in the literature, is the methodological naturalism that evolution presupposes and the ontological materialism it entails. Granted, *belief* (in the popular sense of unproven opinion) in the existence of God is not *logically* inconsistent with materialism, but the *existence* of God— if God is defined as the immaterial self-existent Creator of all that contingently exists—is *inconsistent* with materialism, the view that the natural universe is all that exists and all the entities in it can be accounted for by strictly material processes without resorting to any designer, Creator, or nonmaterial entity as an explanation for either any aspect of the natural universe or the universe as a whole. Given the fact that materialist explanations, according to the naturalists who dominate the academy, are the only ones accorded the privilege of being called "knowledge" (the others are pejoratively called "supernatural" or "miraculous" and are never permitted to count against materialist explanations), to say that *belief* in God's existence is not inconsistent with naturalistic evolution is to imply that God is not really an object of knowledge. Thus, Judge Overton can coherently claim that the existence of God, a nonmaterial reality, is consistent with the truth of evolution only if (1) he defines evolution in such a modest fashion that it is unobjectionable to even hard-line creationists or (2) he takes evolution to entail materialist metaphysics and defines belief in God in such a subjective fashion that God is not a proper object of knowledge.

In order to answer the second question—"Is creation-science really science?"—Judge Overton relied heavily on the expert testimony of scientists and other scholars who testified for the plaintiffs. According to the court, creation science is not really science, for it fails to qualify as science because it is inconsistent with (1) "more general descriptions of 'what scientists think' and 'what scientists do'" and (2) the five "essential characteristics of science."[123]

Concerning the first point, Judge Overton asserts:

> The scientific community consists of individuals and groups, nationally and internationally, who work independently in such varied fields as biology, paleontology, geology and astronomy. Their work is published and subject to review and testing by their peers. The journals for publication are both numerous and varied. There is, however, not one recognized scientific journal which has published an article espousing the creation science theory.[124]

It is interesting to note that this criticism would not apply to design theorists, for, as we have seen,[125] ID proponents have developed highly sophisticated arguments, have had their works published by prestigious presses and in academic journals, have aired their views among critics in the corridors of major universities and other institutions, and have been recognized by leading periodicals, both academic and nonacademic. Also, there are published peer-reviewed works (1986–2001) by non-ID scientists that raise questions about, and pose challenges to, aspects of evolution in three areas of study from which some ID proponents begin their case:[126] questions of pattern,[127] questions of process,[128] and questions about the central issue (i.e., the origin and nature of biological complexity).[129]

Moreover, the Supreme Court eleven years after *McLean,* in *Daubert v. Merrell Dow Pharmaceuticals, Inc.* (1993), held that "[t]he fact of publication (or lack thereof) in a peer reviewed journal thus will be a relevant, though not dispositive, consideration in assessing the scientific validity of a particular technique or methodology on which an opinion is premised."[130] "[Peer review p]ublication," according to the Court, "is not a sine qua non of admissibility; it does not necessarily correlate with reliability. . . , and in some instances well-grounded but innovative theories will not have been published." Those viewpoints that "are too particular, too new, or of too limited interest" may suffer the same fate.[131] In *Daubert* the Court rejected the widely held evidential standard of the D.C. Circuit case *Frye v. United States* (1923): a scientific opinion is reliable and therefore admissible if it is generally accepted within the scientific community.[132] The Supreme Court held in *Daubert* that the Frye standard, "absent from, and incompatible with, the Federal Rules of Evidence, should not be applied in federal trials."[133] This, of course, does not mean that there are no standards by which to assess scientific opinion; rather, it means that polling scientists, though relevant, is no longer sufficient or necessary. According to the Court, "[p]roposed testimony must be supported by appropriate validation— i.e., 'good grounds,' based on what is known." That is, "the requirement that an expert's testimony pertain to 'scientific knowledge' establishes a standard of evidentiary reliability."[134] This means that "the test of scientific legitimacy comes from the validation of the empirical research supporting the evidence."[135] It is, very simply and sensibly, a matter of arguments and their soundness and not a matter of popularity.

Concerning his second point, Judge Overton argues that creation science is inconsistent with the following definition of science:

(1) It is guided by natural law;
(2) It has to be explanatory by reference to natural law;
(3) It is testable against the empirical world;
(4) Its conclusions are tentative, i.e., are not necessarily the final word;
(5) It is falsifiable.[136]

This is an example of a *demarcation theory,* a theory by which one is able to demarcate science from nonscience. When Judge Overton applied this demarcation theory to creation science he concluded that because creation science postulates non-natural explanations for the existence of the universe, life, and the immutability of species (failing points 1, 2, and 3), relies exclusively on creationist writings (failing points 1, 2, and 4), and is "dogmatic, absolutist and never subject to revision" (failing points 4 and 5),[137] creation science is not science.

Although relying on expert testimony of philosopher of biology Michael Ruse,[138] Judge Overton's use and application of a demarcation theory was, and is, anachronistic.[139] In fact, some philosophers of science, though agreeing that creationism ought not to be part of public school science curricula, were highly critical of this aspect of his opinion.[140] Ruse himself has since tempered,[141] though it is difficult to say whether he has actually repudiated, his Arkansas testimony.[142] For these reasons, as well as the fact that this demarcation theory may be employed against design theory in a future court case, I summarize some, but by no means all, of the problems one may raise against Overton's analysis.

Judge Overton's Demarcation Theory Is Self-Refuting.[143] If these five characteristics are essential to science, then Overton's demarcation theory is itself not science, and thus, on its own grounds, ought not to be taught in public school science classes or employed by public school educators, state legislatures, or judges as a means to distinguish science from nonscience. After all, Overton's standard is not "guided by natural law," not "explanatory by reference to natural law," and not "testable against the empirical world." For it is a theory *about* science resulting, presumably, from thoughtful and sustained philosophical reflection. And its conclusions are not tentative and it is not falsifiable, for it is being employed as the absolute standard by which to assess the scientific status of other theories.

If, however, the supporter of this demarcation theory were to concede that it may not be the final word on the matter and is thus falsifiable, then it is unclear why one could not reject this demarcation theory and replace it with a better one on the grounds that one has good philosophical and scientific reasons to reject methodological naturalism and ontological materialism, as design theorists claim they have, and thus jettison (or at least amend) points 1, 2, and perhaps 3.

If, of course, the defender of this demarcation theory were to reply to this criticism and concede that her theory is not scientific, but philosophical, that it is a theory *about* rather than *of* science, then she would be admitting that it is not inappropriate to bring into the study and analysis of scientific theories philosophical arguments and other considerations when assessing the conceptual fruitfulness, empirical fitness, and/or rationality of any theory.[144] But this would mean that ID, for example, could not be dismissed as unscientific simply because it does not presuppose the materialism presupposed in, and the ontological materialism entailed by points 1, 2, and 3 of Judge Overton's demarcation theory, for the arguments for ID challenge that very presupposition (and its entailment), a presupposition (and entailment) that is philosophical and not scientific.

Judge Overton's Criteria Are Seriously Flawed. In addition to the above conceptual problem with Judge Overton's criteria, the work of philosopher of science Larry Laudan is instructive. He is one of many scholars who has challenged the criteria themselves as well as the prospect of developing any demarcation criteria at all.[145]

(1) Concerning points 3 ("It is testable against the empirical world"), 4 ("Its conclusions are tentative, i.e., are not necessarily the final word"), and 5 ("It is falsifiable"), Laudan maintains that "they are of dubious merit."[146]

First, he points out that creation science makes empirical claims and predictions: the earth is remarkably young, the geological features of earth are the result of Noah's flood, variability of species is limited, human fossils "must be plaeontologically co-extensive with the record of lower animals," and so on. "In brief," writes Laudan, "these claims are testable, they have been tested, and they failed the tests."[147] Applying Laudan's observation to design theory,

> ID is empirical insofar as its proponents claim that it is able to account for certain phenomena in the natural world and that empirical data may count against it. Of course, design theorists admit that their view is inconsistent with methodological naturalism and ontological materialism. But that fact has no bearing whatsoever on the plausibility of the arguments for ID. (*See* chapter 3.)

Second, Judge Overton's concern about the dogmatism of creation science and its unrevisability in the face of contrary evidence is flawed as well. For example, "[i]f the claims of modern-day creationists are compared with those of their nineteenth-century counterparts, significant shifts in orientation and assertion are evident." Citing the fact that creationists now allow for greater variability of species changes, "[c]reationists do, in fact, change their minds from time to time."[148] Even if Judge Overton were referring only to some of creation science's core assumptions (e.g., there was a worldwide flood, a Supreme Being created the universe out of nothing, and humans did not descend from lower life forms), its resistance to theoretical modification is not unique in the history of science. "[H]istorical and sociological researches on science," Laudan points out, "strongly suggest that the scientists of any epoch likewise regard some of their beliefs as so fundamental as not to be open to repudiation or negotiation." Laudan cites some examples:

> Would Newton, for instance, have been tentative about the claim that there were forces in the world? Are quantum mechanicians willing to contemplate giving up the uncertainty relation? Are physicists willing to specify circumstances under which they would give up energy conservation? Numerous historians and philosophers of science (e.g., Kuhn, Mitroff, Feyerabend, Lakatos) have documented the existence of a certain degree of dogmatism about core commitments in scientific research and have argued that

such dogmatism plays a constructive role in promoting the aims of science. I am not denying that there may be subtle but important differences between the dogmatism of scientists and that exhibited by many creationists; but one does not even begin to get at those differences by pretending that science is characterized by an uncompromising openmindedness.[149]

The work of the highly influential historian and philosopher of science Thomas Kuhn is critical in this regard. Although Laudan makes a brief mention of Kuhn's work, it is essential that the reader understand the importance of Kuhn's views as they pertain to demarcation theories in general and Judge Overton's criteria in particular.

According to Kuhn, scientific investigation of any kind must take place within the framework of a paradigm. A paradigm, explains Kuhn, is that which the community of scientists has tacitly accepted in order to perform, what he calls, normal science. Examples of paradigms include "'Ptolemaic astronomy' (or 'Copernican'), 'Aristotelian dynamics' (or 'Newtonian'), 'corpuscular optics' (or 'wave optics'), and so on."[150] Within these frameworks, the scientist conducts experiments, makes predictions, proposes explanations of phenomena, etc. This is normal science.

Within normal science, experiments and predictions succeed and fail, but the paradigm remains intact. As long as scientists remain within the confines of the paradigm, all is well. For Kuhn, a paradigm determines the nature of the problems that normal science must solve. The paradigm is the "jaundiced eye" of the scientist by which he "sees" everything as yellow (i.e., the problems that are important).[151]

However, paradigms have not remained constant, but have shifted (i.e., from Ptolemy to Copernicus, Newton to Einstein, etc.). When scientists shift from one paradigm to another, Kuhn calls this revolutionary science (in contrast to normal science). These revolutions are preceded by a period of scientific crisis, which occurs whenever there is continued failure in the normal problem-solving activity within a paradigm structure. Writes Kuhn: "Furthermore, except for the case of Copernicus in which factors external to science played a particularly large role, that breakdown and the proliferation of theories that is its sign occurred no more than a decade or two before the new theory's enunciation. The novel theory seems a direct response to crisis."[152]

What makes Kuhn's distinction between revolutionary and normal science problematic for demarcation theories, such as Judge Overton's, is due to what Kuhn calls the incommensurability of rival paradigms and their resistance to falsification. For Kuhn, "[p]hilosophers of science have repeatedly demonstrated that more than one theoretical construction can always be placed upon a given collection of data." In addition, "[n]o process yet disclosed by the historical study of scientific development at all resembles the methodological stereotype of falsification with direct comparison with nature."[153] And whenever anomalies arise that appear to falsify the paradigm, scientists "will devise numerous articulations and *ad hoc* modifications of their theory in order to eliminate any apparent conflict."[154]

Thus, supporters of ID may argue that normal science's resistance to ID may be more the result of a prior commitment to a materialist paradigm and an embracing of ad hoc and promissory note hypotheses to protect that paradigm when discordant data are recognized, rather than a result of critical analysis of the arguments proposed by design theorists.[155]

(2) Concerning points 1 ("It is guided by natural law") and 2 ("It has to be explanatory in reference to natural law") of Judge Overton's criteria, Laudan understands these points to mean "that it is inappropriate and unscientific to postulate the existence of any process or fact which cannot be explained in terms of some known scientific laws—for instance, the creationists' assertion that there are outer limits to the change of species 'cannot be explained by natural law.'"[156] According to Laudan, the flaw in this reasoning lies with its mistaken notion "that an existence claim (e.g., there was a worldwide flood) is unscientific until we have found the laws on which the alleged phenomenon depends."[157] He cites a number of examples:

> Galileo and Newton took themselves to have established the existence of gravitational phenomena, long before anyone was able to give a causal or explanatory account of gravitation. Darwin took himself to have established the existence of natural selection almost a half-century before geneticists were able to lay out the law of heredity on which natural selection depended. If we took the *McLean* opinion criterion seriously, we should have to say that Newton and Darwin were unscientific; and, to take an example from our own time, it would follow that plate tectonics is unscientific because we have not yet identified the laws of physics and chemistry which account for the dynamics of crustal motion.[158]

For Laudan, what makes the creationist claims wrong is that there is no evidence for them, not whether these claims cannot be accounted for or explained by scientific laws. But, ironically, in order for one to make this charge one must abandon the charges that creationism is neither testable nor falsifiable.[159] Along the same lines, other philosophers of science have argued that *historical sciences,* such as geology, archeology, and paleontology, are no less sciences than physics or chemistry simply because the former do not rely on laws as explanations for phenomena

but rather reconstruct the past grounded in inferences based on knowledge of the causal powers and forces of particular entities. Historical sciences are sciences.[160]

Although there are other objections, not raised by Laudan,[161] that one
may raise against points 1 and 2 of Judge Overton's criteria, what we
have covered so far should suffice. Nevertheless, it is important to note
that design theorists affirm that if their arguments are correct, then material nonagent causes cannot account for all the phenomena in the natural world. But in order to evaluate the plausibility of their case, they
suggest that their arguments be weighed on their own merits rather than
rejected a priori because they are inconsistent with a particular demarcation theory. To paraphrase Laudan: the core issue is not whether Intelligent Design satisfies some undemanding and highly controversial definitions of what is scientific; the real question is whether the existing
evidence provides stronger arguments for materialism than for Intelligent Design.[162]

In any event, Judge Overton concludes, based on two reasons (the second
of which we just extensively covered), that creation science is religion because it is not science.[163] And given the court's conclusion that Act 590 has
no secular purpose (that is, it fails the first prong of the Lemon test), the Act
advances religion and therefore violates the second prong of the Lemon test
as well.

Judge Overton ends his Lemon test analysis by concluding that Act 590 violates the third prong as well—does the statute foster an excessive government entanglement with religion? He argues that because creation science is
derived from the Bible, "[t]here is no way teachers can teach the Genesis account of creation in a secular manner." And if the State attempted to enforce
this statute it would involve the State in constant monitoring of classrooms in
order to make sure there was no religious instruction going on. And because
it would also require the State to extract and remove religious references from
possible texts and curricula, it would "require State officials to make delicate
religious judgments."[164] In sum, "[t]hese continuing involvements of State officials in questions and issues of religion create an excessive and prohibited
entanglement with religion."[165]

C. SUMMARY OF CHAPTER ONE

In section A of this chapter, we defined the terms *creationism, evolution,* and
intelligent design. These definitions are important, for much of the confusion

over the teaching of origins in public schools is the result of the participants not clearly defining or understanding what the others mean when they use these terms.

In section B we reviewed three court cases as well as the Supreme Court's Establishment Clause jurisprudence (including the Lemon test). We discovered, among other things, that the near absolute deference to state authority concerning matters of education that one finds in *Scopes* is rejected in both *Epperson* and *McLean*. Although the latter two courts conceded the presumption of state authority, they both concluded that such deference may be trumped if the state has policies whose primary (or overriding) purpose is to advance religion. There were four concerns that were important to both courts in their assessing of these statutes:

The statute's historical continuity with *Scopes* as well as the creation/evolution battles throughout the twentieth century.

How closely the curricular content required by the statute paralleled the creation story in Genesis, and/or how closely the curricular content prohibited by the statute is proscribed because it is inconsistent with the creation story in Genesis.

The motives of those who supported the statutes in the legislature and/or the public square.

Whether the statutes were legitimate means to achieve appropriate state ends.

In applying these four concerns, both courts concluded that the statutes they were evaluating were inconsistent with the Supreme Court's First Amendment jurisprudence. The pre-Lemon test *Epperson* Court held that the statute in question violated state neutrality on religion; the statute also employed an illegitimate means (criminalizing the teaching of a scientific theory) in order to achieve an inappropriate end (establishing religion in public school curricula). In *McLean,* the federal district court, applying the Lemon test, also evaluated the statute in light of the four concerns listed above, concluding that the statute failed every prong of the Lemon test; and since the statute had no secular purpose, the state's ends were inappropriate (teaching a religious doctrine as part of public school curricula) and its means illegitimate (by requiring that creationism be taught for the sake of "balance"). We also carefully assessed the *McLean* definition of science (i.e., a demarcation theory to distinguish between science from nonscience), for it may be employed in a future court case to argue that ID is not science and thus religion. We concluded, however, that the *McLean* definition is seriously flawed and has been challenged and rejected by philosophers of science who are not sympathetic to either ID or creationism. In chapter 3 we briefly return to this issue and examine the possibility of ID opponents proposing a demarcation theory to exclude design theory.

As we shall see, the above four concerns are the basis by which the Supreme Court strikes down the Louisiana statute in *Edwards*. However, unlike the judge in *McLean*, the Court is much more circumspect and does not delve into questions concerning the scientific status of either creationism or evolution. In addition, the Court seems to leave open the possibility that if a statute were crafted in a way that would adequately answer the four concerns listed above, that statute would pass constitutional muster.

NOTES

1. For Aristotle, "God" was a theoretical entity, an Unmoved Mover, he posited to explain the motion of the universe. God was not an object of worship. *See* Aristotle, *Physics,* VII, 311, a, 4; Aristotle, *Metaphysics,* XII, 6, 1071, b, 2.

2. Phillip E. Johnson, *Darwin on Trial* (Chicago: Regnery/Gateway, 1991), 4. For a defense of young-earth creationism, *see* Paul Nelson and John Mark Reynolds, "Young Earth Creationism," in *Three Views on Creation and Evolution,* ed. J. P. Moreland and John Mark Reynolds (Grand Rapids, MI: Zondervan, 2000).

3. Robert C. Newman, "Progressive Creationism ('Old Earth Creationism')," in *Three Views on Creation and Evolution,* 105.

4. Walter L. Bradley, "Response to Robert C. Newman," in *Three Views on Creation and Evolution,* 135 (emphasis added).

5. For a defense of theistic evolution, *see* Howard J. Van Till, "The Fully Gifted Creation ('Theistic Evolution')," in *Three Views on Creation and Evolution.*

6. *See* William A. Dembski, "Introduction: Mere Creation," in *Mere Creation: Science, Faith and Intelligent Design,* ed. William A. Dembski (Downers Grove, IL: InterVarsity Press, 1998), 19–23.

7. *See* chapter 2 of this present text.

8. There are disputes among scientists and other scholars over the precise meaning of Darwinism and neo-Darwinism (or what is called the "Darwinian synthesis"). Because this is not a book on the complexities and schools of thought on that important topic, let me suggest the following works for further study: Stephen Jay Gould, "Darwinism and the Expansion of Evolutionary Theory," in *Philosophy of Biology,* ed. Michael Ruse (Amherst, NY: Prometheus, 1998); Michael Ruse, *The Darwinian Paradigm: Essays on Its History, Philosophy, and Religious Implications* (New York: Routledge, 1989), 118–145 (critically examining Gould's theory of "punctuated equilibrium," an alternative to Darwinian gradualism); Douglas J. Futuyama, *Science on Trial: The Case for Evolution* (New York: Pantheon Books, 1983), 23–43; Antony Flew, *Darwinian Evolution,* 2nd ed. (New Brunswick, NJ: Transaction Books, 1997), 1–72; Michael Ruse, *Can a Darwinian Be a Christian?: The Relationship between Science and Religion* (New York: Cambridge University Press, 2001), 28–32 (Ruse points out that "[t]here are some who argue that selection is fine as far it goes but that

there is much in the living world that lies beyond the scope of this mechanism. In particular, it is claimed at the molecular level, below the grasp of selection, one has a great deal of random, directionless change. Evolution in this respect is 'non-Darwinian'" [31]); and Michael Ruse, *The Evolution Wars: A Guide to the Debates* (Santa Barbara, CA: ABC-CLIO, 2000), 231–260.

9. Charles Darwin, *The Origin of Species,* a facsimile of the 1st ed. (1859), intro. Ernst Mayr (Cambridge, MA: Harvard University Press, 1964).

10. *See* Darwin, *The Origin of Species,* 80–130.

11. Darwin, *The Origin of Species,* 61.

12. Richard Dawkins, *The Blind Watchmaker* (New York: Norton, 1986), 5–6.

13. Flew, *Darwinian Evolution,* 42.

14. Futuyama, *Science on Trial,* 95, quoting from Darwin, *The Origin of Species,* 484 (emphasis added).

15. The "Big Bang" is the dominant theory of the origin of the universe in cosmology: "The presently accepted view . . . suggests that at a distant time in the past the whole universe was a small sphere of concentrated energy/matter. This substance then exploded in a big bang to form hydrogen first and then eventually all the galaxies and stars" (Monroe W. Strickberger, *Evolution,* 3rd ed. [Sudbury, MA: Jones & Bartlett, 2000], 76).

16. Strickberger, *Evolution,* 3rd ed. In this widely used textbook, now in its 3rd edition, the author presents in great detail in twenty-five chapters this grand materialist explanation.

17. Futuyama, *Science on Trial,* 114.

18. James Rachels, *Created from Animals: The Moral Implications of Darwinism* (New York: Oxford University Press, 1990), 110.

19. Paul Churchland, *Matter and Consciousness: A Contemporary Introduction to the Philosophy of Mind* (Cambridge, MA: M.I.T. Press, 1984), 12.

20. See Michael Ruse, "Creation-Science Is Not Science," in *Creationism, Science, and the Law: The Arkansas Case,* ed. Marcel C. LaFollette (Cambridge, MA: M.I.T. Press, 1983).

21. Michael Ruse, *Philosophy of Biology Today* (Albany, NY: State University of New York Press, 1988), 74.

22. Michael Ruse, "The New Evolutionary Ethics," in *Evolutionary Ethics,* ed. Matthew H. Nitecki and Doris V. Nitecki (Albany, NY: State University of New York Press, 1993), 148.

23. Ruse, *The Darwinian Paradigm,* 268–269. (citations omitted).

24. George Gaylord Simpson, *The Meaning of Evolution: A Study of the History of Life and of Its Significance for Man,* rev. ed. (New Haven, CT: Yale University Press, 1967), 279. It is interesting to note that Simpson concedes that there could be a First Cause, or God, but that such a Being has no explanatory value in accounting for life's origin nor intervenes in history: "There is neither need nor excuse for postulation of nonmaterial intervention in the origin of life, the rise of man, or any other part of the long history of the material cosmos. Yet the origin of that cosmos and the causal principles of its history remain unexplained and inaccessible to science. Here is hidden the First Cause sought by theology and philosophy. The First Cause is not known and

I suspect it will never be known to living man. We may, if we are so inclined, worship it in our own ways, but we certainly do not comprehend it" (Simpson, *The Meaning of Evolution,* 344–345).

25. Strickberger, *Evolution,* 3rd ed., 70.

26. Francis Crick, *The Astonishing Hypothesis: The Scientific Search for the Soul* (New York: C. Scribner's Sons, 1994), 5–7.

27. For example, Futuyama writes: "By providing materialistic, mechanistic explanations, instead of miraculous ones, for the characteristics of plants and animals, Darwin brought biology out of the realm of theology and into the realm of science. For miraculous spiritual forces fall outside the province of science; all of science is the study of material causation" (Futuyama, *Science on Trial,* 37). What Futuyama is suggesting is that Darwin's theory resulted in a shift in the dominant "scientific episteme." According to J. P. Moreland, "a scientific episteme is not just a view within science about the nature of living organisms and their development. It is also a second-order philosophical view about science that defines the nature, limits, metaphysics, and epistemology of 'good' science" (J. P. Moreland, *Christianity and the Nature of Science* [Grand Rapids, MI: Baker Book House, 1989], 215).

28. See Crick, *The Astonishing Hypothesis,* 7 ("Many educated people, especially in the Western world, also share the belief that the soul is a metaphor and that there is no personal life either before conception or after death"); Ruse, *Can a Darwinian Be a Christian,* 153 ("If evolution be true, then in some very real sense we humans are all part of one big family, no matter what our numbers. For the Christian, is this not the fulfillment of God's promise to Abraham? 'I will make of you a great nation'. . . . Christians should not read this literally. Rather, as one could read the creation stories metaphorically—as telling us of God's relationship to humans and our obligations to nature—so one could read this promise metaphorically, as referring to the family status of humankind.")

29. "God-of-the-gaps," the philosophical equivalent of Lochnerizing in Supreme Court jurisprudence, is said to occur when a scientist, unable to develop a natural explanation for an observation or event, resorts to God or some other supernatural agency or power as an explanation. When the scientist or a future scientist discovers a natural explanation, God is no longer needed to fill the gap and so is discarded as an explanation. So, according to conventional wisdom, a God-of-the-gaps strategy short-circuits scientific investigation. For analyses of this problem, *see* John Mark Reynolds, "God of the Gaps: Intelligent Design and Bad Apologetic Advice," in *Mere Creation,* 313–331; and J. P. Moreland, "Theistic Science and Methodological Naturalism," *The Creation Hypothesis: Scientific Evidence for an Intelligent Designer,* ed. J. P. Moreland (Downers Grove, IL: InterVarsity Press, 1994), 59–60.

30. An implicit example of this is John Searle's candid comments about why just about every philosopher of mind embraces some view of the mind that relies on a materialist (or physicalist) construal of the human person, even though it seems inconsistent with our well-grounded intuitions: "How is it that so many philosophers and cognitive scientists can say so many things that, to me at least, seem obviously false? . . . I believe one of the unstated assumptions behind the current batch of views is that they represent the only scientifically acceptable alternatives to the antiscientism that went

with traditional dualism, the belief in the immortality of the soul, spiritualism, and so on. Acceptance of the current views is motivated not so much by an independent conviction of their truth as by a terror of what are apparently the only alternatives. That is, the choice we are tacitly presented with is between a 'scientific' approach, as represented by one or another of the current versions of 'materialism,' and an 'unscientific' approach, as represented by Cartesianism or some other traditional religious conception of the mind" (John Searle, *The Rediscovery of the Mind* [Cambridge, MA: M.I.T. Press, 1992], 3–4).

31. In the preface to a 1984 pamphlet published by the National Academy of Sciences, its then-president Dr. Frank Press writes, "It is false . . . to think that the theory of evolution represents an irreconcilable conflict between religion and science. A great many religious leaders accept evolution on scientific grounds without relinquishing their belief in religious principles. As stated in a resolution by the Council of the National Academy of Sciences in 1981, however, 'Religion and science are separate and mutually exclusive realms of human thought whose presentation in the same context leads to misunderstanding of both scientific theory and religious belief'" (National Academy of Sciences, *Science and Creationism: A View for the National Academy of Sciences* (1984), 5–6, *available at* http://stills.nap.edu/books/030903440X/html/ [February 8, 2001] [NAS]). I respond to a version of this argument in chapter 4, section B, part 1.a.

32. National Association of Biology Teachers, *Statement on Teaching Evolution,* available at http://www.nabt.org/sub/position_statements/evolution.asp (June 30, 2002).

33. According to Ronald Numbers, "[a]lthough individually [design theorists] have espoused a wide range of views on origins (from [Michael] Denton's and Behe's virtual theistic evolution to Nelson's young-earth creationism), collectively they have staked out a position between theistic evolutionism . . . and scientific creationism, American Fundamentalism's ill-conceived effort to base science on Scripture" (Ronald L. Numbers, *Darwinism Comes to America* [Cambridge, MA: Harvard University Press, 1998], 18). Design theorist William Dembski maintains that "[i]ntelligent design is logically compatible with everything from utterly discontinuous creation (e.g., God intervening at every conceivable point to create new species) to the most far-ranging evolution (e.g., God seamlessly melding all organisms together into one great tree of life). For intelligent design the first question is not how organisms came to be (though . . . this is a vital question for intelligent design) but whether organisms demonstrate clear, empirically detectable marks of being intelligently caused. In principle an evolutionary process can exhibit such marks of intelligence as much as any act of special creation. That said, intelligent design is incompatible with what typically is meant by theistic evolution. . . . When boiled down to its scientific content . . . theistic evolution is no different from atheistic evolution, treating only undirected natural processes in the origin and development of life" (Dembski, "Introduction: Mere Creation," 19–20).

34. *See* introduction, section A of this present volume.

35. Chapter 27, Tenn. Acts 1925; Tenn. Code Ann. s. 49—1922 (1966 Repl. Vol.).

36. Edward J. Larson, *Trial and Error: The American Controversy over Creation and Evolution* (New York: Oxford University Press, 1985), 58, 60 (notes omitted).

37. The American Civil Liberties Union, *The Fight for Free Speech* (New York: American Civil Liberties Union, 1921), 17–18.

38. For an overview of the prosecution and defense arguments, *see* Larson, *Trial and Error,* 58–72.

39. The Court stated that Louisiana defended its statute by appealing to the secular purpose of furthering academic freedom (*Edwards v. Aguillard*, 482 U.S. 578, 586–589 [1987]). The Court, however, rejected this argument because (1) Louisiana teachers already had academic freedom, and thus, the statute as a means to that noble end was inadequate, and (2) the Court did not think that this claimed purpose was the real purpose, which was to advance religion (*Edwards,* 482 U.S., 586–589). Nevertheless, the Court affirmed in *Epperson v. Arkansas* that academic freedom is a vital liberty grounded in the Constitution (*Epperson v. Arkansas,* 393 U.S. 97, 104–106 [1968]).

40. *See* chapter 2 of this book.

41. Larson, *Trial and Error,* 67 (note omitted).

42. *Scopes v. State,* 289 S.W. 363, 363 (1927).

43. Larson writes: "Both sides went to Dayton seeking to use a judicial forum to influence public opinion. Their arguments addressed the world. The world listened. Hundreds of reporters descended on Dayton from across America and Europe. Pioneering live radio broadcasts and newsreel footage carried the event with unprecedented intimacy to a fascinated public. Millions followed the progress of the eight-day trial, which was billed as a battle between religion and science. . . . When the *Scopes* court convened on July 10, 1925, the Dayton town fathers could only marvel at the success of their little publicity stunt" (Larson, *Trial and Error,* 63).

44. George Marsden, *Fundamentalism and American Culture: The Shaping of Twentieth-Century Evangelicalism: 1870–1925* (New York: Oxford University Press, 1980), 185–186.

45. Russell D. Owen, "Issues and Personalities, in the Significance of the Scopes Trial," *Current History Illustrated,* 22 (1925), 883.

46. Initiated Act No. 1, Ark. Acts 1929; Ark. Stat. Ann. §§ 80—1627, 80–1628 (1960 Repl. Vol.).

47. Ark. Stat. Ann. §§ 80–1627.

48. Ark. Stat. Ann. §§ 80–1628.

49. *Epperson v. Arkansas,* 393 U.S. 97, 99 (1968) (no citation for quoted text).

50. It should be noted, however, when *Epperson* was decided in 1968 there was "no record of any prosecutions in Arkansas under this statute. It is possible that the statute is presently [in 1968] more of a curiosity than a vital fact of life" (*Epperson,* 393 U.S., 101).

51. *Epperson,* 393 U.S., 100.

52. *Epperson,* 393 U.S., 100.

53. From the opinion of the Chancery Court, as quoted in *Epperson,* 393 U.S., 100. There is no specific citation, for according to the *Epperson* Court, "the opinion of the Chancery Court is not officially reported" (*Epperson,* 393 U.S., 100).

54. 242 Ark. 922, 416 S.W. 2d 322 (1967), as quoted in *Epperson,* 393 U.S., 101 n. 6.

55. "I would either strike down the Arkansas Act as too vague to enforce, or remand to the State Supreme Court for clarification of its holding and opinion" (*Ep-

person, 393 U.S., 114 [Black, J. concurring]); "Since I believe that no State could constitutionally forbid a teacher 'to mention Darwin's theory at all,' and since Arkansas may, or may not, have done just that, I conclude that the statute before us is so vague as to be invalid under the Fourteenth Amendment" (*Epperson,* 393 U.S., 116 [Stewart, J. concurring]).

56. *Epperson,* 393 U.S., 103 (Fortas, J.) (explaining the vagueness of the statute but concluding that "we do not rest our decision upon the asserted vagueness of the statute. On either interpretation of its language, Arkansas' statute cannot stand").

57. *Epperson,* 393 U.S., 103.

58. *Epperson,* 393 U.S., 107 (note omitted); *Epperson,* 393 U.S., 108 (note omitted).

59. The Court admitted that the Arkansas statute had less explicit language than the one in Tennessee. That is, there were no references to the Bible or the Book of Genesis in the statute itself (*Epperson,* 393 U.S., 108–109). However, "in its brief, the State admits that the Arkansas statute was passed with the holding of the Scopes case in mind" (*Epperson,* 393 U.S., 109 n. 18). In addition, the Court cites a 1928 advertisement as well as 1928 newspaper letters from the public showing the religious underpinnings of the Arkansas statute (*Epperson,* 393 U.S., 109 n. 16).

60. *Epperson,* 393 U.S., 113. (Black, J., concurring). In support of this contention, Justice Black cites *United States v. O'Brien,* 391 U.S. 367, 382–383 (1968). Justice Antonin Scalia takes up the same argument in his dissent in *Edwards,* 482 U.S., 636–639.

61. *Epperson,* 393 U.S., 107.

62. *John Burstyn, Inc v. Wilson,* 343 U.S. 495, 505 (1952), quoted in *Epperson,* 393 U.S. at 107.

63. *Epperson,* 393 U.S., 104–106. Justice Fortas writes: "Today's problem is capable of resolution in the narrower terms of the First Amendment's prohibition of laws respecting an establishment of religion or prohibiting the free exercise thereof" (*Epperson,* 393 U.S., 106).

64. *Epperson,* 393 U.S., 103–104 (note omitted). In the note following this quote, Justice Fortas cites a series of prior cases that are well-known for their call for government neutrality on matters of religion: *Everson v. Board of Education,* 330 U.S. 1 (1947); *People of State of Ill. ex rel McCollum v. Board of Education,* 333 U.S. 203 (1948); *Zorach v. Clauson,* 343 U.S. 306 (1952); *Fowler v. State of Rhode Island,* 345 U.S. 67 (1953); and *Torcaso v. Watkins,* 367 U.S. 488. (1961).

65. *Epperson,* 393 U.S., 109.

66. *Epperson ,* 393 U.S., 113 (Black, J., concurring).

67. *Segraves v. California Bd. of Educ.,* No. 278978 (Cal. Super. Ct. June 12, 1981). *See* Peter Gwynne et al., "'Scopes II' in California," *Newsweek* (March 16, 1981), 67; and Kenneth M. Pierce, "Putting Darwin Back in the Dock; 'Scientific' Creationists Challenge the Theory of Evolution," *Time* (March 16, 1981), 80. A special thank you to one of my M.A. students at Trinity International University, Daniel J. DeWitt, J.D., who was able to track down the text of the Segraves case on the Internet.

68. Gwynne, "Scopes II," 67.

69. *Segraves*, n. p.

70. Bill Carlson, "Antidogmatism Policy: But What about Their Rights?" *EducationNews.org: The World's Leading Source of EducationNews,* available at http://www.educationnews.org/antidogmatism_policy_but_what _ab.htm (April 13, 2002).

71. Alvin Plantinga, "Creation and Evolution: A Modest Proposal," in *Intelligent Design Creationism and Its Critics: Philosophical, Theological, and Scientific Perspectives,* ed. Robert T. Pennock (Cambridge, MA: M.I.T. Press, 2001). For a reply to this essay, see Robert T. Pennock, "Reply to Plantinga's 'Modest Proposal'," in *Intelligent Design Creationism.*

72. Citing the testimony of Dr. Mayer (no first name given) in support of its holding, the *Segraves* court seems to accept, with Plantinga, that epistemology is doing all the intellectual work. Unfortunately, Dr. Mayer's presentation, though superficially consistent with Plantinga's view, seems to imply that "knowledge" not derived from the hard sciences cannot count against the apparent deliverances of the hard sciences. For example, Mayer asserts, "I would not like to see my theology and my science to get mixed. I have never dealt with a scientific process where somebody says, 'I believe.' I have dealt with theological processes where one believes. In short, I think at that point you begin to mix epistemologies" (*Segraves,* n. p.). But what happens when "science" conflicts with "theology" when each is describing the exact same phenomenon, event, or entity? For example, the claim that there is an immaterial ground to the human being, such as a soul, is *inconsistent with* the claim of materialist philosophers of mind who argue that an exhaustive materialist accounting of the human person is in principle possible. Suppose I have good reasons to believe in the existence of the soul, a conclusion inconsistent with the deliverances of materialist science? Who wins? I suspect that Dr. Mayer would say that they are not in conflict but are two "different ways" of "knowing." He may *say* that, just as one may *say* that Fred is both married and a bachelor. But it is not clear how contrary accountings of precisely the same entity can *both be* accurately described as knowledge. Granted, one may offer categorically different descriptions of the same entity—e.g., an aesthetic one ("Mt. Rushmore contains the sculptures of four U.S. presidents") and a geological one ("Mt. Rushmore is composed of rock, sand, and granite and some vegetation")—but that is different than offering metaphysically inconsistent descriptions of the same entity— e.g., a materialist one ("Abraham Lincoln's person consisted entirely of matter") and an immaterial one ("Abraham Lincoln's person consisted of both soul and matter"). The conflicts arising in the debate over origins are more often than not like the latter rather than the former. Moreover, Dr. Mayer's distinction between theological and scientific knowledge is something he claims to know that is neither theology nor science, for it is a distinction arrived at through philosophical reflection.

73. *Segraves*, n.p.

74. State Board of Education, *Science Framework for California Public Schools Kindergarten through Grade Twelve* (Adopted February 6, 2002), 5 (*CSF* hereafter).

75. It does, however, mention "divine creation" (*CSF,* 5).

76. *See,* for example, Phillip E. Johnson, *Darwin on Trial* (Chicago: Regnery/Gateway, 1991), 140–144.

77. *CSF,* 5.

78. *CSF,* 5.

79. *CSF,* 5.

80. For example, *Smith v. Mississippi,* 242 So. 2d 692 (Miss. 1970) (similar to *Epperson*; struck down on First Amendment Establishment grounds Mississippi statute prohibiting the teaching of evolution in public schools); *Wright v. Houston Independent School District,* 366 F. Supp. 1208 (S. D. Tex. 1972) (ruled that students' complaint to enjoin the school district and state board from teaching evolution-only curriculum and requiring evolution-only textbooks failed to state a cause of action for which the court may grant relief, since the state did not deny plaintiffs free exercise of religion or equal protection and because the state did not prohibit them from opting out of the evolution-only lessons); *Daniels v. Waters,* 515 F. 2d 485 (6th Cir. 1975) (struck down on Establishment grounds a Tennessee statute that required that public school textbooks contain a disclaimer that all views of human origins are "theories" rather than "facts" and that textbooks must afford equal treatment to alternative theories and must include the Genesis account of creation as one of those theories; and if the Bible is used as a reference work rather than a textbook, no "theory" disclaimer shall be required to be placed in the Bible); and *Steel v. Waters,* 527 S. W. 2d 72 (Tenn. 1975) (concerns same Tennessee statute struck down in *Daniels,* and concurs with *Daniels* that the statute violates both the U.S. and Tennessee Constitutions).

81. *See Moore v. Gaston County Board of Education,* 357 F. Supp. 1037 (W.D. N.C. 1973). The Court ruled that an unpaid student teacher's dismissal violated his First Amendment right to academic freedom, and that the basis of his dismissal—the local parents' and teachers' objections to his agreement with Darwinism, disbelief in biblical literalism, and affirmation of personal agnosticism—violated the Establishment Clause of the First Amendment. I conscript this case for my purposes in chapter 2, section B, part 4 of this book.

82. Although the original purpose of the First Amendment was to restrain Congress ("*Congress* shall make no law respecting an establishment of religion"), the Supreme Court has incorporated the First Amendment through the Fourteenth Amendment and now applies the former to the states as well. The Court first incorporated the freedom of speech and press clauses, eventually incorporating the entire First Amendment. *See Gitlow v. New York,* 268 U.S. 652, 666 (1925) (freedom of speech and press "are among the fundamental personal rights and 'liberties' protected by the Due Process Clause of the Fourteenth Amendment from impairment by the states"); *Near v. Minnesota,* 283 U.S. 697, 707 (1931) ("It is no longer open to doubt that the liberty of the press and of speech is within the liberty safeguarded by the due process clause of the Fourteenth Amendment from invasion by state action"); *De Jorge v. Oregon,* 299 U.S. 353, 364 (1937) ("The right of peaceable assembly is a right cognate to those of free speech and free press as fundamental"); *Cantwell v. Connecticut,* 310 U.S. 296, 303–304 (1940) ("The First Amendment declares that Congress shall make no law respecting an establishment of religion or prohibiting the free exercise thereof. The Fourteenth Amendment has rendered legislatures of the States as incompetent as Congress to enact such laws"); and *Everson v. Board of Education,* 330 U.S. 1 (1947) (Justices unanimously agreed that the Establishment Clause applies to the states through the Fourteenth Amendment).

83. An informative and accessible essay on this topic is Douglas Laycock, "Formal, Substantive, and Disaggregated Neutrality toward Religion," *DePaul Law Review*, 39 (1990).

84. *Lemon v. Kurtzman*, 403 U.S. 602 (1971) (striking down as unconstitutional statutes in Pennsylvania and Rhode Island that involved public aid programs to private school teachers including parochial school teachers).

85. *Lemon*, 403 U.S., 612–613. Kern Alexander and M. David Alexander point out that "prior to 1970, the Supreme Court sought to determine state neutrality [concerning religion] with a two-part test which required that: (1) the action of the state not be intended to aid one religion or all religions and (2) the principle of primary effect of the program be one that 'neither advances nor inhibits religion.' In 1970 the Supreme Court added a third prong to the test, that the state must not foster 'an excessive government entanglement with religion [*Walz*, 397 U.S., 668]'" (Kern Alexander and M. David Alexander, *The Law of Schools, Students, and Teachers in a Nutshell* [St. Paul, MN: West Publishing, 1984], 100–101).

86. *Roemer v. Board of Public Works*, 426 U.S. 736, 747 (1976) (emphasis added).

87. *See*, for example, Steven V. Monsma, *Positive Neutrality: Letting Religious Freedom Ring* (Westport, CT: Greenwood Press, 1993); Robert Cord, *The Separation of Church and State: Historical Fact and Current Fiction* (New York: Lambeth Press, 1982), 169–211; Carl H. Esbeck, "Equal Treatment: Its Constitutional Status," in *Equal Treatment in a Pluralistic Society*, ed. Stephen V. Monsma and J. Christopher Soper (Grand Rapids, MI: Eerdmans, 1998); Michael W. McConnell, "The Origins and Historical Understanding of Free Exercise of Religion," *Harvard Law Review*, 103 (May 1990); Michael W. McConnell, "Should Congress Pass Legislation Restoring the Broader Interpretation of Free Exercise of Religion?" *Harvard Journal of Law & Public Policy*, 15 (1992); Michael W. McConnell, "Accommodation of Religion: An Update and a Response to the Critics," *George Washington Law Review*, 60 (March 1992).

88. *See*, for example, *Marsh v. Chambers*, 436 U.S. 783 (1983) (upheld "the Nebraska Legislature's practice of opening each legislative session with a prayer by a chaplain paid by the State," but did not apply the Lemon Test); *Lynch v. Donnelly*, 465 U.S. 668, 687–694 (1984) (O'Connor, J., concurring) (suggesting an "endorsement test"); *Mueller v. Allen*, 463 U.S. 388 (1983) (upheld Minnesota's policy that allowed taxpayers to deduct from gross income actual expenses incurred for textbooks, tuition, and transportation for dependents attending elementary and secondary schools whether public or nonpublic, maintaining that Lemon is settled law but is "no more than a signpost"); *Meek v. Pittinger*, 421 U.S. 349, 374 (1975) (Brennan, J., dissenting) (finding a fourth prong to the Lemon Test: "four years ago, the Court, albeit without express recognition of the fact, added a significant *fourth factor* to the test: 'A broader base of entanglement of yet a different character is presented by the divisive political potential of these state programs' [*Lemon*, 403 U.S., 622]"); *Wallace v. Jaffree*, 472 U.S. 38, 112 (1985) (Rehnquist, J., dissenting) (arguing that the Lemon test is "a constitutional theory [that] has no basis in the history of the amendment it seeks to interpret, it is difficult to apply, and yields unprincipled results");

Edwards, 482 U.S., 636–637 (Scalia, J., dissenting) (criticizing the "purpose" prong of the Lemon test).

89. *Lynch,* 465 U.S., 688 (O'Connor, J., concurring). O'Connor's endorsement test and versions of it defended by legal scholars have been criticized as well. *See,* for example, Steven D. Smith, "Symbols, Perceptions, and Doctrinal Illusions: Establishment Neutrality and the 'No Endorsement' Test," *Michigan Law Review,* 86 (November 1987); and Derek H. Davis, "Equal Treatment: A Christian Separationist Perspective," in *Equal Treatment,* 136–157.

90. *Wallace,* 472 U.S., 67 (O' Connor, J., concurring).

91. "Lemon's first prong focuses on the purpose that animated adoption of the Act. 'The purpose prong of the Lemon test asks whether government's actual purpose is to endorse or disapprove of religion' [*Lynch,* 465 U.S., 690] (O'Connor, J., concurring)" (*Edwards,* 482 U.S., 585).

92. *Lee v. Weisman,* 505 U.S. 577 (1992).

93. *Lee,* 505 U.S., 578, citing *Engel v. Vitale,* 370 U.S. 421 (1962) and *School District of Abington Township v. Schempp,* 374 U.S. 203 (1963).

94. "We can decide the case without reconsidering the general constitutional framework by which public schools' efforts to accommodate religion are measured. Thus we do not accept the invitation of petitioners and *amicus* the United States to reconsider our decision in *Lemon.* . . . The government involvement with religious activity in this case is pervasive, to the point of creating a state-sponsored and state-directed religious exercise in a public school. Conducting this formal religious observance conflicts with settled rules pertaining to prayer exercises for students, and that suffices to determine the question before us" (*Lee,* 505 U.S., 587).

95. "The Establishment Clause was inspired by the lesson that in the hands of government what might begin as a tolerant expression of religious views may end in a policy to indoctrinate and coerce" (*Lee,* 505 U.S., 577).

96. "The 'establishment of religion' clause of the First Amendment means at least this: Neither a state nor the Federal Government can set up a church. . . . Neither can force nor influence a person to go to or to remain away from church against his will or force him to profess a belief or disbelief in any religion. No person can be punished for entertaining or professing religious beliefs or disbeliefs, for church attendance or non-attendance" (*Everson,* 330 U.S., 15, 16).

97. *See,* for example, *Widmer v. Vincent,* 454 U.S. 263 (1981) (finding that a religious student group's free speech and association rights were violated when it was prohibited by a state university from meeting on campus); *Lamb's Chapel v. Center Moriches Union Free School District,* 508 U.S. 384 (1993) (ruling that it does not violate the Establishment Clause for a public school district to permit a church to show, after school hours and on school property, a religiously oriented film on family life); *Zobrest v. Catalina,* 113 U.S. 2462 (1993) (ruling that a school district may not refuse to supply a sign-language interpreter to a student at a religious high school when such government benefits are neutrally dispensed to students without regard to the public-nonpublic or sectarian-nonsectarian nature of the school); *Capitol Square Review Board v. Pinette,* 515 U.S. 753 (1995) (finding that it was content-based discrimination

for the government to prohibit a controversial organization from sponsoring a religious display in a public park); *Rosenberger v. The University of Virginia,* 515 U.S. 819 (1995) (ruling that it was a denial of college students' free speech rights, as well as a risk of nurturing hostility toward religion, to prohibit the students from using student funds for a religiously oriented publication); *Mitchell v. Helms,* 530 U.S. 793 (2000) (finding that direct funding to private schools including religious schools does not violate Establishment Clause, since the distribution is evenhanded and the use of the money to indoctrinate in religious schools cannot reasonably be attributed to government); *Mitchell,* 530 U.S. 836 (O'Connor, J., concurring) (finding that direct funding to private schools including religious schools does not violate Establishment Clause, since the distribution is evenhanded *and* there is no evidence that funds given to religious schools were used to indoctrinate).

98. "[W]e must draw lines with reference to the three main evils against which the Establishment Clause was intended to afford protection: 'sponsorship, financial support, and active involvement of the sovereign in religious activity'" (*Lemon,* 403 U.S., 612, quoting *Walz,* 397 U.S. at 668). *See also, Stone v. Graham,* 449 U.S. 39 (1980) (finding that required public school classroom posting of Ten Commandments, even with a disclaimer stating that it has no religious intent, is unconstitutional); *School District of Abington Township,* 374 U.S. (ruling that required teacher-led Bible-reading in public schools, even while allowing for parental permission not to participate, is unconstitutional); *Lee,* 505 U.S. (finding that public middle school's invitation to a local clergyman to perform an invocation and benediction at graduation ceremony is unconstitutional); and *County of Allegheny v. ACLU,* 492 U.S. 573 (1989) (ruling that a nativity display on city property, not surrounded by secular symbols, is unconstitutional because it sends the message that the county promotes and supports Christianity).

99. The Court writes in *Epperson* (393 U.S. 104, 105):

> Our courts . . . have not failed to apply the First Amendment's mandate in our educational system where essential to safeguard the fundamental values of freedom of speech and inquiry and of belief. By and large, public education in our Nation is committed to the control of state and local authorities. Courts do not and cannot intervene in the resolution of conflicts which arise in daily operation of school systems and which do not directly and sharply implicate basic constitutional values. On the other hand, "[t]he vigilant protection of constitutional freedoms is nowhere more vital than in the community of American schools" [Shelton v. Tucker, 364 U.S. 479, 487 (1960)]. . . . As this Court said in Keyishian v. Board of Regents [385 U.S. 589, 603 (1967)], the First Amendment "does not tolerate laws that cast a pall of orthodoxy over the classroom.". . . The Court . . . [has] acknowledged the State's power to prescribe the school curriculum, but it held [in Meyer v. Nebraska 262 U.S. 390 (1923)] that these were not adequate to support the restriction upon the liberty of teacher and pupil.

See William W. Van Alstyne, "Academic Freedom and the First Amendment in the Supreme Court of the United States: An Unhurried Historical Review," *Law & Contemporary Problems,* 53 (Summer 1990).

100. *See* chapter 2 in this present volume.

101. Gerald Gunther and Kathleen Sullivan, *Constitutional Law,* 13th ed. (Westbury, NY: Foundation Press, 1997), 1501. Cord argues that some version of the endorsement test seems to be more consistent with the views held by the congressional architects of the First Amendment. Granting that the First Amendment now applies to the states, Cord holds that "there appears to be no historical evidence that the First Amendment was intended to preclude Federal government aid to religion when it was provided on a nondiscriminatory basis" (Cord, *Separation of Church and State,* 15).

102. *See,* for example, Norman L. Geisler, A. F. Brooke II, and Mark J. Keough, *Creator in the Courtroom: Scopes II* (Milford, MI: Mott Media, 1982); *Creationism, Science, and the Law*; Langdon Gilkey, *Creationsim on Trial: Evolution and God at Little Rock* (Minneapolis: Winston Press, 1985); Robert V. Gentry, *Creation's Tiny Mystery,* 2nd ed. (Knoxville, TN: Earth Science Associates, 1988).

103. According to one account of the trial by an expert witness, "The Arkansas trial was appropriately billed by many as 'Scopes II.' Media attended from all over the world" (Geisler, *Creator,* ix).

104. Among the witnesses were theologians Langdon Gilkey and Francis Bruce Vawter, philosophers Michael Ruse and Norman L. Geisler, geneticist Francisco J. Ayala, paleontologist Stephen Jay Gould, biochemist William Scot Morrow, physicist Robert V. Gentry, astronomer and mathematician N. Chandra Wickramasinghe, and historian George Marsden.

105. Ark. Stat. Ann. s 80-1663, et seq. (1981 Supp.).

106. *McLean v. Arkansas Board of Education,* 529 F. Supp. 1255, 1255 (1982), quoting from the first sentence of the act.

107. "It is under this three part test that the evidence in this case must be judged. Failure on any of these grounds is fatal to the enactment" (*McLean,* 529 F. Supp., 1258).

108. There were four arguments, two proposed by the plaintiffs and two by the defendants, for which, the judge reasoned, there was "no need to reach legal conclusions" (*McLean,* 529 F. Supp., 1272–1273), even though he does comment on them in dicta. The two plaintiffs' arguments were: (1) The word "balanced" in the act is too vague, and (2) the act violates the academic freedom of teachers. The two defendants' arguments were: (1) Evolution is itself a religion and thus the teaching of it in public schools violates the free exercise rights of students, and (2) a sizable majority of Americans believe that creation science should be taught if evolution is taught. See *McLean,* 529 F. Supp., 1273–1274.

109. The court argued that "the State of Arkansas, like a number of states whose citizens have relatively homogeneous religious beliefs, has a long history of official opposition to evolution which is motivated by adherence to Fundamentalist beliefs in the inerrancy of the book of Genesis. This history is documented in Justice Fortas' opinion in *Epperson,* 393 U.S. at 89" (*McLean,* 529 F. Supp., 1263).

110. The judge is referring to Paul Ellwanger, founder of Citizens for Fairness in Education (Anderson, South Carolina), a respiratory therapist who drafted the model act that became Act 590. Ellwanger, on a number occasions, including in

42   *Chapter One*

correspondence with people in politics, clergy, and the press, revealed, according to the judge, that he was "motivated by his opposition to the theory of evolution and his desire to see the Biblical version of creation taught in the public schools" (*McLean,* 529 F. Supp., 1263).

111. According to Judge Overton, Senator James L. Holsted, "a self-described 'born again' Fundamentalist, introduced the act in the Arkansas Senate" (*McLean,* 529 F. Supp., 1262).

112. *McLean,* 529 F. Supp.,1263. Judge Overton writes in a note: "Senator Holsted testified that he holds to a literal interpretation of the Bible; that the bill was compatible with his religious beliefs; that the bill does favor the position of literalists; that his religious convictions were a factor in his sponsorship of the bill; and that he stated publicly to the Arkansas Gazette (though not on the floor of the Senate) contemporaneously with the legislative debate that the bill does presuppose the existence of a divine creator. There is no doubt that Senator Holsted knew he was sponsoring the teaching of a religious doctrine. His view was that the bill did not violate the First Amendment because, he saw it, it did not favor one denomination over another" (*McLean,* 529 F. Supp., 1263 n. 14).

113. *McLean,* 529 F. Supp., 1264.

114. *McLean,* 529 F. Supp., 1263, citing *Committee for Public Education & Religious Liberty v. Nyquist,* 413 U.S. 756, 773 (1973) and *McGowan v. Maryland,* 366 U.S. 420, 445 (1961); *McLean,* 529 F. Supp., 1263, citing *United States v. Emmons,* 410 U.S. 396 (1973); *Chrysler Corp. v. Brown,* 441 U.S. 281 (1979); *McLean,* 529 F. Supp., 1263, citing *Stone,* 449 U.S., *Abington Township,* 374 U.S.

115. *McLean,* 529 F. Supp., 1263, citing *Epperson,* 393 U.S., 89; *McLean,* 529 F. Supp., 1263, citing *Village of Arlington Heights v. Metropolitan Housing Corp.,* 429 U.S. 252 (1977); *McLean,* 529 F. Supp., 1263–1264, citing *Fed. Energy Admin. v. Algonquin SNG, Inc.,* 426 U.S. 548, 564 (1976).

116. *McLean,* 529 F. Supp., 1264.

117. *McLean,* 529 F. Supp., 1264.

118. *McLean,* 529 F. Supp., 1264–1265.

119. *McLean,* 529 F. Supp., 1265 n. 19. Judge Overton does not cite a parallel for 4(a)(2): "The insufficiency of mutation and natural selection in bringing about development of all living things from a single organism." I suspect that the reason why he does not offer a biblical parallel is twofold: (1) it is implied in the other five parallels, (2) two witnesses for the plaintiffs—Ayala and Gould—agreed that mutation and natural selection are insufficient. However, they did testify that "such phenomena as recombination, the founder effect, genetic drift and the theory of punctuated equilibrium . . . are believed to play important evolutionary roles" (*McLean,* 529 F. Supp., 1267).

120. *McLean,* 529 F. Supp., 1267, 1266.

121. *McLean,* 529 F. Supp., 1266 (note omitted).

122. *See* chapter 1 section A, part 2 and accompanying notes of this present text.

123. *McLean,* 529 F. Supp., 1268, 1267.

124. *McLean,* 529 F. Supp., 1267.

125. *See* introduction, section A of this present volume.

Because ID's project strikes at the philosophical core of evolutionary theory—its unchallenged epistemological and metaphysical presuppositions—ID proponents have published most of their pro-ID essays in peer-reviewed periodicals that specialize in the *philosophy* of science or in anthologies produced by respected university presses. In addition, as noted in the text (introduction, section A), ID proponents have made significant inroads in publishing monographs with prestigious presses. The ID movement has found more success in these venues rather than in traditional scientific journals, for the latter typically do not have reviewers and editors adequately trained to assess the soundness of arguments—both empirical and philosophical—that challenge the core presuppositions of the entrenched paradigm.

However, design theorists' publication in peer-reviewed biology journals *is* thin, and cannot be entirely attributed to hostile editorial boards who want to suppress ID (though that sometimes is the case). According to a personal email from Dembski,

> I would say there are two things going on: (1) Much of biological research is frankly engineering (genetic engineering, molecular machines, etc.) and thus already frameable in ID terms; the problem is that Darwinists are framing this work in Darwinian terms, seeing the Darwinian mechanism as the great engineer of biology. Thus work that should be considered design-theoretic research has been co-opted for a materialist agenda. (2) We are just getting off the ground with a biological research program that is uniquely design-theoretic (i.e., which cannot be co-opted by Darwinians). The number of researchers who presently see how to employ design-theoretic concepts to inspire fruitful biological research is merely a handful. (Personal email to Francis J. Beckwith from William A. Dembski, July 10, 2002).

Nevertheless, it should be stressed that ID opponents are *mistaken* when they claim that design theorists have not published peer-reviewed works. In addition, as I point out below in this chapter, as a matter of constitutional law, peer-review publication, though relevant, is not necessary in order for a viewpoint to be considered "scientific" by a court of law.

126. The citations in the following three notes come from a list of publications and their summaries submitted on March 11, 2002, by Stephen C. Meyer and Jonathan Wells to the Ohio Board of Education in support of the modifications of its science curriculum discussed earlier (introduction, section B) (The Discovery Institute, *Bibliography of Supplementary Resources for Ohio Science Instruction* [March 11, 2002], *available at* http://www. discovery.org/viewDB/index.php3?/program=CRSC%20 Responses&command=view&id=1127 [April 24, 2002]). Meyer and Wells are careful to say that "the publications are not presented either as support for the theory of intelligent design, or as indicating that the authors cited doubt evolution."

127. According to the Discovery Institute staff, pattern "concerns the large-scale geometry of biological history: how are organisms related to each other, and how do we know that?" (Discovery Institute, *Bibliography of Supplementary Resources*.) *See* Ying Cao, Axel Janke, Peter J. Waddell, Michael Westerman, Osamu Takenaka, Shigenori Murata, Norihiro Okada, Svante Pääbo, and Masami Hasegawa, "Conflict among Individual Mitochondrial Proteins in Resolving the Phylogeny of Eutherian Orders," *Journal of Molecular Evolution*, 47 (1998); Simon Conway Morris, "Evolution: Bringing Molecules into the Fold," *Cell*, 100 (2000); W. Ford Doolittle, "Tempo, Mode, the

Progenote, and the Universal Root," in *Tempo and Mode in Evolution,* ed. W. Fitch and F. Ayala (Washington, DC: National Academy Press, 1995); W. Ford Doolittle, "At the Core of the Archaea," *Proceedings of the National Academy of Sciences USA,* 93 (1996); W. Ford Doolittle, "Uprooting the Tree of Life," *Scientific American* (February 2000); W. Ford Doolittle, "Phylogenetic Classification and the Universal Tree," *Science,* 284 (1999); W. Ford Doolittle, "The Nature of the Universal Ancestor and the Evolution of the Proteome," *Current Opinion in Structural Biology,* 10 (2000); Douglas H. Erwin, "Early Introduction of Major Morphological Innovations," *Acta Palaeontologica Polonica,* 38 (1994); Trisha Gura, "Bones, Molecules . . . or Both?" *Nature,* 406 (2000); Michael S. Y. Lee, "Molecular Clock Calibrations and Metazoan Divergence Dates," *Journal of Molecular Evolution,* 49 (1999); Michael S.Y. Lee, "Molecular Phylogenies Become Functional," *Trends in Ecology and Evolution,* 14 (1999); Detlef D. Leipe, L. Aravind, and Eugene V. Koonin, "Did DNA Replication Evolve Twice Independently?" *Nucleic Acids Research,* 27 (1999); Peter J. Lockhart and Sydney A. Cameron, "Trees for Bees," *Trends in Ecology and Evolution,* 16 (2001); David P. Mindell, Michael D. Sorenson, and Derek E. Dimcheff, "Multiple Independent Origins of Mitchondrial Gene Order in Birds," *Proceedings of the National Academy of Sciences USA,* 95 (1998); Paul Morris and Emily Cobabe, "Cuvier Meets Watson and Crick: The Utility of Molecules as Classical Homologies," *Biological Journal of the Linnean Society,* 44 (1991); Arcady R. Mushegian, James R. Garey, Jason Martin, and Leo X. Liu, "Large-Scale Taxonomic Profiling of Eukaryotic Model Organisms: A Comparison of Orthologous Proteins Encoded by the Human, Fly, Nematode, and Yeast Genomes," *Genome Research,* 8 (1998); Gavin J. P. Naylor and Wesley M. Brown, "Amphioxus Mitochondrial DNA, Chordate Phylogeny, and the Limits of Inference Based on Comparisons of Sequences," *Systematic Biology,* 47 (1998); Colin Patterson, David M. Williams, and Christopher J. Humphries, "Congruence between Molecular and Morphological Phylogenies," *Annual Review of Ecology and Systematics,* 24 (1993); Michael K. Richardson et al., "There Is No Highly Conserved Stage in the Vertebrates: Implications for Current Theories of Evolution and Development," *Anatomy and Embryology,* 196 (1997); Kensal E. van Holde, "Respiratory Proteins of Invertebrates: Structure, Function and Evolution," *Zoology: Analysis of Complex Systems,* 100 (1998); Kenneth Weiss, "We Hold These Truths to Be Self-Evident," *Evolutionary Anthropology,* 10 (2001); and Carl Woese, "The Universal Ancestor," *Proceedings of the National Academy of Sciences USA,* 95 (1998).

128. Process "concerns the mechanisms of evolution, and open problems in that area" (Discovery Institute, *Bibliography*). *See* Robert L. Carroll, "Towards a New Evolutionary Synthesis," *Trends in Ecology and Evolution,* 15 (2000); Douglas Erwin, "Macroevolution Is More Than Repeated Rounds of Microevolution," *Evolution & Development,* 2 (2000); Scott F. Gilbert, Grace A. Loredo, Alla Brukman, and Ann C. Burke, "Morphogenesis of the Turtle Shell: The Development of a Novel Structure in Tetrapod Evolution," *Evolution & Development,* 3 (2001); Olivier Rieppel, "Turtles as Hopeful Monsters," *BioEssays,* 23 (2001); Scott F. Gilbert, John M. Opitz, and Rudolf A. Raff, "Resynthesizing Evolutionary and Developmental Biology," *Developmental Biology,* 173 (1996); George L. Gabor Miklos, "Emergence of Organizational Complexities during Metazoan Evolution: Perspectives from Molecular Biology, Palaeontology

and Neo-Darwinism," *Mem. Ass. Australas. Palaeontols.,* 15 (1993); Neil H. Shubin and Charles R. Marshall, "Fossils, Genes, and the Origin of Novelty," in *Deep Time: Paleobiology's Perspective: A Special Volume Commemorating the twenty-fifth Anniversary of the Journal* Paleobiology, ed. Douglas W. Erwin and Scott L. Wing (Lawrence, KS: The Paleontological Society, 2000); Keith Stewart Thomson, "Macroevolution: The Morphological Problem," *American Zoologist,* 32 (1992); Bärbel M. R. Stadler, Peter F. Stadler, Günther P. Wagner, and Walter Fontana, "The Topology of the Possible: Formal Spaces Underlying Patterns of Evolutionary Change," *Journal of Theoretical Biology,* 213 (2001); and Günther P. Wagner, "What Is the Promise of Developmental Evolution? Part II: A Causal Explanation of Evolutionary Innovations May Be Impossible," *Journal of Experimental Zoology (Mol Dev Evol),* 291 (2001).

129. Biological complexity "concerns the origin of what makes organisms distinctively what they are: the source of the specified complexity of biological information" (Discovery Institute, *Bibliography*). See Philip Ball, "Life's Lessons in Design," *Nature,* 409 (2001); Rodney Brooks, "The Relationship between Matter and Life," *Nature,* 409 (2001); David W. Deamer, "The First Living Systems: A Bioenergetic Perspective," *Microbiology and Molecular Biology Reviews,* 61 (1997); Michael J. Katz, *Templets and the Explanation of Complex Patterns* (Cambridge: Cambridge University Press, 1986) (first usage of the term *irreducible complexity* ten years prior to Behe's use of it); Claire M. Fraser et al., "The Minimal Gene Complement of *Mycoplasma genitalium*," *Science,* 270 (1995); Clyde A. Hutchison et al., "Global Transposon Mutagenesis and a Minimal *Mycoplasma* Genome," *Science,* 286 (1999); Eugene V. Koonin, "How Many Genes Can Make a Cell: The Minimal-Gene-Set Concept," *Annual Review of Genomics and Human Genetics,* 1 (2000); Jack Maniloff, "The Minimal Cell Genome: 'On Being the Right Size,'" *Proceedings of the National Academy of Sciences USA,* 93 (1996); Arcady R. Mushegian and Eugene V. Koonin, "A Minimal Gene Set for Cellular Life Derived by Comparison of Complete Bacterial Genomes," *Proceedings of the National Academy of Sciences USA,* 93 (1996); Scott N. Peterson and Claire M. Fraser, "The Complexity of Simplicity," *Genome Biology,* 2 (2001); Leslie E. Orgel, "Self-Organizing Biochemical Cycles," *Proceedings of the National Academy of Sciences,* 97 (2000); and Eörs Szarthmáry, "The Evolution of Replicators," *Philosophical Transactions of the Royal Society of London B,* 335 (2000).

130. *Daubert v. Merrell Dow Pharmaceuticals, Inc.,* 509 U.S. 579, 594 (1993).

131. *Daubert,* 509 U.S., 593 (citations omitted).

132. *Frye v. United States,* 293 F. 1013, 104 (D.C. Cir. 1923).

133. *Daubert,* 509 U.S., 589 (note omitted).

134. *Daubert,* 509 U.S., 590 (note omitted).

135. David K. DeWolf, Stephen C. Meyer, and Mark Edward DeForrest, "Teaching the Controversy: Science, or Religion, or Speech?" *Utah Law Review* (2000), 77, citing *Daubert,* 509 U.S., 594.

136. *McLean,* 529 F. Supp., 1267.

137. *McLean,* 529 F. Supp., 1267–1269.

138. Ruse, "Creation-Science Is Not Science."

139. For example, Larry Laudan writes that the "victory in the Arkansas case was hollow" and that "no one familiar with the issues can really believe that anything important

was settled through anachronistic efforts to revive a variety of discredited criteria for distinguishing between the scientific and the non-scientific" (Larry Laudan, "Commentary on Ruse: Science at the Bar—Causes for Concern," in *Creationism, Science, and the Law,* 166). For a reply to Laudan's analysis, *see* Ruse, "Creation-Science Is Not Science."

140. See, for example, Laudan, "Commentary on Ruse," 161–166. Another philosopher, Phillip Quinn, maintains that expert testimony in *McLean* was "fallacious" and did not accurately represent "settled consensus of opinion in the relevant community of scholars" (Phillip Quinn, "The Philosopher of Science as Expert Witness," in *But Is It Science?: The Philosophical Question in the Creation/Evolution Controversy,* ed. Michael Ruse [Buffalo, NY: Prometheus Books, 1988], 388).

141. Ruse asserted in a 1993 talk at the annual meeting of the American Association for the Advancement of Science:

> And to a certain extent, I must confess, in the ten years since I performed, or I appeared, in the creationism trial in Arkansas, I must say that I've been coming to this kind of position myself. And, in fact, when I first thought of putting together my collection *But Is It Science?,* I think Eugenie [Scott] was right, I was inclined to say, well, yes, creationism is not science and evolution is, and that's the end of it, and you know just trying to prove that.
>
> Now I'm starting to feel—I'm no more of a creationist now than I ever was, and I'm no less of an evolutionist now than I ever was—but I'm inclined to think that we should move our debate now onto another level, or move on. And instead of just sort of, just— I mean I realize that when one is dealing with people, say, at the school level, or these sorts of things, certain sorts of arguments are appropriate. But those of us who are academics, or for other reasons pulling back and trying to think about these things, I think that we should recognize, both historically and perhaps philosophically, certainly that the science side has certain metaphysical assumptions built into doing science, which—it may not be a good thing to admit in a court of law—but I think that in honesty that we should recognize, and that we should be thinking about some of these sorts of things. (Speech by Michael Ruse to the annual meeting of the American Assoc. for the Advancement of Science [February 13, 1993], *available at* http://www.arn.org/docs/ orpages/or151/ mr93tran.htm [February 10, 2001].)

142. For example, in *Can a Darwinian Be a Christian?* (101), Ruse claims that he was not providing the Court with a prescriptive definition of science, but rather a descriptive one, that is, what scientists in fact do and what scientists typically mean when they use the term *science.* He writes: "As a Darwinian, I myself am named a major culprit in this respect, and my Arkansas testimony is highlighted as particularly offensive. . . . It would indeed be very odd were I and others to simply characterize 'science' as something which, by definition, is based on a (methodologically) naturalistic philosophy and hence excludes God, and then simply leaving things like that. Our victory . . . would be altogether too easily won. We would indeed simply be ruling religion out by fiat. But this is not quite what is happening. . . . What is going on— what I was trying to do in Arkansas—is the offering of a lexical definition: that is to say, we are giving a characterization of the use of the term 'science.'"

143. It is interesting to note that the California Board of Education's definition of science in its Science Framework, which I briefly analyzed above (section B, part 2), suffers from problems similar to Judge Overton's theory.

144. For example, Larry Laudan argues that external conceptual problems—e.g., philosophical, logical, theological, and mathematical—may provide, and have provided in the history of scientific progress, negative evidence for the acceptance of scientific theories. *See* Larry Laudan, *Progress and Its Problems: Towards a Theory of Scientific Growth* (Berkeley: University of California Press, 1977), 45–69.

145. *See* Laudan, "Commentary on Ruse"; Quinn, "The Philosopher of Science as Expert Witness"; Moreland, *Christianity and the Nature of Science,* 23–35; and Stephen C. Meyer, "The Methodological Equivalence of Design and Descent," in *The Creation Hypothesis: Scientific Evidence for an Intelligent Designer,* ed. J. P. Moreland (Downers Grove, IL: InterVarsity Press, 1994), 72–88.

146. Laudan, "Commentary on Ruse," 162.

147. Laudan, "Commentary on Ruse," 162. Laudan points out the irony of the "friends of science" employing Overton's criteria to dismiss creation science:

By arguing that the tenets of Creationism are neither testable nor falsifiable, Judge Overton . . . deprives science of its strongest argument against Creationism. Indeed, if any doctrine in the history of science has ever been falsified, it is the set of claims associated with "creation-science." Asserting that Creationism makes no empirical claims plays directly, if inadvertently, into the hands of creationists by immunizing their ideology from empirical confrontation. The correct way to combat Creationism is to refute the empirical claims it does make, not to pretend that it makes no such claims at all. (Laudan, "Commentary on Ruse," 162)

148. Laudan, "Commentary on Ruse," 163.

149. Laudan, "Commentary on Ruse," 163.

150. Thomas Kuhn, *The Structure of Scientific Revolutions,* 2nd ed. (Chicago: University of Chicago Press, 1970), 10.

151. Kuhn, *The Structure of Scientific Revolutions,* 2nd ed., 1–51.

152. Kuhn, *The Structure of Scientific Revolutions,* 2nd ed., 75.

153. Kuhn, *The Structure of Scientific Revolutions,* 2nd ed., 76, 77.

154. Kuhn, *The Structure of Scientific Revolutions,* 2nd ed., 78. Citing the work of the most ardent defender of the falsification theory, Karl Popper, Paul R. Thagard points out the problem of saying in advance what would count as a falsification of a theory:

Popper himself noticed early that no observation ever guarantees falsification: a theory can always be retained by introducing or modifying auxiliary hypotheses, and even observation statements are not incorrigible. . . . Methodological decisions about what can be tampered with are required to block the escape from falsification. However, [Imre] Lakatos has persuasively argued that making such a decision in advance of tests is arbitrary and may often lead to overhasty rejection of a sound theory which ought to be saved by anti-falsificationist stratagems. (Paul R. Thagard, "Why Astrology Is a Pseudoscience," in *Introductory Readings in the Philosophy of Science,* ed. E. D. Klemke, Robert Hollinger, and A. David Kline [Buffalo, NY: Prometheus, 1980], 69)

Popper's views can be found in Karl Popper, *Conjectures and Refutations: The Growth of Scientific Knowledge* (London: Routledge & Kegan Paul, 1963). For more on Lakatos, *see* Imre Lakatos, *The Methodology of Scientific Research Programmes,* ed. John Worrall and Gregory Currie (New York: Cambridge University Press, 1978). For an overview of the demarcation debates within philosophy of science, *see* Imre Lakatos and Alan Musgrave, eds., *Criticism and the Growth of Knowledge* (New York: Cambridge University Press, 1970); and W. H. Newton-Smith, *The Rationality of Science* (Boston : Routledge & Kegan Paul, 1981).

155. *See* chapter 3 of this present text.

156. Laudan, "Commentary on Ruse," 164, quoting from *McLean,* 529 F. Supp., 1268.

157. Laudan, "Commentary on Ruse," 164.

158. Laudan, "Commentary on Ruse," 164. Stephen C. Meyer makes a similar point when he writes that "insofar as both creationist and evolutionary theories constitute historical theories about past causal events, neither explains exclusively by reference to natural law" (Meyer, "The Demarcation of Science and Religion," in *The History of Science and Religion in the Western Tradition: An Encyclopedia,* ed. Gary B. Ferngren, Edward J. Larson, Darrel W. Amundsen, and Anne-Marie E. Nakhla [New York: Garland, 2000], 22).

159. Laudan, "Commentary on Ruse," 164.

160. *See* Elliot Sober, *Reconstructing the Past* (Cambridge, MA: M.I.T. Press, 1988), 4–5; Michael Scriven, "Causes, Connections, and Conditions in History," in *Philosophical Analysis and History,* ed. W. Dray (New York: Harper & Row, 1966), 238–264 (especially 249–250); and Stephen C. Meyer, "DNA and the Origin of Life: Information, Specification, and Explanation," in *Debating Design: From Darwin to DNA,* ed. William A. Dembski and Michael Ruse (New York: Cambridge University Press, forthcoming 2004) and in *Darwinism, Design, and Public Education,* ed. John A. Campbell and Stephen C. Meyer (East Lansing: Michigan State University Press, forthcoming 2003). Special thanks to Steve Meyer for providing to me a pre-publication copy of his essay, which led me to the works of Sober and Scriven.

161. *See,* for example, Moreland, *Christianity and the Nature of Science,* 23–28.

162. This is what Laudan actually said: "The core issue is not whether Creationism satisfies some undemanding and highly controversial definitions of what is scientific; the real question is whether the existing evidence provides stronger arguments for evolutionary theory than for Creationism" (Laudan, "Commentary on Ruse," 165).

163. Writes Overton: "Since creation science is not science, the conclusion is inescapable that the only real effect of Act 590 is the advancement of religion" (*McLean,* 529 F. Supp., 1272). For a judge who decried "contrived dualism," (*McLean,* 529 F. Supp., 1266 [note omitted]), this seems to be a textbook example of a contrived dualism. After all, because creation science is not science, it does not follow that it is religion. It could be both nonscience and nonreligion. The Rules of Civil Procedure, for example, are not "science" according to Judge Overton's definition, but it hardly follows from that that the judicial system is a religious magisterium.

164. *McLean,* 529 F. Supp., 1272.

165. *McLean,* 529 F. Supp., 1272 (footnote omitted).

Chapter Two

Edwards v. Aguillard and After

The legal conflict over the teaching of evolution in public schools reached its culmination in the U.S. Supreme Court in the 1987 case *Edwards v. Aguillard*.[1] Unlike *Epperson*—the only other Supreme Court ruling on the issue—*Edwards* did not concern a statute that banned evolution from the public school classroom, but rather, like *McLean,* it concerned a statute that sought to expand, rather than narrow, the curriculum by requiring balanced treatment.

Given the precedential significance of *Edwards* for answering the question of the constitutional permissibility of teaching Intelligent Design in public schools, this chapter is devoted largely to providing a judicial history of the case as well as an exegesis of the Court's majority, concurring, and dissenting opinions. After *Edwards* there have been a number of lower court cases that have dealt with public schools and evolution. In the second part of this chapter we critically review four of those cases: *Webster v. New Lenox School District* (1990), *Peloza v. Capistrano School District* (1992), *Freiler v. Tangipahoa Parish Board of Education* (1999), and *LeVake v. Independent School District* (2001).[2]

A. *EDWARDS v. AGUILLARD*

1. Background

In *Edwards* the Court struck down a Louisiana statute that was similar, though not identical, to the one struck down in *McLean*.[3] The Louisiana statute, the "Balanced Treatment for Creation-Science and Evolution-Science in Public School Instruction"[4] (hereafter, Balanced-Treatment Act or act), prohibited "the teaching of the theory of evolution in public schools unless accompanied by instruction in 'creation science.'" Although no school was obligated to teach creation science or evolution, if one was taught, the other had to be taught as well.[5] The act defined the theories of creation science and evolution as "the scientific evidences for [creation or evolution] and inferences from those scientific evidences."[6] This is in contrast to the definitions of creation science and evolution found in the Arkansas Act struck down in *McLean,* which were far more detailed and the object of much criticism by both the district court and a number of expert witnesses.[7] Justice Powell, in his concurring opinion in *Edwards,* points out that the elaborate definitions of creation science and evolution that were in the original Louisiana bill, and that paralleled those found in the Arkansas statute struck down in *McLean,* were removed by a Louisiana Senate committee on May 28, 1981, the day after the complaint in *McLean* was filed in Federal District Court.[8] Also, unlike the statute struck down in *McLean,* the Balanced-Treatment Act was more specific and detailed on how it defined balanced treatment.[9] This amended bill, which emerged as the Balanced-Treatment Act, then became the subject of legislative hearings.

The judicial history of this case began soon after the act became law in 1981, when "a group of Louisiana educators, religious leaders[,] parents of children in Louisiana public schools" and others "challenged the constitutionality of the Act in district court, seeking an injunction and a declaration that the Act violated the Louisiana Constitution and the first amendment of the United States Constitution."[10] This action was originally stayed pending the resolution of another Federal District Court case initiated by the bill's sponsor (Senator Bill Keith) and others who requested that the Court declare the act constitutional as well as enforce the act by injunction. The case was dismissed on jurisdictional grounds.[11] The stay in the initial case was then lifted. The Court in that case ruled that the act violated the Louisiana Constitution.[12] The State then appealed to the U.S. Court of Appeals in the Fifth Circuit. That court certified to the Louisiana Supreme Court the question of whether the act violated the Louisiana Constitution. The Supreme Court ruled that the act did not violate the state constitution.[13] The Fifth Circuit then remanded with instructions to the District Court to answer whether the act violated the federal Constitution.[14] The District Court granted the plaintiffs' motion for summary judgment and enjoined the act's implementation. According to the Fifth Circuit, "the district court reasoned that the doctrine of creation-science necessarily entailed teaching the existence of a divine creator and the concept of a creator was an inherently religious tenet. The court thus held that the purpose of the Act was to promote religion and the implementation of the Act would have the effect of establishing religion."[15]

The State appealed that district court judgment to the Fifth Circuit, which maintained that the central question in this case was "whether the Act has a secular legislative purpose." After carefully outlining the principles by which it made its judgment (i.e., the Lemon test), the court assessed whether the act embodied a secular purpose in light of two questions: (1) Is the theory of creation a religious belief? and (2) What is "the plain language of the Act?" The Court answered the first question in the affirmative, claiming to base its answer on the historical facts surrounding the creation-evolution debate,[16] which, as we have seen, was an important factor for the courts in *Epperson* and *McLean* when they evaluated and struck down the statutes in those cases.[17]

In answering the second question, the court first looked at the portion of the acts's language that stated that its purpose was "to 'protect academic freedom.'" Although such a state end is legitimate, the Court found that the act did not promote the end of academic freedom, for two reasons: (1) "the compulsion inherent in the Balanced Treatment act is, on its face, inconsistent with the idea of academic freedom as it is universally understood," and (2) "[n]o court of which we are aware has prohibited voluntary instruction concerning scientific evidence that happens, incidentally, to be consistent with a religious doctrine or tenet."[18] Evidently, according to this court, a teacher sympathetic to creation science may inform her students of scientific facts, and perhaps other sorts of objective arguments and insights, that lend support to, but do not entail the state establishment of, that religious belief. If that is the case, then the act was unnecessary.[19]

The Court then looked at other aspects of the act's language, arguing that the statute's scheme, "focusing on the religious bete noire of evolution, demonstrates the religious purpose of the statute. Indeed, the Act continues the battle William Jennings Bryan carried to his grave. The Act's intended effect is to discredit evolution by counterbalancing its teaching at every turn with the teaching of creationism, a religious belief." Thus, "the statute . . . is a law respecting a particular religious belief." Based on the above reasons, the Court concluded "that the Act fails to satisfy the first prong of the Lemon test and thus is unconstitutional."[20] The State petitioned for a rehearing en banc. The court denied the request.[21] The State appealed to the U.S. Supreme Court.

2. The Majority Opinion

Compared to Judge Overton's opinion in *McLean*, the majority opinion in *Edwards* is far less complex and much more straightforward. This is largely because of three reasons: (1) the Court had the benefit of a well-written and clearly reasoned Fifth Circuit opinion, (2) because the initial ruling in district court on the act's compliance with the federal Constitution was a summary judgment, the Court did not have to wade through and evaluate the veracity of reams of conflicting courtroom testimony by expert witnesses (as Judge Overton did in *McLean*), and (3) much of the Court's jurisprudential spade work was done in *Epperson, McLean,* and the courts below in *Edwards*.

Although the Court's opinion overlaps much of what was said in the Fifth Circuit's opinion, it has some unique features. Justice Brennan, writing for the majority, evaluates the Balanced-Treatment Act in light of the Lemon test, though his analysis focuses exclusively on the first prong, for "if the law was enacted for the purpose of endorsing religion, 'no consideration of the second or third criteri[on] [of Lemon] is necessary.'"[22] Justice Brennan begins his analysis by placing the issue under the rubric of the importance of public education and the special place it has in our pluralistic society:

> The Court has been particularly vigilant in monitoring compliance with the Establishment Clause in elementary and secondary schools. Families entrust public schools with the education of their children, but condition their trust on the understanding that the classroom will not purposely be used to advance religious views that may conflict with the private beliefs of the student and his or her family. . . . Therefore, in employing the three-pronged Lemon test, we must do so mindful of the particular concerns that arise in the context of public elementary and secondary schools.[23]

Thus, the ordinary deference accorded states in shaping and regulating their public educational institutions is set aside when state policies that appear to transgress the Establishment Clause are at issue. That is, the level of scrutiny is heightened when a fundamental liberty is at stake.[24]

The Court first evaluates the relationship between Louisiana's declared ends ("academic freedom") and its means (Balanced-Treatment Act). It agrees with, and cites in a footnote, the Fifth Circuit's reasons for concluding that "the Act was not designed to further" the goal of academic freedom.[25] The Court then rejects the State's oral "argument that the 'legislature may not [have] use[d] the terms "academic freedom" in the correct legal sense. They might have [had] in mind, instead, a basic concept of fairness; teaching all of the evidence.'"[26] But, the Court reasoned, even if it were to accept this definition of academic freedom offered in oral argument, "the goal of providing a more comprehensive science curriculum is not furthered either by outlawing the teaching of evolution or by requiring the teaching of creation science."[27] So, even if we were to assume that the act's ends were clear and legitimate, the means was not.

The Court continues its means-end analysis by asking whether the secular purpose claimed by the State "is sincere and not a sham."[28] It first cites the act's legislative history, showing that the purpose of the act's sponsor, Senator Bill Keith, was to "narrow the science curriculum."[29] At the legislative hearings, Senator Keith asserted that his "preference would be that neither [creationism nor evolution] be taught."[30] According to the Court, "[s]uch a ban on teaching does not promote—indeed, it undermines—the provision of a comprehensive scientific education."[31] In addition, the act did not give teachers any more academic freedom than what they already had in supplanting "the present science curriculum with the presentation of theories, besides evolution, about the origin of life."[32] Since "[t]he Act provides Louisiana school teachers with no new authority[,] . . . the stated purpose is not furthered by it." Along the same lines, the Court maintains that the act did not encourage "the teaching of all scientific theories about the origins of humankind,"[33] which would be consistent with expanding both the curriculum and academic freedom. Ironically, "under the Act's requirements, teachers who were once free to teach any and all facets of this subject are now unable to do so."[34] And to make matters worse, as the Court of Appeals pointed out, "the Act fails even to ensure that creation science will be taught, but instead requires the teaching of this theory only when the theory of evolution is taught."[35]

Furthermore, the Court argues that fairness is not "furthered by the Act's discriminatory preference for the teaching of creation science and against evolution."[36] The Court points out that the act requires "curriculum guides be developed for creation science" though nothing similar is required for evolution; "resource services are supplied for creation science but not for evolution"; "[o]nly 'creation scientists' can serve on the panel that supplies the resource services"; and the act prohibits school boards from discriminating against those who embrace or teach creationism, though no such protections are afforded those who embrace or teach evolution.[37] So, the Court agrees with the Court of Appeals "that the Act does not serve to protect academic freedom, but has the distinctly different purpose of discrediting 'evolution by counterbalancing its teaching at every turn with the teaching of creationism.'"[38] So, even though academic freedom is a legitimate end, the statute was unlikely to achieve that end.

The Court then went on to divine what it believes was the true purpose of the act: to advance a particular religious viewpoint, the Genesis account of creation. Like the courts in *Epperson* and *McLean,* the Court looked at the "historic and contemporaneous link between the teachings of certain religious denominations and the teaching of evolution." According to the Court, the legislative history, including the testimonies of both Senator Keith and his creation science expert, Edward Boudreaux, "reveals that the term 'creation science,' as contemplated by the legislature that adopted this Act, embodies the religious belief that a supernatural creator was responsible for the creation of humankind."[39] In addition, the senator's opposition to evolution was fueled by his belief that the theory "incidentally coincided with what he characterized as religious beliefs antithetical to his own."[40] Also, the act targeted one scientific theory, evolution, which people in a particular theological tradition believe is hostile to their religious faith.[41] This, according to the Court, is inconsistent with the Constitution, which "'forbids alike the preference of a religious doctrine or the prohibition of a theory which is deemed antagonistic to a particular dogma.'"[42] Given these factors, the Court concluded that the real purpose of the act was to advance a particular religious viewpoint, creation science, and thus the act violated the Establishment Clause.

However, the Court was careful to point out that its opinion does "not imply that the legislature could never require that scientific critiques of prevailing scientific theories be taught." The Court maintains that "teaching a variety of scientific theories about the origins of humankind to schoolchildren might be validly done with the clear secular intent of enhancing the effectiveness of science instruction."[43] In addition, Justice Powell writes in his concurring opinion that "a decision respecting the subject matter to be taught in public schools does not violate the Establishment Clause simply because the material to be taught 'happens to coincide or harmonize with the tenets of some or all religions.'"[44] These qualifications are important, for they may allow that an alternative view, such as Intelligent Design, be taught in public schools.

Justice Brennan made some concluding remarks about the State's argument that the District Court's summary judgment did not allow the State to include expert affidavits to show that an issue of material fact can be raised. Justice Brennan concluded that the District Court made no errors in its judgment, for "it rested on the plain language of the Creationism Act, the legislative history and historical context of the Act, the specific sequence of events leading to the passage of the Act, the State Board's report on a survey of school superintendents, and the correspondence between the Act's legislative sponsor and its key witnesses."[45]

3. The Concurring Opinions

There are two concurring opinions in this case, one by Justice Powell (with whom Justice O'Connor joined) and the other by Justice White. Of the two opinions, Justice Powell's is longer and more detailed. Because Justice White's one-and-one-half page opinion deals almost exclusively with procedural matters, I focus only on Justice Powell's.[46]

Justice Powell reiterates the importance of the Lemon test in matters of public education. He then makes the point that when interpreting a statute one must interpret its words, "'unless otherwise defined, . . . as taking their ordinary, contemporary, common meaning.'"[47] So, he defines the words "creation" and "evolution" by citing their definitions as found in *Webster's Third New International Dictionary*. It defines creation "as 'holding that matter, various forms of life, and the world were created by a transcendent God out of nothing.'"[48] "'Evolution' is defined as 'the theory that the various types of animals and plants have their origin in other preexisting types, the distinguishable differences being due to modifications in successive generations.'"[49] He concludes from these definitions that the "Act mandates that public schools present the scientific evidence to support a theory of divine creation whenever they present the scientific evidence to support the theory of evolution."[50] However, in order to draw his final conclusion that the statute's prima facie purpose is to advance a religious belief, Justice Powell adds another premise, a quote from a 1977 District Court case, *Malnak v. Yogi*: "[C]oncepts concerning God or a supreme being of some sort are manifestly religious. . . . These concepts do not shed that religiosity merely because they are presented as a philosophy or as a science."[51]

It is interesting to note that *Malnak I*'s holding may actually be *inconsistent* with Justice Powell's assessment. First, Justice Powell left out and replaced with ellipses the comments "when they appear as tenets of Christianity or Buddhism or Hinduism."[52] This is important because it shows that the district court merely claimed that the tenets of these religions, *when they appear as tenets,* are *paradigm cases* (or sufficient conditions) of religious belief, not *necessary* conditions for a belief to be religious when they do not appear as tenets. The rest of the opinion seems to bear this out.

Second, given this correction, the quote in its context is far from useful for Justice Powell's purposes. The case in *Malnak I* concerned the constitutionality of the teaching of Science of Creative Intelligence/Transcendental Meditation (SCI/TM) in New Jersey public schools. The SCI/TM lessons were disguised in the language of science and philosophy in order to make their clear religious nature difficult to detect (SCI/TM is a version of Hindu spirituality). The Court ruled that the teaching of SCI/TM violated the Establishment Clause and was therefore unconstitutional.[53] Thus, the Court in *Malnak I* was saying that religious tenets are still religious tenets even when they are transparently cloaked in the language of philosophy and/or science. However, the Court was not saying that *actual* philosophical and scientific positions and arguments that lend credence and support to belief in God are de facto religious. It is the *inculcation* of religion, cloaked in apparently nonreligious language, that the court found repugnant.[54] For example, the *Malnak II* court writes that "[c]ertain isolated answers to 'ultimate' questions . . . are not necessarily 'religious' answers. . . . Thus, the so-called 'Big Bang' theory, an astronomical interpretation of the creation of the universe, may be said to answer an 'ultimate' question, but it is not, by itself, a 'religious' idea." Patriotic and moral perspectives, though "not by themselves 'religious,'" *may* be "if they are presented as divine law or a part of a comprehensive belief-system that presents them as 'truth.'"[55] Particularly relevant to the purpose of this book is *Malnak II*'s insight that "a science course may touch on many ultimate concerns, but it is unlikely to proffer a systematic series of answers to them that might begin to resemble a religion."[56]

Third, when the *Malnak I* court was speaking about *all religions* and their concepts of a *supreme being* (i.e., that which is self-existent and for which no explanation is necessary) it included those belief systems that are nontheistic and/or materialist.[57] Thus, if Justice Powell had defined evolution in terms of its epistemological commitment (i.e., methodological naturalism) and ontological entailment (i.e., materialism)[58] rather than its application to biology, and if he had done the same in defining creationism as well, he could have depicted Louisiana's Balanced-Treatment Act more sympathetically as concerning two conflicting perspectives (materialism versus intelligent design) about the same subject (the nature of reality, i.e., metaphysics) rather than merely two different subjects, one of which is "science" (biological evolution) and the other "religion" (creationism).[59] Such a rendering of the act still may not have passed constitutional muster, but it is unlikely that *Webster's Dictionary* would have been able to resolve the issue so neatly for Justice Powell. However, in fairness to the justice, the language of the act as well as the rhetoric of its supporters did not make such a sympathetic reading easy to come by.

Nevertheless, Justice Powell concedes that even if the act has a religious purpose, that "alone is not enough to invalidate" it. "The religious purpose must predominate."[60] Although he is suspicious of the state's argument that the act's purpose is to promote academic freedom, he thinks that it is "at least ambiguous."[61] So, unlike the majority, he believes that the state's argument may have some merit. However, like the majority, Justice Powell carefully examines the legislative history, as well as the broader judicial history of the creation/evolution conflict, and concludes that the motivation of its sponsors and supporters is sufficient to conclude that the act's predominate purpose is to advance religion and that it, therefore, violates the Establishment Clause. As part of his case he also includes an analysis in which he connects the act with the Genesis-inspired statutes in *McLean* and *Epperson*.[62]

Justice Powell writes that nothing in his opinion should be interpreted to undermine the traditional constitutional doctrine that the Court defer to state and local officials concerning matters of public education. He points out that the Establishment Clause only applies "when the purpose for [the] decision" of these officials "is clearly religious,"[63] not "simply because the material to be taught 'happens to coincide with the tenets of some or all religions.'"[64] Justice Powell concludes with some comments about the importance of exposing public school students to America's religious traditions and the significance of religion in the lives and ideas of the American Founders.[65]

4. The Dissenting Opinion

Justice Scalia, in his lengthy dissenting opinion[66] (joined by Chief Justice Rehnquist), criticizes the majority on a number of points, three of which seem to be especially relevant to this book's purpose:[67] (i) the majority's use of the legislature's motivation in assessing the religious purpose of the statute, (ii) the majority's notion of advancing religion, and (iii) the majority's analysis of the alleged academic freedom purpose.[68] Although Justice Scalia's opinion is not the Court's holding, it is important because it may be used by a future court that seeks to employ persuasive, rather than precedential, reasons in order to *discard* the *Edwards* standard.

(i) Concerning the majority's use of the legislature's motivation in assessing the religious purpose of the statute, Justice Scalia makes several points.

  First, in order for the majority's charge to stick, they have to ignore the lengthy legislative process that resulted in the act. This process included many hearings and much study over several months that resulted in significant revisions as well as a "specifically secular purpose [the legislators] meant it to serve." Despite the record's "abundant evidence of the sincerity of that purpose (the only issue pertinent to this case), the Court today holds . . . that the members of the Louisiana Legislature knowingly violated their oaths and then lied about it."[69]

  Second, Justice Scalia argues that the Court relies on the stereotypes and folk history of the evolution/creation debate (going all the way back to *Scopes*) in order to discover the act's purpose rather than relying on the announced purpose of the legislature.[70] In fact, the "history" is employed to label the legislature's announced purpose "a sham." This, according to Justice Scalia, is not an appropriate way to interpret a statute.[71]

Third, he challenges the notion of whether the Court is capable of un-
covering a statute's purpose from the motivation of the legislature.[72] He
argues that the motivations of individual legislators, and the governor
who eventually signs a bill, are often disparate and largely undetectable.[73] Although he does not mention this explicitly, it seems that one
could read Justice Scalia as saying that the Court confuses motivation
with purpose. For example, my motivation for defending the Free Exercise Clause may be religious; that is, I support it because it affords me
the opportunity to convert others to my faith. Nevertheless, I publicly
announce to my fellow citizens, with all sincerity, that the *purpose* of the
Free Exercise Clause is to allow religious liberty to people from all
faiths including ones hostile to mine. Yet, it would seem foolish to argue
that based on my motivation one may reasonably infer that the Free Exercise Clause's "real" purpose is to advance my sectarian beliefs and
thus, paradoxically, one may conclude that the Free Exercise Clause violates the Establishment Clause.

In order to appreciate the fallaciousness of such reasoning, suppose
that another person defends the Free Exercise Clause because she is motivated by a desire for religious liberty. And, like me, she publicly an-
nounces to her fellow citizens, with all sincerity, that the purpose of the
Free Exercise Clause is to allow religious liberty to people from all
faiths including ones hostile to hers. Her motivation, unlike mine, coin-
cides with the clause's purpose. But since the text and announced purpose of the Free Exercise Clause in each scenario are identical to those
found in the other, it would seem that the motivation of its supporters is
at best a curiosity and at worst a logically fallacious basis for discarding
a statute.[74] It is interesting to note that "the distinction between motive
and purpose is elementary in criminal law."[75] Whether or not a defendant
is guilty is not contingent on whether he was motivated by beneficence
or malevolence, but rather, "whether he acted with the purpose of ac-
complishing a particular result."[76]

Perhaps this is why, according to Justice Scalia, the Court, in cases involving a question of religious establishment, "[a]lmost invariably . . .
[has] effortlessly discovered a secular purpose for measures challenged
under the Establishment Clause, typically devoting no more than a sentence or two to the matter."[77] And in the three cases prior to *Edwards,* in
which the Court did strike down "laws under the Establishment Clause
for lack of a secular purpose," the Court "found that the legislature's sole
motive was to promote religion."[78]

(ii) Justice Scalia argues that the majority's notion of advancing religion is con-
fused and thus unhelpful. He makes several arguments to defend this point.

First, he maintains that the Court's holdings in this area "no way imply that the Establishment Clause forbids legislators merely to act upon their religious convictions." To illustrate this, he writes that "political activism by the religiously motivated is part of our heritage" and that "we surely would not strike down a law providing money to feed the hungry or shelter the homeless if it could be demonstrated that, but for the religious beliefs of the legislators, the funds would not have been approved."[79]

Second, the Court "will not presume that a law's purpose is to advance religion merely because it 'happens to coincide or harmonize with the tenets of some or all religions,' . . . or because it benefits religion substantially."[80] Concerning the latter, the Court "turned back challenges to restrictions on abortion funding"[81] and "Sunday closing laws,"[82] and upheld "tax deduction for expenses of religious education,"[83] "aid to religious schools,"[84] "tax exemption for church property,"[85] and "textbook loans to students in religious schools."[86]

Third, according to Justice Scalia, the Court has held that there are at least two situations in which the government *must* advance religion and it *may* do so in a third. One circumstance is when the state is hostile to religion and thus inhibits its free exercise. In such a circumstance the government must advance religion if doing so is necessary to protect free exercise and/or government neutrality toward religion.[87] Therefore, "if the Louisiana Legislature sincerely believed that the State's science teachers were being hostile to religion, [the Court's] cases indicate that it could act to eliminate that hostility without running afoul of Lemon's purpose test." Another circumstance in which the government must advance religion is when the State is obligated to "accommodate the beliefs of religious citizens by exempting them from generally applicable regulations."[88] (Some examples include exemption from restrictions on unemployment benefits and the right of parents to educate their children in religious schools.[89]) Finally, the government may accommodate religion, even if it is not required by the First Amendment. "We have implied," writes Justice Scalia, "that voluntary governmental accommodation is not only permissible, but desirable." For example, because "Title VII of the Civil Rights Act, which both forbids religious discrimination by private sector employers . . . , and requires them reasonably to accommodate the religious practices of their employees," is not required by the Free Exercise Clause, its "'purpose' is . . . to advance religion."[90] Yet, few, if any, would say that Title VII violates the Establishment Clause. Thus, even if the act's purpose "were exclusively to advance religion, some of the well-established exceptions to the impermissibility of that purpose might be applicable—the validating intent to eliminate a perceived discrimination against a particular religion, to facilitate its free exercise, or to accommodate it."[91]

(iii) Justice Scalia is also critical of the majority's analysis of the act's alleged academic freedom purpose. He accuses the Court of not carefully evaluating this alleged purpose in light of the act's genesis including the hearings, debates, and expert testimonies that eventually resulted in an overwhelming number of legislators voting for an act "which explicitly stated a secular purpose." "[W]hat is crucial," according to Justice Scalia, "is not their wisdom in believing that purpose would be achieved by the bill, but their sincerity in believing it would be."[92] The justice maintains that the Court ignored reams of testimonial evidence—including testimony by experts whose credentials the legislature thought impressive—that made a secular case for a balanced treatment curriculum that included creationism. [93]

Justice Scalia makes these observations because he believes that what the legislature primarily meant by academic freedom is "students' freedom from indoctrination."[94] According to the justice, "the legislature wanted to ensure that students would be free to decide for themselves how life began, based upon a fair and balanced presentation of the scientific evidence—that is, to protect 'the right of each [student] voluntarily to determine what to believe (and what not to believe) free of any coercive pressures from the State.'"[95] In addition, the statute's bias toward the teaching of creationism, which the majority took as evidence that the state had no real interest in academic freedom, Justice Scalia cites as evidence *for* that purpose. He maintains that the legislature did not unreasonably believe that discrimination and marginalization of creationists and their views by the educational and scientific establishments required a statute that could protect members of this group, their views, and their students.[96]

B. AFTER *EDWARDS*

Although there has been much public debate about evolution, religion, and the law in the 1990s and early twenty-first century (see, e.g., introduction, section A), actual litigation has been rare. However, there are four cases after *Edwards* that are noteworthy in respect to our analysis of whether ID can be taught in public schools without violating the Establishment Clause.

1. *Webster v. New Lenox School Distrtict*[97]

In 1990 the Seventh Circuit Court of Appeals affirmed a District Court decision to dismiss the complaint of a public school teacher, Ray Webster. The circuit court ruled that Mr. Webster, who taught junior high, had not had his First and Fourteenth Amendment rights violated when the superintendent, writing on behalf of the school board, instructed Mr. Webster by letter "that he should restrict his classroom instruction to the curriculum and refrain from advocating a religious viewpoint."[98] He "was specifically instructed not to teach creation science, because the teaching of this theory had been held by the federal courts to be religious advocacy."[99] The reason for disciplinary action arose from Mr. Webster including in his lesson plans "nonevolutionary theories of creation" for the purpose of rebutting "a statement in the social studies textbook indicating the world is over four billion years old." Mr. Webster defended himself against the charge of having violated the Establishment Clause by arguing that "at most, he encouraged students to explore alternative viewpoints."[100]

The Court's holding dealt with the narrow question of whether Mr. Webster "has a first amendment right to determine the curriculum content of his junior high class."[101] Given the controversial nature of Mr. Webster's extracurricular lessons—creation-science, a view repudiated as inherently religious by a number of other courts—and the school board's responsibility in shaping curriculum and avoiding establishment clause violations in its institutions, Mr. Webster's First and Fourteenth Amendment rights were not violated. That is, the court held that a school may censor classroom instruction that seeks to promote or advance a particular religious belief such as creation science. On the other hand, the Court admits that "this case does not present the issue of whether, or under what circumstances, a school board may completely eliminate material from the curriculum," but rather, what is dispositive in this case is "the principle that an individual teacher has no right to ignore the directives of duly appointed education authorities."[102]

For the purposes of this book, this is an important qualification, for other cases, apparently consistent with this qualification, have affirmed that the First Amendment does support some notion of academic freedom for public school teachers[103] including the principle that a "school may not flatly prohibit teachers from mentioning relevant material."[104] Given these opinions, it seems that a statue allowing (or even requiring) the teaching of ID in public schools may pass constitutional muster if it is carefully crafted in order to address the assorted judicial concerns we have extracted from the cases presented in chapters 1 and 2.

2. *Peloza v. Capistrano School District*[105]

In this 1994 case, the Ninth Circuit Court of Appeals affirmed in part a District Court opinion. John E. Peloza, a high school biology teacher, brought action against his school district and others, complaining "that the school district requires him to teach 'evolutionism' and that evolutionism is a religious belief" and that he was prohibited from sharing his religious beliefs with his students.[106] The former charge is germane to this book.

Although the Court ruled against Peloza, its opinion is not inconsistent with the Fifth Circuit's claim in *Aguillard*—an analysis echoed in Justice Powell's concurrence in *Edwards*[107]—that "[n]o court of which we are aware has prohibited voluntary instruction concerning scientific evidence that happens, incidentally, to be consistent with a religious doctrine or tenet."[108] For in *Peloza* the plaintiff never "taught creationism in his classroom,"[109] and was not reprimanded for the content of his class lectures, which may have included critical comments about evolution.

In addition, the *Peloza* Court defined evolution as a theory of how living organisms change over time—vague enough to refer to either microevolution, macroevolution, or both—rather than as a cosmological theory or one presupposing methodological naturalism and entailing ontological materialism. Thus, the court, not surprisingly, concluded that evolution "has nothing to do with whether or not there is a divine Creator (who did or did not create the universe or did or did not plan evolution as part of a divine scheme)."[110] But, as we saw earlier,[111] evolution, as understood in the professional literature, is naturalistic (or materialist) and does not allow for an intelligent designer of any sort. It is interesting to note that Mr. Peloza "might make out a claim," the Court reasoned, "[o]nly if we define 'evolution' and 'evolutionism' . . . as a concept that embraces the belief that the universe came into existence without a Creator."[112]

Consequently, although some may see *Peloza* as a blow against the teaching of ID in public schools, such a reading is unwarranted, for this decision, like *Webster,* concerned the narrow question of the right of a teacher in his lesson plan to alter without permission a public school curriculum required by a legitimate state authority. Mr. Webster wanted to add creation science to his curriculum, something the courts had already concluded would be advancing religion and thus in violation of the Establishment Clause. Mr. Peloza, on the other hand, wanted to subtract evolution from his curriculum, something he thought violated the Establishment Clause and that he believed required him to be an unwilling instrument of that violation. But the *Peloza* Court concluded that evolution is not a theory that provides answers inconsistent with either the existence or nonexistence of God. Thus, both the *Webster* and *Peloza* Courts saw creation and evolution as two different subjects (one religion, the other science) rather than two different metaphysical perspectives on the same subject. Hence, they were able to dismiss, without fear of inconsistency, the complaints of both Mr. Peloza and Mr. Webster. This is not to say that the *Webster* and *Peloza* courts did not have a myriad of other reasons at their disposal by which they may rule against the plaintiffs.[113] Rather, the point is that both courts were relying on unchallenged, and philosophically controversial, premises concerning the nature of metaphysical claims about origins and theological claims in general,[114] premises deeply embedded in the public culture and reinforced by prior cases (e.g., *Epperson, McLean, Edwards*), that if jettisoned would open the door for the teaching of ID in public schools. For the Intelligent Design movement, and the numerous and diverse aspects of its project, defy and challenge these embedded and unchallenged notions in a highly sophisticated way (*see* chapters 3 and 4).

3. Freiler v. Tangipahoa Parish Board of Education

This 1999 case was heard by the Fifth Circuit Court of Appeals and denied certiario by the U.S. Supreme Court in 2000 after the Fifth Circuit in 2000 denied a rehearing en banc.[115] In the 1999 case, the Fifth Circuit affirmed the District Court opinion against the defendant,[116] Tangipahoa Parish Board of Education (Louisiana), which had in 1994 passed a resolution that required the following:

> Whenever, in classes of elementary or high school, the scientific theory of evolution is to be presented, whether from textbook, workbook, pamphlet, other written material, or oral presentation, the following statement shall be quoted immediately before the unit of study begins as a disclaimer from endorsement of such theory.
>
> It is hereby recognized by the Tangipahoa Board of Education, that the lesson to be presented, regarding the origin of life and matter, is known as the Scientific Theory of Evolution and should be presented to inform students of the scientific concept and not intended to influence or dissuade the Biblical version of Creation or any other concept.
>
> It is further recognized by the Board of Education that it is the basic right and privilege of each student to form his/her own opinion and maintain beliefs taught by parents on this very important matter of the origin of life and matter.[117] Students are urged to exercise critical thinking and gather all information possible and closely examine each alternative toward forming an opinion.[118]

In assessing the resolution, the Fifth Circuit applied the first two prongs of the Lemon test. According to the first prong, the resolution must have a secular purpose. The Court maintained that the school board asserted three purposes for the disclaimer: "(1) to encourage informed freedom of belief, (2) to disclaim any orthodoxy of belief that could be inferred from the exclusive placement of evolution in curriculum, and (3) to reduce offense to the sensibilities and sensitivities of any student or parent caused by the teaching of evolution." If only one of these purposes is furthered by the disclaimer and that purpose is secular, the resolution passes the first prong of the Lemon test.[119]

According to the Court, the resolution passes Lemon's first prong because the second and third purposes are secular and are furthered by the disclaimer.[120] Disclaiming orthodoxy and reducing offense are legitimate secular purposes. The first purpose, however, though secular, is not furthered by the disclaimer because the resolution does not really encourage freedom of belief or critical thinking, but rather "the disclaimer as a whole furthers a contrary purpose, namely the protection and maintenance of a particular religious viewpoint."[121] Because the disclaimer, according to the Court, instructs schoolchildren "that evolution as taught in the classroom need not affect what they already know," and "[s]uch a message is contrary to an intent to encourage critical thinking, which requires that students approach new concepts with an open mind and a willingness to alter and shift existing viewpoints,"[122] freedom of thought is not furthered by the disclaimer.

This is a curious argument. For it is not clear how the advocation of freedom of thought and critical thinking is inconsistent with reminding school children that they need not believe the state-endorsed metaphysics taught to them by their science teachers, and that these children in fact have a right to believe otherwise, whether they are beliefs held by their parents or ones arrived at through extended and critical reflection. It seems to me that the authors of the resolution were dismayed by the poverty of their science curriculum's metaphysical offerings. For it offered only one point of view, materialism, a view that by its very nature excludes certain points of view from the privileged status of "knowledge." And in reply to this metaphysical monopoly—this ontological imperialism—the school board was more than gracious and tolerant, for it did not coerce its teachers to offer another point of view as part of its curriculum. Rather, the board took an overly modest strategy: it required its teachers to merely mention to their students, for a few moments, that the students have a right to disagree with the only permissible viewpoint that will be presented without rebuttal, reply, or counterargument for the remainder of the course. Yet, this unpretentious prerequisite, according to the Court, was inconsistent with freedom of thought and critical thinking, for *it* and not its removal "furthers a contrary purpose, namely the protection and maintenance of a particular religious viewpoint."[123]

Nevertheless, the Court may still have a defensible point to its reasoning in light of both the line of cases we have looked at so far (*Scopes, Epperson, McLean, Edwards*) and the language employed in the resolution to convey the school board's advocation of critical thinking. In order to see this point, we must look to why the Court concluded that the resolution failed Lemon's second prong, its sole basis for rejecting the disclaimer as unconstitutional. It failed, according to the Court, for *precisely the same reason* why the first purpose failed Lemon's first prong: "the primary effect of the disclaimer is to protect and maintain a particular religious viewpoint, namely belief in the Biblical version of creation." The Court provided three reasons for this: "(1) the juxtaposition of the disavowal of endorsement of evolution with an urging that students contemplate alternative theories of life; (2) the reminder that students have the right to maintain beliefs taught by their parents regarding the origin of life; and (3) the 'Biblical version of Creation' as the only alternative theory is referenced in the disclaimer."[124] According to the Court, "[t]he disclaimer, taken as a whole, encourages students to read and meditate upon religion in general and the 'Biblical version of Creation' in particular,"[125] and this "impermissibly advances religion."[126] So, it is not that the court opposes a disclaimer in principle, but rather, that this particular disclaimer mentions by name only one option to evolution, even if only illustratively,[127] creation science, the view rejected in *Epperson, McLean,* and *Edwards.*

Edward McGlynn Gaffney Jr. replies to the Court's reasoning by arguing that the "chief difficulty with this move is that it conveniently ignored the next four words in the disclaimer: 'or any other concept.'"[128] I disagree. I do not think it is accurate to say that the Court ignored this phrase in its analysis, for it does address the phrase in three places.[129] In addition, the resolution's claim that what is taught in the classroom need not alter the beliefs one learns at home could reasonably be seen as *inconsistent* with critical thinking. Moreover, the school board did nothing to further its case when it chose to include in the resolution the phrase "Biblical version of Creation," especially in light of the judicial history of the concept. This is why Gaffney is mistaken when he claims that the Court is saying that "promoting critical thinking about the origins of the universe must be equated with advancing religion."[130] Rather, the Court is saying that it is inconsistent to call for critical thinking and at the same time say that what is learned in the classroom need not alter one's beliefs *including* religious beliefs. Granted, there are deep philosophical questions about belief and rationality that are percolating beneath the Court's reasoning in this case.[131] Nevertheless, as I argue below, the school board did not help matters much by employing language that reinforces the widely held, though defeasible, view that creation and evolution are not two perspectives on the same subject, but two different subjects, religion and science respectively (*see* chapters 3 and 4).

Although an argument could be made that the Court's decision was flawed and that it exaggerates the extent to which such a mild and modest disclaimer impermissibly advances religion,[132] it seems to me that the Court, given the genre of case it was given, had little wiggle room to rule otherwise. Moreover, the school board did not seem to have an overabundance of insight or cleverness among its well-meaning members. And here, I'd like to make two points that are germane for the case for teaching Intelligent Design in public schools.

First, in drafting its resolution the school board seemed oblivious to the four issues that the Courts have focused on when assessing creation science statutes (see section C below). By placing in its resolution "Biblical version of Creation" it raised a red flag that could not be argued away, especially given Louisiana's historical connection to *Edwards*. Such a resolution (as I suggest in greater detail in chapter 4) should have focused on the underlying metaphysical dispute in the debate over origins—materialism versus design— rather than on viewpoints that the Courts have already declared, whether rightly or wrongly,[133] religious (creation science) and scientific (evolution). Consequently, given the jurisprudential hand dealt to the school board, it should have opted for a more circumspect strategy, one that addressed the deeper philosophical issues for which the concepts of critical thinking and freedom of thought were likely designed.

Second, though the resolution is no doubt the result of the deliberations of well-meaning religious people, it seems to presuppose that religion or theology is not a branch of real knowledge, and that evolution is in fact real knowledge, for the latter is labeled as "scientific": "[T]he lesson to be presented, regarding the origin of life and matter, is known as the Scientific Theory of Evolution and should be presented to inform students of the scientific concept and not intended to influence or dissuade the Biblical version of Creation or any other concept."[134] But to imply to students that something that is scientific ought not to interfere with their religious beliefs seems to denigrate the epistemological status of those beliefs. For the message being conveyed is that science, which presupposes materialism, is the highest (and perhaps the only) form of knowledge, and because religious beliefs cannot touch, or be touched by, that knowledge, religious beliefs are not really knowledge. This is why, for example, in the preface to a 1984 pamphlet published by the National Academy of Sciences, its then-president Dr. Frank Press can write without fear of affirming an inconsistency,

> It is false . . . to think that the theory of evolution represents an irreconcilable conflict between religion and science. A great many religious leaders accept evolution on scientific grounds without relinquishing their belief in religious principles. As stated in a resolution by the Council of the National Academy of Sciences in 1981, however, "Religion and science are separate and mutually exclusive realms of human thought whose presentation in the same context leads to misunderstanding of both scientific theory and religious belief."[135]

Even though this view is widely held, it is philosophically controversial (*see* chapter 3). When the Courts accept this epistemology of religious belief—as apparently the *McLean* and *Peloza*[136] Courts (as well as the Tangipahoa school board) have—they are in fact proposing a meta-theory on how to understand the nature of religious beliefs, which comes perilously close to violating the Supreme Court's rule against assessing the truth of a religion or the interpretation of doctrines and creeds.[137] Ironically, the *Freiler* Court may have rejected the view of religion and science found in *McLean* and *Peloza*. For the *Freiler* Court said that *it was wrong* for the school board to say that evolution, a scientific theory, should not be considered by the students to count against creationism and other concepts they may have learned from their parents. This implies that evolution and other views on origins including creationism (and perhaps ID) are contrary perspectives on the same subject rather than separate spheres as the *McLean* and *Peloza* Courts seem to think. The *Freiler* Court's subsequent opinion on the matter seems to bear this out:

> [W]e emphasize that we do not decide that a state-mandated statement violates the Constitution simply because it disclaims any intent to communicate to students that the theory of evolution is the only accepted explanation of the origin of life, informs students of their right to follow their religious principles, and encourages students to evaluate all explanations of life's origins, including those taught outside the classroom. We decide only that under the facts and circumstances of this case, the statement of the Tangipahoa Parish School Board is not sufficiently neutral to prevent it from violating the Establishment Clause.[138]

As I argue in chapters 3 and 4, Intelligent Design, because it is based on philosophical and empirical arguments rather than on appeals to special revelation, poses few if any of the delicate problems of religious epistemology inadvertently (and perhaps inappropriately) raised by creation science in the Courts. However, ID, because it challenges the materialist paradigm, could be dismissed by a court as religious or nonscientific because the Court may naively think that methodological naturalism is a necessary precondition for science and ontological materialism its appropriate entailment. This is addressed in chapters 3 and 4.

The *Freiler* Court limited its "analysis to the precise language of the disclaimer and the context in which it was adopted." It did "not confront the broader issue of whether the reading of any disclaimer before the teaching of evolution would amount to an unconstitutional establishment of religion."[139] For that reason, the Court's holding, though important, poses no significant legal impediments to the teaching of ID in public schools.

However, in the case below, the District Court committed an unfortunate gaffe that seems to some to define Intelligent Design as synonymous with

Creation Science: "Creation Science, as the term shall be used herein, is the theory that the universe, including all forms of life, was created literally in the manner described in the Bible by a higher Being, or, as alternately described, the theory of intelligent design or creation by a Divine Creator."[140] Although this statement lacks clarity and rigor, it nevertheless has been employed by a number of ID opponents to dismiss ID as nothing more than "Creation Science." For example, the National Center for Science Education (NCSE) writes that Freiler "is also noteworthy for recognizing that curriculum proposals for 'intelligent design' are equivalent to proposals for teaching creation science." It goes on to say that "the Fifth Circuit Court of Appeals affirmed the ruling."[141] There are several problems with this argument.

First, although it is true that the Fifth Circuit affirmed the ruling of the District Court, it does not follow that it affirmed the appropriateness of the Lower Court's use of the term *Intelligent Design,* since Creation Science has a definitive meaning in Federal Court cases, as we have seen in this chapter and in chapter 1.

Second, at best the District Court is saying that Creation Science is *sometimes* called Intelligent Design. It does not follow from this, however, that every claim of affirming Intelligent Design is ipso facto a claim of affirming Creation Science. For example, what if the state of Louisiana, by statute, were to rename Evolution "Intelligent Design," and require all its teachers and textbooks to do likewise, would it now mean that Evolution (at least in Louisiana) is the same as Creation Science and that "Intelligent Design" (alias "Evolution") must be banned from classrooms, since, after all, the District Court said that ID is the same as Creation Science (at least according to the NCSE)? This is, of course, silly. For one must examine the content of the view defended, e.g., Michael Behe's argument for irreducible complexity, rather than dismissing it by semantic fiat not held in appeal. Because we already know the meaning of Creation Science from prior Federal Court cases, therefore, when the District Court says Creation Science may "be alternately described [as] the theory of intelligent design," it is simply informing us of what should be obvious to any rational mind committed to legal principle: renaming curriculum that has already been repudiated in prior court cases does not now make the unconstitutional curriculum constitutional (as if renaming slavery "employment" bypasses the requirements of the thirteenth Amendment). But since this truth is based on legal *principle,* the inverse follows inexorably: renaming Intelligent Design "Creation Science," as the NCSE has tried to do in its misuse of a quote from the District Court case, does not make ID *unconstitutional* (as if renaming employment "slavery" requires that the attorney general prosecute employers for violating the thirteenth Amendment). As we shall see in chapters 3 and 4, ID, when correctly understood, and as defended and supported by the leading theorists in the field, is *not* the Creation Science repudiated in the cases assessed in this book.[142]

4. *LeVake v. Independent School District*[143]

This 2001 Minnesota Court of Appeals case, like *Webster* and *Peloza,* concerned a conflict between a science teacher and a school district's required curriculum. This is an important case for the purposes of this book, for its holding, and the reasoning on which it is based, serves as a nice foil by which to explore the question of the extent to which public school teachers have academic freedom, apart from statutory requirement or permission, to voluntarily include criticisms of evolution and/or ID *in addition to* teaching the required curriculum.

Rodney LeVake, who was hired as a math and science teacher by his school district in 1984, was offered in summer 1997 an opportunity to teach tenth-grade biology during the forthcoming school year. Prior to teaching the class, he conferred with both the principal and the cochair of the science department about the required curriculum as well as the course itself. According to the requirements, "upon the completion of the class, students will be able to understand that evolution involves natural selection and mutations, which constantly cause changes in living things." The required text included three chapters on evolution, only one of which the teacher was obligated to cover. These chapters contained no criticisms of evolution, and neither did they offer any alternative theories. Knowing the curriculum and what was expected of him, LeVake agreed to teach the course.[144.]

When he taught the course in spring 1998, LeVake dedicated only one day to the topic of evolution (including a lab). Although the other biology teachers also did not spend a lot of time covering the topic because of a shortened school year, the cochair of the science department told the principal as well as LeVake that he was concerned that LeVake's teaching of evolution had been inadequate. LeVake, the court writes, "essentially told" the cochair "that he could not teach evolution according to the prescribed curriculum."[145] At an April 1, 1998, meeting with the science department cochair, principal, and curriculum director, "LeVake indicated that he did not regard evolution as a viable scientific concept," and was asked by the curriculum director whether LeVake "mentioned God or the Bible in class," for "she wanted to be sure that [he] was not discussing religion in a manner that would give the impression that the school was not religiously neutral." At an April 7 department meeting, whose purpose was to discuss LeVake's teaching of the curriculum, LeVake was asked by his principal to compose an essay on how he planned in the future to instruct his biology students on the topic of evolution. Turning it in eight days later, LeVake claimed in his essay that there is no evidence for evolution and that the theory is impossible biologically, anatomically, and physiologically.[146] LeVake maintained "that the 'complexity of life that we see around us is a testimony that evolution, as it is currently handled in our text, is impossible.'"[147] He went on to say:

> I don't believe an unquestioning faith in the theory of evolution is foundational to the goals I have stated in teaching my students about themselves, their responsibilities, and gaining a sense of awe for what they see around them. I will teach, should the department decide that it is appropriate, the theory of evolution. I will also accompany that treatment of evolution with an honest look at the difficulties and inconsistencies of the theory without turning my class into a religious one.[148]

After conferring with the school district's attorneys, the curriculum director, and others, the principal made a decision to remove LeVake from teaching tenth-grade biology and to appoint him to teach a ninth-grade natural science course instead. The following day LeVake was told of his reassignment. The principal based his decision on his "concern that a basic concept of biology, meaning the theory of evolution, would be diluted and that students would 'lose the gist' of the theory."[149] Soon afterward LeVake appealed this decision to the superintendent, who subsequently rejected LeVake's appeal because he "believed that LeVake differed fundamentally with the 'commonly held principles of the curriculum outlined,'"[150] and "that LeVake's insistence on teaching the inconsistencies of evolution was not an appropriate method for teaching the approved curriculum."[151] In a lawsuit filed on May 24, 1999, against the school district, its superintendent, LeVake's principal, the science department cochair, and the curriculum director, "LeVake alleged that respondents violated his right to free exercise of religion, free speech, due process, freedom of conscience, and academic freedom"[152] The District Court granted the Respondents' motion for summary judgment. LeVake appealed that ruling to the Minnesota Court of Appeals. The Appeals Court affirmed the District Court ruling.

There are several aspects of the Court of Appeals' ruling that are worth exploring for the purposes of this book. The Court divided its analysis into three parts: freedom of religion, free speech, and due process. In order for LeVake to have had prevailed on appeal he would have had to raise a genuine issue of material fact concerning at least one of the fundamental rights he claims the defendants violated.

Of the three, LeVake's due process claim is the weakest, for LeVake was provided with "sufficient notice about what he could and could not teach through the established curriculum and the syllabus" and his contract "required him to 'faithfully perform the teaching . . . prescribed by the School Board.'"[153] In deposition LeVake confessed that "in essence [he] said to [the science department cochair] that [he could not] teach evolution."[154] In addition, LeVake's argument relied on teacher termination cases, but "he was not even demoted."[155]

Suppose, however, LeVake had been told in advance that the curriculum requires that he publicly deny his Christian faith while affirming a belief in atheism or face reassignment or possibly demotion but only after a hearing. Even if LeVake had agreed to these terms, the fact that he was given advance notice and afforded a hearing does not speak to the substance of the terms to which he agreed. Consequently, even though the Court is correct that LeVake's claim of procedural malfeasance has little merit, it does not follow that the school did not violate his *substantive* rights. The Court assesses these alleged violations under two general categories, freedom of religion and freedom of speech.

The Court rejects LeVake's freedom of religion claim on the grounds that "[h]e does not contend that the respondents prohibited him from practicing the religion of his choice" or "demanded that he refrain from practicing his religion outside the scope of his duties as a public school teacher in order to retain his teaching position, and he does not assert that the curriculum requirements incidentally infringed on his religious practice."[156] However, it seems to me that LeVake is *not* arguing that the school interfered with his religious practice, but rather that he was reassigned *because of* his religious *beliefs*. The Court concedes as much when it points out that LeVake had used "employment discrimination cases to argue that circumstantial evidence of discrimination based on his religious belief exists." Aside from the question of whether it is appropriate to analogize from employment discrimination cases when LeVake had not brought an employment discrimination action, the Court maintains that LeVake had "not provided authority demonstrating how the use of this standard raised a genuine issue of material fact regarding his free exercise."[157] This last statement is particularly odd, since the Court, under its free speech analysis, seems implicitly to concede that LeVake had raised a genuine issue of material fact concerning free exercise, that LeVake was in fact *reassigned because of his belief,* when it writes that the school's "concern about [LeVake's] inability to teach the prescribed curriculum was well-founded" because it is "based on LeVake's *belief* that evolution is not a viable theory."[158]

The Court's free exercise analysis is terribly confusing, for it seems to use the terms *belief* and *practice* interchangeably when in fact the Supreme Court has recognized a clear distinction between the two. State action that discriminates against someone because of his or her religious belief is de facto unconstitutional,[159] whereas a state action that discriminates against a citizen because of his or her religious practice is prima facie constitutional if it is the result of a generally applicable law.[160] Thus, since the Court concedes that Mr. LeVake's reassignment was based on his beliefs, an act that is de facto unconstitutional, therefore, the Court should have ruled in his favor on those grounds.[161]

The Court rejects LeVake's freedom of speech claim as well. It relies on cases that focus on "a public employee's free speech rights"[162] including two cases that involved conflicts between a teacher's freedom of expression and his employer: *Clark v. Holmes*[163] and *Webster*. Because these cases are intermingled by the Court in its analysis, I first make a few comments about *Webster* and *Holmes* and then discuss the general question of the extent to which a particular set of public employees, schoolteachers, possess freedom of speech in their primary workplace, the classroom, and how it applies to the concern of this book.

As we saw in our analysis of *Webster* above, it was the *content* of Mr. Webster's extracurricular lessons—Creation Science, a view repudiated as inherently religious by a number of other courts—and the school board's statutory responsibility in shaping curriculum and avoiding Establishment Clause violations in its public school institutions that led the Court to conclude that Mr. Webster's First and Fourteenth Amendment rights were not violated. The *Webster* Court, however, admits that "this case does not present the issue of whether, or under what circumstances, a school board may completely eliminate material from the curriculum," but rather what is dispositive in this case is "the principle that an individual teacher has no right to ignore the directives of duly appointed education authorities."[164] Given that Mr. LeVake did not teach, and was not trying to teach, Creation Science, *Webster* is not quite to the point.

The *Clark* case concerned a temporary full-time faculty member at Northern Illinois University (NIU). L. Verdelle Clark was offered a two-year appointment in 1962 by the Department of Biological Sciences, but he was warned in the department's letter of offer "that his acceptance . . . should be made with the understanding that he should remedy certain deficiencies in his professional conduct: he counseled an excessive number of students instead of referring them to NIU's professional counselors; he overemphasized sex in his health survey course; he counseled students with his office door closed; and he belittled other staff members in discussions with students." Germane to our analysis of *LeVake* is Clark's claim that his academic freedom (as a species of freedom of speech) was violated by the university when it did not offer him another contract because, in its judgment, he did not remedy the professional deficiencies he agreed to remedy when he accepted the offer of appointment. The Court rejected Clark's claim on the grounds that "academic freedom" is not "a license for uncontrolled expression at variance with established curricular contents and internally destructive of the proper functioning of the institution. First Amendment rights must be applied in light of the special characteristics of the environment in the particular case."[165] The Court relied on a balancing test extracted from *Pickering v. Board of Education* (1968),[166] a case to which both plaintiff and defendants appealed in *Clark*[167] and which the *LeVake* Court cites in its analysis of the free speech rights of public employees:[168]

> It cannot be gainsaid that the State has interests as an employer in regulating the speech of its employees that differ significantly from those it possesses in connection with regulation of the speech of the citizenry in general. *The problem in any case is to arrive at a balance* between the interests of *the teacher, as a citizen,* in commenting upon matters of *public concern* and the interests of the State, as an employer, in promoting the efficiency of the public services it performs through its employees.[169]

Consequently, the question for the Court in *LeVake* is whether the school's reassignment of Mr. LeVake violated his freedom of speech given (1) his prior performance of not teaching the curriculum adequately, (2) his claim to not believe in evolution, (3) his early assertion that he could not teach the curriculum, and (4) his promise in his essay that he would teach evolution in the future *along with* nonreligious criticisms of the theory. Given the totality of these facts (but excluding 2, since it may be a religious belief and thus cannot be the basis for state action), it seems to me that Mr. LeVake was reassigned *because* his superiors were not confident that he would teach the course as required in the curriculum. In light of the deference accorded states in matters of public education, and given the school district's legal duty to teach the curriculum correctly, the Court seems to have balanced the interests of Mr. LeVake and the school district appropriately.

However, under a different set of facts, Mr. LeVake might have had a strong academic freedom claim. Suppose Mr. LeVake had accepted the offer to teach the biology class, agreed to teach the curriculum in precisely the way he is told to do so, and subsequently taught everything required in the curriculum, but in one of his lectures he offered to his students for their consideration nonreligious criticisms of evolution that were neither in the textbook nor in the required curriculum, though relevant to critically assessing the subject matter under study. And suppose that these criticisms of evolution had been developed and defended by qualified and credentialed scholars in respected venues. If Mr. LeVake had *done that* and only that, and if his employer then prohibited him from engaging in such speech during class time, he surely would have had a case, for the law is in his favor.

Given these different set of facts, the other public employee free speech cases on which the Court relies either support or do not address the point of principle that grounds LeVake's free speech rights as a *particular type* of public employee, a high school teacher. *Finch v. Wemlinger* did not deal with a teacher's classroom instruction, but with "an unclassified employee in the Governor's Manpower Office (GMO)"[170] and his firing after he publicly criticized his superiors. Similarly, *Terrell v. University of Texas System Police* dealt with "a public employee" of the university police system who "was fired when his secret diary, which was critical of his supervisor, fell into the supervisor's hands."[171] The case of *Mount Healthy City School District Board of Education v. Doyle* dealt with a nontenured teacher with a history of troublemaking and public altercations who was not rehired after an incident involving his releasing to a local radio station a memo from his principal having to do with the appearance and dress of teachers.[172] The case did not address what is germane to *LeVake:* the extent of a teacher's academic freedom in the classroom. Although the U.S. Supreme Court in *Mount Healthy* accepts "the District Court's finding that the [teacher's] communication was protected by the First and Fourteenth Amendments," it is "not entirely in agreement with that court's manner of reasoning from this finding to the conclusion that Doyle is entitled to reinstatement with backpay."[173] Relying on the *Pickering* balancing test, the Court vacated and remanded the case back to the District Court telling it that it "should have gone on to determine whether the Board had shown by a preponderance of the evidence that it would have reached the same decision as to respondent's reemployment even in the absence of the protected conduct."[174]

The *LeVake* Court cites a case (*Keyishian v. Board of Regents*) involving two faculty members and one librarian who were dismissed by their employer, the State University of New York, for not signing state-mandated loyalty oaths. The faculty members refused to sign a certificate indicating that they were not Communists and the librarian refused to sign a document indicating that he was not a member of a subversive organization that sought or advocated the forceful and violent overthrow of the U.S. government.[175] Ironically, given the different set of facts I proposed, this case would tend to support, rather than undermine, Mr. LeVake's academic freedom to teach criticisms of evolution. For the Court held that the New York statutes on which the firings were based "are invalid insofar as they proscribe mere knowing membership without any showing of specific intent to further the unlawful aims of the Communist Party of the United States or of the State of New York."[176] Thus, the mere fact that Mr. LeVake believes that evolutionary theory is false, or may belong to an organization or group that intends to circumvent the law in order to further this belief,[177] does not show any specific intent on Mr. LeVake's part to teach "religion" (e.g., Creation Science) or to teach the curriculum incorrectly, both of which would be unlawful. In addition, the *Keyishian* case is replete with assertions about the value of academic freedom and that the classroom ought to be a free "marketplace of ideas."[178] For example, in one place, the Court writes:

> Our Nation is deeply committed to safeguarding academic freedom, which is of transcendent value to all of us and not merely to the teachers concerned. That freedom is therefore a special concern of the First Amendment, which does not tolerate laws that cast a pall of orthodoxy over the classroom. "The vigilant protection of constitutional freedoms is nowhere more vital than in the community of American schools."[179]

Clearly the *LeVake* Court is correct that academic freedom in public schools is not absolute and must be balanced by other state interests (*Clark, Pickering, Webster,* and *Mount Healthy* unambiguously affirm this). However, if Mr. Le-Vake would have taught the curriculum adequately and included relevant materials critical of evolution, as in the fictional scenario above, there is much case law on his side in addition to what we have gone over thus far.[180]

First, the Court, in *Epperson,* as quoted in note 103, acknowledges the academic freedom of teachers and students as grounded in their First Amendment right of freedom of expression:

> Our courts . . . have not failed to apply the First Amendment's mandate in our educational system where essential to safeguard the fundamental values of freedom of speech and inquiry and of belief. By and large, public education in our Nation is committed to the control of state and local authorities. Courts do not and cannot intervene in the resolution of conflicts which arise in daily operation of school systems and which do not directly and sharply implicate basic constitutional values. . . . The Court . . . [has] acknowledged the State's power to prescribe the school curriculum, but it held [in *Meyer v. Nebraska* 262] that these were not adequate to support the restriction upon the liberty of teacher and pupil.[181]

According to a U.S. District Court in *Moore v. Gaston County Board of Education,* "that teachers are entitled to First Amendment freedoms is an issue no longer in dispute,"[182] for "the Supreme Court has on numerous occasions emphasized that the right to teach, to inquire, to evaluate and to study is fundamental to a democratic society" even though "academic freedom is not one of the enumerated rights of the First Amendment."[183] This is why, in *Tinker v. Des Moines Independent Community School District,* the Court writes:

> First Amendment rights, applied in light of the special characteristic of the school environment, are available to teachers and students. It can hardly be argued that either students or teachers shed their constitutional rights to freedom of speech or expression at the schoolhouse gate. This has been the unmistakable holding of this Court for almost 50 years.[184]

Second, the *Edwards* Court assumed that teachers had the academic freedom to "supplant the present science curriculum with the presentation of theories, besides evolution, about the origins of life"[185] without needing the Balanced-Treatment Act, which, as we have seen, was struck down by the Court on the grounds that the act's construction would lead to *limiting* rather than advancing the academic freedom of teachers to offer alternative views.[186] The *Webster* Court affirms the principle that a "school may not flatly prohibit teachers from mentioning relevant material."[187] As David K. DeWolf writes, "The Supreme Court has been emphatic in noting that in public schools, the suppression of ideas based upon a disagreement with the ideas themselves is a violation of the First Amendment."[188]

To conclude this analysis of *LeVake,* the Court correctly ruled against the plaintiff, but it should have done so not because of his belief in the falsity of evolution or because he sought to offer his students thoughtful nonsectarian criticisms of evolutionary theory, but rather because of his past performance of teaching the class and his verbal admission that he could not teach the prescribed curriculum. For discriminating against someone because of her religious belief is de facto (not merely prima facie) unconstitutional, and bringing into the classroom relevant material that is supplementary to the curriculum (and not a violation of any other legal duties), when the public school teacher has adequately fulfilled all of her curricular obligations, *is protected speech* under the rubric of academic freedom.

C. SUMMARY OF CHAPTER TWO

Like the Courts in *Epperson* and *McLean,* four issues dominate the majority, concurring, and dissenting opinions in *Edwards*:

The statute's historical continuity with *Scopes* as well as the creation/evolution battles throughout the twentieth century.

How closely the curricular content required by the statute paralleled the creation story in Genesis, and/or whether the curricular content prohibited by the statute is proscribed because it is inconsistent with the creation story in Genesis.

The motives of those who supported the statute in either the legislature or the public square.

Whether the statute was a legitimate means to achieve appropriate state ends.

The *Edwards* opinions, including the dissent, touch on the first, third, and fourth issues in some detail. The second issue is a bit more difficult to assess in *Edwards,* simply because the act was emptied of any clear definition of "Creation Science" prior to passage. This is why both Justice Brennan and Justice Powell in their opinions rely on the contemporaneous and historical connections to the Arkansas statute struck down in *McLean,* as well as to the statutes assessed in *Epperson* and *Scopes.* Justice Powell goes even further and connects the final version of the act with earlier pre-revised versions that were nearly identical to the Genesis-inspired statute struck down in *McLean.* He also connects the act to the literature distributed by the Institute for Creation Research in San Diego (ICR), a young-earth creationist think tank affiliated with Christian Heritage College. Apparently, ICR's "scientists" were cited in the testimony of Dr. Boudreaux.[189]

However, the majority opinion maintains that it is permissible for legislatures to require and/or allow public schools to teach scientific critiques of predominant scientific theories as well as to expose students to a diversity of scientific perspectives on human origins as long as it is done "with the clear secular intent of enhancing the effectiveness of science instruction."[190] The Court also cited positively the Fifth Circuit's finding "that no law prohibited Louisiana public school teachers from teaching any scientific theory."[191] Justice Powell goes a bit further and argues both that a statute may have a religious purpose as long as it does not predominate and that the Establishment Clause is not violated if the material taught in a public school classroom happens to be consistent with the beliefs of some or all religious faiths.

There have been three Federal Court cases and one state case after *Edwards* that are significant to assessing the constitutional permissibility of teaching ID in public schools: *Webster, Peloza, Freiler,* and *LeVake.* The *Freiler* opinion (in the Fifth Circuit) relied on the *Edwards* standard to reject a school board resolution that required public school teachers to present a disclaimer to their students before teaching evolution. The Court employed the Lemon test and concluded that the disclaimer impermissibly advances religion, for the way in which the resolution mentions the biblical doctrine of Creation and other concepts, and the context in which the school board formulated the disclaimer's language, are inconsistent with the resolution's advocacy of critical thinking. The *Freiler* Court dealt with the narrow issue of the disclaimer's language and thus did not propose any legal doctrine that would prohibit the teaching of ID in public schools.

Webster, Peloza, and *LeVake* dealt with the degree to which public school teachers have the liberty to teach alternatives to evolution (*Webster*), criticisms of evolution (*LeVake*), or not to teach evolution at all (*Peloza*) if evolution is the exclusive viewpoint offered in the required curriculum. Although all three cases and their holdings must be taken into consideration when an attorney is defending or counseling a teacher who chooses to incorporate ID in her lesson plan or when a legislator is crafting a statute that permits or requires the teaching of ID in public schools, nevertheless, it seems that nothing in the opinion of either case, when its narrow holding is rightly understood, would prohibit in principle the teaching of ID in public schools.

NOTES

1. *Edwards v. Aguillard,* 482 U.S. 578 (1987)
2. *Webster v. New Lenox School District,* 917 F.2d 1004 (7th Cir. 1990); *Peloza v. Capistrano Unified School District,* 782 Supp. 1412 (C.D. Cal. 1992) (*Peloza I*), *aff'd in part, Peloza v. Capistrano Unified School District,* 37 F.3d 517 (9th Cir. 1994) (*Peloza II*); *Freiler v. Tangipahoa Parish Board of Education,* 185 F.3d 337 (5th Cir. 1999) (*Freiler II*), *reh'g denied en banc,* 201 F.3d 602 (5th cir. 2000) (*Freiler III*), *cert. denied,* 530 U.S. 1251 (2000) (mem.) (*Freiler IV*); *LeVake v. Independent School District,* 625 N.W.2d 502 (2001).
3. "Significantly, the model Act on which the [Louisiana] bill relied was also the basis for a similar statute in Arkansas" (*Edwards,* 482 U.S., 601 [Powell, J., concurring]) (citation omitted).
4. *Edwards,* 482 U.S., 582 (Brennan, J., majority), citing La. Rev. Stat. Ann. § § 17:286.1–17:286.7 (West 1982).
5. *Edwards,* 482 U.S., 581, citing La. Rev. Stat. Ann. § 17:286.4A.
6. *Edwards,* 482 U.S., 581, quoting La. Rev. Stat. Ann.§ 17:286.3(2) and (3) (parenthetical comments inserted by Court).
7. *See* chapter 1, section B, part 4 of this book.
8. *Edwards,* 482 U.S., 601 (Powell, J., concurring).
9. The Arkansas Act, in its section on "Requirements for Balanced Treatment," reads:

> Public schools within this State shall give balanced treatment to creation-science and evolution-science. Balanced treatment to these two models shall be given in classroom lectures taken as a whole for each course, in textbook materials taken as a whole for each course, in library materials taken as a whole for the sciences and taken as a whole for the humanities, and in other educational programs in public schools, to the extent that such lectures, textbooks, library materials, or educational programs deal in any way with the subject of the origin of man, life, the earth, or the universe. (Ark. Stat. Ann. s 80-1663.1 [1981 Supp.])

Louisiana's Balanced-Treatment Act contains the same wording verbatim (La. Rev. Stat. Ann. § 17:286.4A) except it adds a sentence at the end of the paragraph: "When creation or evolution is taught, each shall be taught as a theory, rather than as proven scientific fact." In another section, which is not contained in the Arkansas statute, the Louisiana Act clarifies what it means by "balanced treatment":

> This Subpart does not require any instruction in the subject of origins but simply permits instruction in both scientific models (of evolution-science and creation-science) if public schools choose to teach either. This Subpart does not require each individual textbook or library book to give balanced treatment to the models of evolution-science and creation-science; it does not require any school books to be discarded. This Subpart does not require each individual classroom lecture in a course to give such balanced treatment but simply permits the lectures as a whole to give balanced treatment; it permits some lectures to present evolution-science and other lectures to present creation-science. (La. Rev. Stat. Ann. § 17:286.5)

10. *Aguillard v. Edwards,* 765 F.2d 1251, 1253 (5th Cir. 1985) (*Aguillard III*) (discussing the history of the case prior to July 8, 1985).

11. *Keith v. Louisiana Department of Education,* 553 F.Supp. 295 (M.D. La. 1982).

12. "In an unpublished opinion the district court held that the Act violated the Louisiana constitution, which grants authority over the public school system to the Board of Elementary and Secondary Education" (*Aguillard,* 765 F. 2d, 1254 n. 5).

13. *Aguillard v. Treen,* 440 So.2d 704 (La. 1983) (*Aguillard I*).

14. *Aguillard v. Treen,* 720 F.2d 676 (5th Cir. 1983) (*Aguillard II*).

15. *Aguillard III,* 765 F.2d, 1254.

16. *Aguillard III,* 765 F.2d, 1254, 1256.

17. *See* chapter 1, section B, parts 2 and 4 of this book.

18. *Aguillard III,* 765 F.2d, 1256, 1257.

19. Although it is dicta, the Court makes the important observation that by allowing the teaching of creation-science to be contingent on whether evolution is taught, Louisiana "fails to promote creation science as a genuine academic interest," for if it is something worth imparting to students, the act "would have required its teaching irrespective of whether evolution was taught" (*Aguillard III,* 765 F.2d, 1257).

20. *Aguillard III,* 765 F.2d, 1257.

21. *Aguillard v. Edwards,* 778 F.2d 225 (5th Circuit 1985) (*Aguillard IV*).

22. *Edwards,* 482 U.S., 585, quoting from *Wallace v. Jaffree,* 472 U.S. 38, 56 (1985), 56 (second parenthetical insertion is the Court's).

23. *Edwards,* 482 U.S., 583–584.

24. *Edwards,* 482 U.S., 583–585. The Court cites numerous cases to support this point.

25. *Edwards,* 482 U.S., 586 n. 6, citing and quoting from *Aguillard III,* 765 F.2d, 1257. *See* section A, part 1 of this chapter; *Edwards,* 482 U.S., 586 (note omitted).

26. *Edwards,* 482 U.S., 586, quoting from Tr. of Oral Arg. 60 (parenthetical insertions are the Court's).

27. *Edwards,* 482 U.S., 586.

28. *Edwards,* 482 U.S., 587. The Court cites in support of this standard Justice Powell's and Justice O'Connor's concurring opinions in *Wallace,* 472 U.S.; *Stone v. Graham,* 449 U.S. 39, 41 (1980); and *School District of Abington Township v. Schempp,* 374 U.S. 203, 223–224 (1963).

29. *Edwards,* 482 U.S., 587.

30. 2 App. E-621, as quoted in *Edwards,* 482 U.S., 587.

31. *Edwards,* 482 U.S., 587.

32. *Edwards,* 482 U.S., 587. As noted in section A of this chapter, the Court of Appeals made a similar observation. *See Aguillard III,* 765 F.2d, 1257.

33. *Edwards,* 482 U.S., 587, 588 (note omitted), 588–589.

34. *Edwards,* 482 U.S., 587, 588–589.

35. *Aguillard III,* 765 F. 2d, 1257; *Edwards,* 482 U.S., 589.

36. *Edwards,* 482 U.S., 588.

37. *Edwards,* 482 U.S., 588, citing La.Rev.Stat.Ann. § § 17:286.7A-B, 17:286.4C.

38. *Edwards,* 482 U.S., 588, quoting from *Aguillard III,* 765 F.2d, 1257.

39. *Edwards,* 482 U.S., 590, 592.

40. *Edwards,* 482 U.S., 592 (note omitted).

41. *Edwards,* 482 U.S., 593. The Court writes that "[o]ut of many possible science subjects taught in the public schools, the legislature chose to affect the teaching of the one scientific theory that historically has been opposed by certain religious sects."

42. *Edwards,* 482 U.S., 593, quoting *Epperson v. Arkansas,* 393 U.S. 97, 106–107 (1968).

43. *Edwards,* 482 U.S., 593, 594.

44. *Edwards,* 482 U.S., 605, quoting *Harris v. McRae,* 448 U.S. 297, 319 (1980), quoting *McGowan v. Maryland,* 366 U.S. 420, 442 (1961) (Powell, J., concurring).

45. *Edwards,* 482 U.S., 595 (Brennan, J., majority).

46. *Edwards,* 482 U.S., 597–608 (Powell, J., concurring); *Edwards,* 482 U.S., 608–610 (White, J., concurring).

47. *Edwards,* 482 U.S., 598, quoting *Perrin v. United States,* 444 U.S. 37, 42 (1979) (Powell, J., concurring).

48. *Edwards,* 482 U.S., 598–599, quoting *Webster's Third New International Dictionary* (unabridged 1981), 532.

49. *Edwards,* 482 U.S., 599 (citation omitted).

50. *Edwards,* 482 U.S., 599.

51. *Edwards,* 482 U.S., 599, quoting *Malnak v. Yogi,* 440 F.Supp. 1284, 1322 (NJ 1977) ("*Malnak I*"), *aff'd per curium,* 592 F.2d 197 (CA3 1979) ("*Malnak II*").

52. *Malnak I,* 440 F.Supp., 1322. The complete quote reads: "These concepts concerning God or a supreme being of some sort are manifestly religious when they appear as tenets of Christianity or Buddhism or Hinduism. These concepts do not shed that religiosity merely because they are presented as a philosophy or as a science."

53. For an application of the reasoning of *Malnak I* to establishment problems with "new age religions," see Francis J. Beckwith, "Separation of Guru and State?: The Influence of New Age Thinking on Public Education," in *God and Caesar,* ed. Michael Bauman and David W. Hall (Camp Hill, PA: Christian Publications, 1994). A revised and abridged version was published as "Separation of Guru and State?: The New Age Movement and Public Education," *Deolog: Forum for Beliefs,* 12 (May 1996).

54. "A philosophy may well posit the existence of a supreme being without functioning as a religion in the sense of having clergy and houses of worship. For purposes of the first amendment, these philosophies are the functional equivalent of religions. Surely the prohibition of the establishment clause could not be avoided by governmental aid *to the inculcation of a belief in a supreme being through philosophical instruction instead of through conventionally recognized religious instruction*" (*Malnak I*, 440 F.Supp., 1322 n. 23) (emphasis added).

55. *Malnak II*, 592 F.2d, 208–209.

56. *Malnak II*, 592 F.2d, 209 (citation omitted).

57. Prior to the quote cited by Justice Powell, the *Malnak I* Court presented a detailed analysis of the Supreme Court's jurisprudence concerning the nature of "religion." It writes in one portion of this section:

> The Supreme Court in *Torcaso* [367 U.S. 488] and *Engel* [*v. Vitale* 370 U.S. 421 (1962)] interpreted the word "religion" in the first amendment broadly to encompass "religious concept(s)" and religions which do not propound a belief in the existence of God. In a footnote to Torcaso, the Court listed certain religions which do not hold a belief in the existence of a Supreme Being: "Among religions in this country which do not teach what would generally be considered a belief in the existence of God are Buddhism, Taoism, Ethical Culture, Secular Humanism and others." (*Malnak I*, 440 F.Supp., 1313, quoting *Torcaso*, 367 U.S., 495 n. 11)

In addition, the *Malnak I* Court writes that "[i]t cannot be doubted that concepts of 'God' or an ultimate level of life or ultimate reality are religious concepts" (1322) (note omitted). The Court then cites *Engel* and *Torcaso* as examples.

58. *See* chapter 1, section A, part 2 of this book.

59. *See* Phillip E. Johnson, "Is God Unconstitutional?" *University of Colorado Law Review,* 66 (1995).

60. *Edwards,* 482 U.S., 599 (Powell, J., concurring) (citations omitted).

61. *Edwards,* 482 U.S., 599 (Powell, J., concurring).

62. *Edwards,* 482 U.S., 599–604 (Powell, J., concurring).

63. *Edwards,* 482 U.S., 605 (Powell, J., concurring).

64. *Edwards,* 482 U.S., 605 (Powell, J., concurring), quoting *Harris,* 448 U.S. at 319, quoting *McGowan,* 366 U.S. 442.

65. *Edwards,* 482 U.S., 606–608 (Powell, J., concurring).

66. *Edwards,* 482 U.S., 610–640 (Scalia, J., dissenting).

67. Although it is not one of the three points we cover, it is worth mentioning that Justice Scalia also criticizes the District Court's summary judgment including its rejection of five affidavits filed by appellants. These affidavits are the testimonies of two scientists, one philosopher, a theologian, and an educator. Justice Scalia believes that the District Court's action casts doubt on the soundness of the Supreme Court's majority opinion:

> The case arrives here in the following posture: The Louisiana Supreme Court has never been given an opportunity to interpret the Balanced Treatment Act, State officials have never attempted to implement it, and it has never been the subject of a full evidentiary hearing. We can only guess at its meaning. We know that it forbids instruction in either "creation-science" or "evolution-science" without instruction in the other, . . . but the

parties are sharply divided over what creation science consists of. Appellants insist that it is a collection of educationally valuable scientific data that has been censored from classrooms by an embarrassed scientific establishment. Appellees insist that it is not science at all but thinly veiled religious doctrine. Both interpretations of the intended meaning find considerable support in the legislative history. (*Edwards,* 482 U.S., 611), citation omitted)

68. It should be noted that in the three points we cover, Justice Scalia *assumes* the validity of the Lemon "purpose" test *for the sake of argument* (*Edwards,* 482 U.S., 613). He writes: "I doubt whether that 'purpose' requirement of Lemon is a proper interpretation of the Constitution; but even if it were, I could not agree with the Court's assessment that the requirement was not satisfied" (*Edwards,* 482 U.S., 613).

69. *Edwards,* 482 U.S., 611, 610.

70. *Edwards,* 482 U.S., 634.

71. *Edwards,* 482 U.S., 587 (Brennan, J., majority); *Edwards,* 482 U.S., 634 (Scalia, J., dissenting).

72. *See* David K. DeWolf, "Academic Freedom after *Edwards*," *Regent University Law Review,* 13, 2 (2000–2001), 461–462.

73. *Edwards,* 482 U.S., 636–640 (Scalia, J., dissenting).

74. One could argue that the Court is committing a fallacy of informal logic by confusing motivation with purpose. For by tying the soundness of a claim to its source (i.e., its supporters' motivation) rather than to an assessment of its merits, the Court commits *the genetic fallacy.* So, if we were to apply a rational basis test to the Court's "motivation test," it would not even pass rational basis, for a fallacious argument is necessarily irrational.

75. DeWolf, "Academic Freedom," 461. Frederick Lawrence writes: "Motive can be distinguished from purpose. Purpose concerns a person's conscious object to engage in certain conduct or to cause a certain result. *See,* e.g., Model Penal Code § 2.02(2)(a)(i) (1962). Motive, on the other hand, concerns the cause that drives the action to further that purpose" (Frederick M. Lawrence, "The Punishment of Hate: Toward a Normative Theory of Bias-Motivated Crimes," *Michigan Law Review,* 93 [1994], 381 n. 173, as quoted in DeWolf, "Academic Freedom," 461 n. 86).

76. DeWolf, "Academic Freedom," 461 n. 87, citing Laurence H. Tribe, "The Mystery of Motive, Private and Public: Some Notes Inspired by the Problems of Hate Crime and Animal Sacrifice," *1993 Supreme Court Review.*

77. *Edwards,* 482 U.S., 613 (Scalia, J., dissenting) (citations omitted).

78. *Edwards,* 482 U.S., 614. The three cases cited by Justice Scalia are *Wallace,* 472 U.S., 56, 57, 60 (finding that authorized and state-directed moments of silence for voluntary prayer and/or meditation are unconstitutional); *Stone,* 449 U.S., 43 n. 5 (finding that required public school classroom posting of Ten Commandments, even with a disclaimer stating that it has no religious intent, is unconstitutional); and *Epperson,* 393 U.S., 103, 107–109 (*see* chapter 1, section B, part 2 of this book). Even in this quote of Justice Scalia one finds the motivation/purpose confusion. For it seems that even if the legislature in each of these cited cases had a solely religious motivation, the statutes could have had a secular purpose and still passed constitutional muster.

79. *Edwards,* 482 U.S., 615 (Scalia, J., dissenting).

80. *Edwards,* 482 U.S., 615 (Scalia, J., dissenting), quoting *Harris,* 448 U.S., 319, quoting *McGowan,* 366 U.S. at 442 (citations omitted).

81. *Edwards,* 482 U.S., 615 (Scalia, J., dissenting), citing *Harris,* 448 U.S., 319.

82. *Edwards,* 482 U.S., 615 (Scalia, J., dissenting), citing *McGowan,* 366 U.S., 442

83. *Edwards,* 482 U.S., 616 (Scalia, J., dissenting), citing *Mueller,* 463 U.S., 394–395.

84. *Edwards,* 482 U.S., 616 (Scalia, J., dissenting), citing *Wolman v. Walter,* 433 U.S., 229, 236 (1977) (plurality opinion); *Meek v. Pittinger* 421 U.S. 349, 363 (1975); *Committee for Public Education & Religious Liberty v. Nyquist,* 413 U.S. 756, 773 (1973); and *Lemon v. Kurtzman,* 403 U.S. 602, 613 (1971).

85. *Edwards,* 482 U.S., 616 (Scalia, J., dissenting), citing *Walz v. Tax Commission,* 397 U.S. 664, 672 (1970).

86. *Edwards,* 482 U.S., 616 (Scalia, J., dissenting), citing *Board of Education v. Allen,* 392 U.S. 236, 243 (1968).

87. *Edwards,* 482 U.S., 616–617 (Scalia, J., dissenting), citing several cases including *Lynch v. Donnelly* 465 U.S. 668, 690 (1984) (O'Connor, J., concurring); *Committee for Public Education,* 413 U.S., 788; and *Walz,* 397 U.S., 673.

88. *Edwards,* 482 U.S., 617 (Scalia, J., dissenting).

89. See, for example, *Sherbert v. Verner,* 374 U.S., 398 (1963) (ruling that a statute that denied a woman unemployment benefits because she quit a job that required her to work on a Saturday sabbath violated the Free Exercise Clause by not accommodating her religious beliefs); *see,* for example, *Wisconsin v. Yoder,* 406 U.S., 205 (1972) (ruling that the Free Exercise Clause requires that the government must exempt Amish parents from compulsory school attendance laws for their children).

90. *Edwards,* 482 U.S., 618 (Scalia, J., dissenting) (citation omitted).

91. *Edwards,* 482 U.S., 635 (citation omitted). Justice Scalia does add on the same page: "I am not in any case enamored of those amorphous exceptions, since I think them no more than unpredictable correctives of what is . . . a fundamentally unsound rule. It is surprising, however, that the Court does not address these exceptions, since the context of the legislature's action gives some reason to believe that they may be applicable" (note omitted).

92. *Edwards,* 482 U.S., 621.

93. *Edwards,* 482 U.S., 621–627 (citing and reviewing this testimony).

94. *Edwards,* 482 U.S., 627.

95. *Edwards,* 482 U.S., 627, quoting from *Grand Rapids School District v. Ball,* 473 U.S. 373, 385 (1985) (parenthetical insertion is the Court's).

96. *See Edwards,* 482 U.S., 588 (Brennan, J., majority); 630–636 (Scalia, J., dissenting).

97. For a brief analysis of this opinion, *see* H. Wayne House, "Darwinism and the Law: Can Non-Naturalistic Scientific Theories Survive Constitutional Challenge?" *Regent University Law Review,* 13, 2 (2000–2001), 424–426.

98. *Webster,* 917 F.2d, 1005.

99. *Webster,* 917 F.2d, 1006, citing in footnote *Edwards,* 482 U.S., 592.

100. *Webster,* 917 F.2d, 1006

101. *Webster,* 917 F.2d, 1007.
102. *Webster,* 917 F.2d, 1008, citing *Zykan v. Warsaw Community School Corp.,* 631 F.2d 1300, 1305–06 (7th Cir. 1980).
103. The Court writes in *Epperson* 393 U.S. (104, 105):

Our courts . . . have not failed to apply the First Amendment's mandate in our educational system where essential to safeguard the fundamental values of freedom of speech and inquiry and of belief. By and large, public education in our Nation is committed to the control of state and local authorities. Courts do not and cannot intervene in the resolution of conflicts which arise in daily operation of school systems and which do not directly and sharply implicate basic constitutional values. On the other hand, "[t]he vigilant protection of constitutional freedoms is nowhere more vital than in the community of American schools" [*Shelton v. Tucker,* 364 U.S., 479, 487 (1960)]. . . . As this Court said in *Keyishian v. Board of Regents* [385 U.S., 589, 603 (1967)], the First Amendment "does not tolerate laws that cast a pall of orthodoxy over the classroom. . . . The Court . . . [has] acknowledged the State's power to prescribe the school curriculum, but it held [in *Meyer v. Nebraska* 262 U.S., 390 (1923)] that these were not adequate to support the restriction upon the liberty of teacher and pupil.

See William W. Van Alstyne, "Academic Freedom and the First Amendment in the Supreme Court of the United States: An Unhurried Historical Review," *Law & Contemporary Problems,* 53 (Summer 1990).
104. *Webster,* 917 F.2d, 1008, summarizing a principle enunciated in *Zykan,* 631 F.2d, 1305–1306.
105. *Peloza I,* 782 Supp., *aff'd in part, Peloza II,* 37 F.3d.
106. *Peloza,* 37 F.3d, 519.
107. *Edwards,* 482 U.S., 605 (Powell, J., concurring), quoting *Harris,* 448 U.S., 319, quoting *McGowan,* 366 U.S., 442.
108. *Agillard III,* 765 F.2d, 1257.
109. *Peloza,* 37 F.3d, 520.
110. *Peloza,* 37 F.3d, 521.
111. *See* chapter 1, section A, part 2 of this book.
112. *Peloza,* 37 F.3d, 521.
113. For example, if Mr. Peloza were allowed by the Court to reject the required curriculum based on the federal Constitution, this would raise all sorts of issues about the wide discretion and presumption accorded states on matters of morality and education. Thus, the Court could have dismissed Mr. Peloza's complaint on the grounds that it is a matter that ought to be addressed through the democratic process rather than by the Courts.
114. If, for example, theological claims (e.g., "God is creator of the universe") could in principle be known and just as true as claims usually associated exclusively with science (e.g., "Only material non-agent explanations of natural phenomena count as knowledge"), then the *Peloza* court is mistaken, for it would mean that naturalistic evolution, if it is the most plausible theory of origins, is a defeater against theism.
115. *Freiler II,* 185 F.3d, *reh'g denied en banc, Freiler III,* 201 F.3d, *cert. denied, Freiler IV,* 530 U.S.

116. *Freiler v. Tangipahoa Parish Board of Education,* 97 F. Supp. 819 (E.D. La. 1997) (*Freiler I*).

117. This portion of the sentence is a mistaken quote by the Freiler Court. The original resolution reads "to form his/her own opinion *or* maintain beliefs taught by parents" rather than what the Freiler Court quoted, "to form his/or opinion *and* maintain beliefs taught by parents" (emphasis added). One could argue that whether the resolution says "or" or "and" makes a significant difference. The court, in a denial of rehearing en banc, argued that "the improper substitution of 'and' for 'or' does not affect the outcome of the case" (*Freiler III,* 201 F.3d, 603). The dissent, however, thought it was important: "The first-purpose-is-a-sham conclusion is unwarranted. As noted, the panel misquoted the following portion of the disclaimer: 'it is the basic right and privilege of each student to form his/her opinion or [not "and", as the panel opinion mistakenly quoted] maintain beliefs taught by parents on [the] . . . matter of the origin of life and matter'. This mistaken reading of the disclaimer as conjunctive, rather than disjunctive, perhaps explains why the panel discounted the disclaimer's clear message that, concerning the origin of life and matter, students are free to either maintain their current beliefs, including those taught by their parents, or to form their own, new, independent opinion" (*Freiler III,* 201 F.3d, 605 [Barksdale, J., dissenting]).

118. *Freiler II,* 185 F.3d, 346.

119. *Freiler II,* 185 F.3d, 344.

120. The District Court, in contrast, ruled that the resolution does not pass Lemon's first prong. *See Freiler I,* 97 F. Supp., 826–830.

121. *Freiler II,* 185 F.3d, 344–345.

122. *Freiler II,* 185 F.3d, 345.

123. *Freiler II,* 185 F.3d, 344–345.

124. *Freiler II,* 185 F.3d, 346.

125. *Freiler II,* 185 F.3d, 346 (footnote omitted).

126. *Freiler II,* 185 F.3d, 346 fn. 4.

127. The school board did argue that the disclaimer's mention of "Biblical version of Creation" is merely illustrative. But the Court did not buy it: "[T]he record does not comport with the School Board's characterization of its reason for including 'Biblical version of Creation' in the disclaimer. When the School Board debated the propriety of the proposed disclaimer, a member suggested deleting the reference to the Biblical version of creation. The Board ultimately rejected that suggestion, apparently not because doing so might confuse students who needed an illustrative reference, but because doing so would, in the words of the disclaimer's sponsor, 'gut . . . the basic message of the [disclaimer]'" (*Freiler II,* 185 F.3d, 346 n. 4).

128. Edward McGlynn Gaffney Jr., "Critical Thinking Prohibited," *First Things,* 104 (April 2001), *available at* http://www.firstthings.com/ftissues/ft0104/opinion/gaffney.html (October 28, 2001).

129. *Freiler II,* 185 F.3d, 341–42, 345, 346 n. 4.

130. Gaffney, "Critical Thinking."

131. *See,* for example, Alvin Plantinga and Nicholar Wollterstorff, eds., *Faith and Rationality: Reason and Belief in God* (New York: Oxford University Press, 1984).

132. *See*, for example, M. Drew DeMott, "*Freiler v. Tangipahoa Parish Board of Education*: Disclaiming the Gospel of Modern Science," *Regent University Law Review*, 13, 2 (2000–2001); Gaffney, "Critical Thinking."

133. *See*, for example, Stephen L. Carter, "Evolutionism, Creationism, and Teaching Religion as a Hobby," *Duke Law Journal* (1987).

134. *Freiler II*, 185 F.3d, 346.

135. National Academy of Sciences, *Science and Creationism: A View for the National Academy of Sciences* (1984), 5–6, *available at* http://stills.nap.edu/books/030903440X/html/ (February 8, 2001), 5–6. I respond to a version of this argument in chapter 4, section B, part 1.a.

136. "The idea that belief in a creator and acceptance of the scientific theory of evolution are mutually exclusive is a false premise and offensive to the religious views of many. . . . Dr. Francisco Ayala, a geneticist of considerable renown and a former Catholic priest who has the equivalent of a Ph.D. in theology, pointed out that many working scientists who subscribed to the theory of evolution are devoutly religious" (*McLean*, 529 F. Supp., 1266 n. 23). "Although the subject of origins of life is within the province of biology, the scientific community does not consider origins of life a part of evolutionary theory. The theory of evolution assumes the existence of life and is directed to an explanation of how life evolved. Evolution does not presuppose the absence of a creator or God and the plain inference conveyed by Section 4 is erroneous" (*McLean*, 529 F. Supp., 1266 [note omitted]); Evolution "has nothing to do with whether or not there is a divine Creator (who did or did not create the universe or did or did not plan evolution as part of a divine scheme)" (*Peloza*, 37 F.3d, 521).

137. According to the U.S. Supreme Court, courts may not resolve questions of the truth of religious beliefs. *See U.S. v. Ballard*, 322 U.S. 78 (1944); "It is not within the judicial ken to question the centrality of particular beliefs or practices to a faith or the validity of particular litigants' interpretations of [their] creeds" (*Hernandez v. Commissioner*, 490 U.S. 680, 699 [1989]).

138. *Freiler III*, 201 F.3d, 603.

139. *Freiler II*, 185 F.3d, 342.

140. *Freiler I*, 97 F. Supp., 821.

141. National Center for Science Education, *Seven Significant Court Decisions on the Issue of Evolution versus Creationism*, republished in Niles Eldredge, *The Triumph of Evolution and the Failure of Creationism* (New York: W. H. Freeman & Company, 2000), 184.

142. For a more detailed reply to the District Court's claim, see The Memo Regarding the Freiler Case, from John Calvert, Esq. to Dr. Robert Bowers and the Science Standards Committee, Ohio State Board of Education (February 2, 2002), *available at* http://www.arn.org/docs/ohio/calverttostandardscommittee020402.htm (April 24, 2002).

143. *LeVake*, 625 N.W.2d. The Minnesota Supreme Court declined to hear the case on appeal, and the U.S. Supreme Court declined as well: *LeVake v. Independent School Dist. No. 656*, 122 S.Ct. 814 (Mem) U.S. (2002).

144. *LeVake*, 625 N.W.2d, 505.

145. *LeVake*, 625 N.W.2d, 505.

146. *LeVake*, 625 N.W.2d, 505–506.

147. *LeVake*, 625 N.W.2d, 506, quoting from LeVake's essay.

148. *LeVake*, 625 N.W.2d, 506, quoting from LeVake's essay (Court's emphasis removed).

149. *LeVake*, 625 N.W.2d, 506.

150. *LeVake*, 625 N.W.2d, 506, quoting from a letter to LeVake from Superintendent Keith Dixon.

151. *LeVake*, 625 N.W.2d, 506.

152. *LeVake*, 625 N.W.2d, 506.

153. *LeVake*, 625 N.W.2d, 509, quoting from LeVake's contract with the school district.

154. *LeVake*, 625 N.W.2d, 509, quoting from LeVake's deposition (first and third parenthetical insertions are the Court's; the second is mine).

155. *LeVake*, 625 N.W.2d, 509.

156. *LeVake*, 625 N.W.2d, 507 (citation omitted).

157. *LeVake*, 625 N.W.2d, 507.

158. *LeVake*, 625 N.W.2d, 509 (emphasis added).

159. In *McDaniel v. Paty,* the Supreme Court refers to the "Free Exercise Clause's absolute prohibition of infringements on the 'freedom to believe'" (435 U.S. 618, 627 [1978]). It asserts in *Everson v. Board of Education,* "No person can be punished for entertaining or professing religious beliefs or disbeliefs, for church attendance or non-attendance" (330 U.S. 1, 15–16 [1947]). According to Eugene Volokh, "The government generally may not prosecute someone or otherwise burden them for their religious *beliefs*" (*The First Amendment: Problems, Cases and Policy Arguments* [New York: Foundation Press, 2001], 670). See also, *Cantwell v. State of Connecticut,* 310 U.S. 296 (1940); and *Torcaso,* 367 U.S.

160. *See*, for example, *Employment Division v. Smith,* 494 U.S. 872 (1990).

161. Someone may reply that Mr. LeVake's belief in evolution's falsity is not *religious* but merely secular, and thus is not protected under the First Amendment's Free Exercise Clause. After all, did not LeVake admit that he would critique evolution in the classroom in an entirely nonsectarian manner? Nevertheless, the Court has ruled that freedom of religious belief is grounded in a more general liberty of belief: "If there is any fixed star in our constitutional constellation, it is that no official, high or petty, can prescribe what shall be orthodox in politics, nationalism, religion, or other matters of opinion or force citizens to confess by word or act their faith therein" (*West Virginia State Bd. of Educ. v. Barnette,* 319 U.S. 624, 642 [1943]).

162. *LeVake*, 625 N.W.2d, 508.

163. *Clark v. Holmes,* 474 F. 2d 928 (7th Cir. 1972).

164. *Webster,* 917 F.2d, 1008, citing *Zykan,* 631 F.2d, 1305–06 (7th Cir. 1980).

165. *Clark,* 474 F. 2d, 930; 931 (citations omitted).

166. *Pickering v. Board of Education,* 391 U.S. 563 (1968).

167. The Court writes: "Both parties claim to find support in *Pickering v. Board of Education* . . . , a major pronouncement of the First Amendment rights of public school teachers. There, the Supreme Court reversed the dismissal of a teacher who

had written a letter to a local newspaper in which he, as a citizen, criticized the Board of Education's allocation of school funds and its method of informing the district's taxpayers about the need for additional tax revenue" (*Clark,* 474 F. 2d, 930).

168. *LeVake,* 625 N.W.2d, 508.

169. *Pickering,* 391 U.S., 568, as quoted in *Clark,* 474 F. 2d, 931.

170. *Finch v. Wemlinger,* 361 N.W.2d 865 (Minn.,1985). This is cited in *LeVake,* 625 N.W.2d, 508

171. *Terrell v. University of Texas System Police,* 792 F.2d 1360, 1362 (5th Cir. 1986), *cert. denied,* 479 U.S. 1064 (1987). This is cited in *LeVake,* 625 N.W.2d, 508.

172. *Mount Healthy City Sch. Dist. Bd. of Educ. v. Doyle,* 429 U.S. 274 (1977). This is cited in *LeVake,* 625 N.W.2d, 508.

173. *Mount Healthy,* 429 U.S., 284.

174. *Mount Healthy,* 429 U.S., 284, 287.

175. *Keyishian v. Board of Regents,* 385 U.S. 589 (1967). This is cited in *LeVake,* 625 N.W.2d, 508.

176. *Keyishian,* 385 U.S., 609–610.

177. The curriculum director's request that Mr. LeVake answer questions about his religious beliefs so that she may infer whether or not Mr. LeVake would unlawfully teach the prescribed curriculum seems analogous to trying to find out if a faculty member is a Communist and inferring from it that the faculty member intends to engage in an unlawful overthrow of the government. One press account of LeVake's case reads:

> LeVake was even more amazed when the curriculum director asked him whether he ever mentioned God or the Bible in his science class. He said no.
>
> Then she asked whether his students knew he was a Christian.
>
> "That was one that I couldn't answer right away. I would like to have said, 'Yes, they do know, just because of the way I act.' But I didn't want to say it that way because she would probably think that I was proselytizing in my classroom. So I said, 'I would hope so because I don't curse, and I don't do things that would make people think I'm not a Christian.'"
>
> Although he was surprised by the questions, LeVake said, "It gave me some light on where they were coming from. Those questions betrayed what they were thinking." (Frank York, "No Admittance," in *Teachers in Focus* [2000], *available at* http://www.family.org/ cforum/ teachersmag/features/a0009437.html [April 29, 2002].)

178. Keyishian, 385 U.S., 603.

179. Keyishian, 385 U.S., 603, quoting *Shelton v. Tucker,* 364 U.S. 479, 487 (1960).

180. Much of what follows is gleaned from portions of two outstanding articles on this subject: DeWolf, "Academic Freedom after *Edwards*"; and David K. DeWolf, Stephen C. Meyer, and Mark Edward DeForrest, "Teaching the Controversy: Science, or Religion, or Speech?" *Utah Law Review* (2000), 98–110. Both these articles, however, go into more detail than what I am covering here.

181. *Epperson,* 393 U.S., 104, 105. *See* Van Alstyne, "Academic Freedom and the First Amendment."

182. *Moore v. Gaston County Board of Education,* 357 F. Supp. 1037, 1039 (W.D. N.C. 1973). The *Moore* Court held that to "discharge a teacher without warning because his answers to scientific and theological questions do not fit the notions of the local parents and teachers is a violation of the Establishment Clause of the First Amendment" (1043).

183. *Moore,* 357 F. Supp., 1039–40, citing *Wiemen v. New Hampshire* by Wyman, 354 U.S. 589, 603 (1967) and cross-referencing that with *Meyer,* 262 U.S.

184. *Tinker v. Des Moines Independent Community School District* 393 U.S. 503, 506 (1969).

185. *Edwards,* 482 U.S., 587. The Court below made a similar observation. *See Aguillard III,* 765 F.2d, 1257.

186. "Under the Act's requirements, teachers who were once free to teach any and all facets of this subject are now unable to do so" (*Edwards,* 482 U.S., 588–589). Moreover, "the Act fails even to ensure that creation science will be taught, but instead requires the teaching of this theory only when the theory of evolution is taught" (589).

187. *Webster,* 917 F.2d, 1008, summarizing a principle enunciated in *Zykan,* 631 F.2d, 1305–1306.

188. DeWolf, "Academic Freedom after *Edwards,*" 479 (citing *Pico v. United States,* 457 U.S. 853 [1982]).

189. *See Edwards,* 482 U.S., 600–604 (Powell, J., concurring).

190. *Edwards,* 482 U.S., 594 (Brennan, J., majority).

191. *Edwards,* 482 U.S., 587, citing *Aguillard III,* 765 F.2d, 1257.

Chapter Three

Intelligent Design

Intelligent Design (ID) is an intellectual movement that challenges the widely held viewpoint that methodological naturalism is a necessary precondition for, and ontological materialism (or naturalism)[1] an entailment of, the practice of natural science. ID proponents maintain that this philosophical commitment is the primary reason for the intellectual dominance of naturalistic evolution. Unlike the creation scientists whose views were rebuffed in *Epperson, McLean,* and *Edwards,* design theorists defend a perspective that is grounded in an array of arguments, both empirical and philosophical, that attempt to unseat both methodological naturalism and ontological materialism. Design theorists maintain that their perspective is not the result of a literal reading of Genesis, though they concede that their case lends support to theism generally. Also, unlike the literature, proponents, and history that formed the ideological nexus that supported the statutes struck down in *Epperson, McLean,* and *Edwards,* the ID movement's literature, proponents, and history are respectively of high quality, well credentialed, and largely unconnected to the Scopes Trial and the cultural and legal squabbles that flowed from them.[2]

Although the ID movement is far from monolithic, there are particular strands of thought within the movement, and types of arguments by its proponents, that are important for the purpose of assessing whether ID would pass constitutional muster if a statute were to permit (or perhaps require) it to be taught in public schools. We look at three strands of ID that are relevant to this assessment: (A) The Case against Methodological Naturalism, (B) The Case for Intelligent Design, and (C) The Case for the Illiberality of Teaching Naturalistic Evolution in Public Schools. The first two dominate the literature on design theory. The third, though mentioned rarely in the literature, has a bearing on the Establishment Clause and current understandings of state and legal neutrality. Because the literature supporting ID is sophisticated, vast, and growing,[3] my presentation of its case is cursory.

As I said in the introduction, my primary concern in this book is not with the soundness or persuasive power of the scientific and philosophical arguments of ID proponents, even though we touch on those arguments and their strengths. Rather, my chief focus is answering a question of constitutional jurisprudence. This is an important distinction. For if one finds the ID arguments unpersuasive, that is not a reason to deny students and teachers in public science education access to these arguments.[4] In fact, I believe that all that is legally necessary to permit (or require) ID in public school science classes is that it does not unconstitutionally advance religion, that its proponents make a reasonable and intellectually respectable case for their position, that the state have a legitimate interest in exposing students and faculty to ID,[5] and that the state have legitimate means by which to accomplish this.[6]

A. THE CASE AGAINST METHODOLOGICAL NATURALISM

ID proponents maintain that there is a fundamental reason why naturalistic evolution seems to most scholars in the humanities and sciences to be the only real legitimate explanation for the origin of the universe and life: a prior commitment to methodological naturalism (MN), "the view that science must be restricted solely to undirected natural processes."[7] According to Phillip Johnson, "[a] methodological naturalist defines science as the search for the best naturalistic theories. A theory would not be naturalistic if it left something out (such as the existence of genetic information or consciousness) to be explained by a supernatural cause." Therefore, "all events in evolution (before the evolution of intelligence) are assumed attributable to unintelligent causes. The question is not *whether* life (genetic information) arose by some combination of chance and chemical laws, to pick one example, but merely *how* it did so."[8] Thus, according to design theorists, once one defines science as a discipline that allows only naturalistic explanations, and if one maintains that science is the only field that provides truth on the question of origins, then naturalistic evolution *must be true* even if there are many unanswered questions that seem incapable of being adequately addressed under the evolutionary paradigm. In the words of William Dembski, "So long as methodological naturalism sets the ground rules for how the game of science is to be played, intelligent design has no chance of success."[9] Consider, for example, the remarks of Richard Lewontin, professor of genetics at Harvard University:

We take the side of science in spite of the patent absurdity of some of its constructs, in spite of its failure to fulfill many of its extravagant promises of health and life, in spite of the tolerance of the scientific community for unsubstantiated just-so stories, because we have a prior commitment, a commitment to materialism. It is not that the methods and institutions of science somehow compel us to accept a material explanation of the phenomenal world, but, on the contrary, that we are forced by our a priori adherence to material causes to create an apparatus of investigation and a set of concepts that produce material explanations, no matter how counter-intuitive, no matter how mystifying to the uninitiated. Moreover, that materialism is an absolute, for we cannot allow a Divine Foot in the door.[10]

Consequently, it is no wonder why ID proponents maintain that what should be a rigorous intellectual debate has become, in the hands of more hostile partisans, a question-begging street fight over metaphysical turf.

This is all well and good, but how do ID supporters critique MN? Or more properly, why would they want to? After all, it seems as though science, as we all learned in high school and college, deals exclusively with natural causes and explanations. Sneaking in "God" or some disembodied intelligence to account for a particular phenomenon seems to most of us like a science-stopper that cheats us out of a *real* account of what happened. This "God-of-the-gaps" strategy, as it is pejoratively called, is the antithesis of good science, and hence, any talk of non-natural, nonmaterial accounts of natural phenomena immediately elicits the accusation (and perhaps bellicose laughter) that such talk is the disreputable "God-of-the-gaps" strategy.[11] Thus, it seems to many that MN is a necessary condition for science to function properly.

However, design theorists maintain that there may be times at which an intelligent designer better accounts for certain phenomena than do material causes. And if that is the case, then the naturalist's appeal to possible future materialist accounts of the phenomena is driven not by the data, but by MN and thus is a type of "naturalism-of-the-gaps."[12] Design theorists, as we shall see, do not employ intelligent design as a mere "gap" when all natural explanations fail. But rather they present criteria that they believe are useful in detecting and falsifying design. (Whether such criteria actually work, of course, is another question entirely.)

Because the critiques of MN in the ID literature are sophisticated and plentiful,[13] there is no way I can present all the arguments, or even detailed presentations of some of them, in this book. So, I briefly go over a few points made by design theorists that I believe are pertinent to my objective: (1) Methodological Naturalism Is Not a Claim *of* Science, (2) The Failure of Demarcation Theories, and (3) Science and External Conceptual Problems.

1. Methodological Naturalism Is Not a Claim *of* Science

According to ID proponents, MN is not a claim *of* natural science—e.g., Einstein's Theory of Relativity—but a claim *about* natural science. According to J. P. Moreland, the claim that natural science must adopt MN is a "second-order philosophical" claim *"about"* science."[14] That is, the question of whether MN is necessary for natural science is a philosophical claim that must be justified *philosophically;* it cannot be justified *by* natural science, if it is alleged to be a presupposition for the practice of natural science. No doubt natural science assumes certain preconditions, some of which appear to be essential to its practice. But none of them is derived *from* science; they are philosophical presuppositions that make science possible. This is why, for example, as I pointed out in chapter 1 (section B, part 2), the California Board of Education's definition of science in its Science Framework cannot, on its own grounds, be part of any science curriculum, for it is a claim that is either self-refuting (i.e., it is a claim *of* science that is inconsistent with itself) or it is a philosophical claim (i.e., it is a claim *about* science and thus cannot be part of the science curriculum because it is not a claim *of* science).

The words of philosopher John Kekes, who is not an ID proponent, are instructive here:

> Science is committed to several presuppositions: that nature exists, that it has discoverable order, that it is uniform, are existential presuppositions of science; the distinctions between space and time, cause and effect, the observer and the observed, real and apparent, orderly and chaotic, are classificatory presuppositions; while intersubjective testability, quantifiability, the public availability of data, are methodological presuppositions; some axiological presuppositions are the honest reporting of results, the worthwhileness of getting the facts right, and scrupulousness in avoiding observational or experimental error. If any one of these presuppositions were abandoned, science, as we know it, could not be done. Yet the acceptance of the presuppositions cannot be a matter of course, for each has been challenged and alternatives are readily available.[15]

ID proponents raise the question of whether MN is like the presuppositions Kekes summarizes. If it is, then there is nothing wrong in challenging it, for "each has been challenged and alternatives are readily available." But ID proponents maintain that unlike these other presuppositions—that do appear for the present time necessary for natural science—MN's status as a necessary precondition is weak and is only sustained as such by the ideological infrastructure of the scientific establishment. Thus, the real question, according to design theorists, is whether their arguments for ID work, not whether ID conflicts with MN. After all, if their arguments work and they conflict with MN, then one may conclude, quite reasonably, that MN is not a necessary precondition of natural science after all.[16] For to exclude nonmaterialist (or ID) accounts of natural phenomena by merely defining science as requiring MN does not count either as a philosophical argument against ID or an argument for MN; it is, at best, circular reasoning, and at worst, intellectual imperialism. As Stephen C. Meyer points out:

> [A]sserting mechanism [or materialism] as necessary to the scientific status of origin theories begs the question. In particular, it assumes without justification that all scientifically acceptable causes are *mechanistic* causes. To insist that all causal explanations in science must be mechanistic is to insist that all causal theories must refer only to material entities (or their energetic equivalent). . . . This argument clearly assumes the point at issue, which is whether or not there are independent—that is, metaphysically neutral—reasons for preferring exclusively materialistic causal explanations of origins over explanations that invoke putatively immaterial entities such as creative intelligence, mind, mental action, divine action or intelligent design. While philosophical naturalists may not regard the foregoing as real or (if real) immaterial, they certainly cannot deny that such entities could function as causal antecedents if they were.
>
> Thus, we return to the central question: What noncircular reason can be offered for prohibiting the postulation of nonmechanistic (e.g., mental or intelligent) causes in scientific origins theories? Simply asserting that such entities may not be considered, whatever the empirical justification for their postulation, clearly does not constitute a justification for an exclusively naturalistic definition of science. Theoretically there are at least two possible types of causes: mechanistic and intelligent.[17]

If Meyer is correct, then MN is not a necessary precondition for the practice of natural science. It follows then that science can be practiced without presupposing MN, which means that ID cannot in principle be excluded as a legitimate scientific research program.

2. The Failure of Demarcation Theories

The purpose of demarcation theories is to distinguish science from nonscience. So, for example, assuming MN is a necessary condition to label something science, any theory that does not assume MN is not science. Consequently, ID, because it rejects MN, is not science, if this demarcation theory is sound. But, as we have seen (chapter 3, section A, part 1) and will see (chapter 3, section A, part 3; section B), ID theorists and others have marshaled an impressive array of reasons to reject MN as a necessary precondition of natural science.

Moreover, as we saw in our analysis of *McLean* (chapter 1, section B, part 4), demarcation theories in general have fallen on hard times, even though one such theory found its way into Judge Overton's opinion. Thus, there is no need to repeat what has already been covered in my evaluation of demarcation theories in my analysis of that opinion.

Nevertheless, one can raise the question of whether there are any other demarcation theories that are noncircular and at the same time may work legitimately to exclude ID. To my knowledge, there are none. The overwhelming consensus in philosophy of science is that demarcation theories are doomed to failure for many of the reasons we covered above (*see* chapter 1, section B, part 4; chapter 3, section A, part 1).[18] However, this does not mean that ID should not be subject to strict philosophical and scientific analysis. For instance, if ID arguments lack certain theoretical virtues that are considered earmarks of good theories or explanations—e.g., explanatory power, empirical adequacy, simplicity, predictive and/or retrodictive success (as broadly construed in the historical sciences), testability,[19] clarity of concepts—and/or exhibit the vices of bad theories—e.g., "God-of-the-gaps" strategy, heavy reliance on ad hoc hypotheses, lack of explanatory power—and if there are better alternatives, then perhaps one could reject ID as an explanation and/or theory for apparent design in nature. But one would be doing so not because ID is unable to pass a metaphysical litmus test, but rather because it fails as a hypothesis qua hypothesis. That is, whether ID fits some a priori definition of "science" or "pseudo-science" is a red herring, for such definitions tell us nothing about whether a theory and/or explanation, such as ID, provides us with real knowledge of the order and nature of things. In the words of Larry Laudan, who is not an ID supporter: "If we could stand up on the side of reason, we ought to drop terms like 'pseudo-science.' . . . They do only emotive work for us."[20]

3. Science and External Conceptual Problems

If science is contingent upon second-order philosophical claims (*see* chapter 3, section A, part 1), and if demarcation theories fail (*see* chapter 1, section B, part 4; and chapter 3, section A, part 2), then it is perfectly appropriate to bring into the assessment of scientific theories external conceptual concerns. Laudan has argued that external conceptual problems—e.g., philosophical, logical, theological, and mathematical—may provide, and have provided, in the history of scientific progress, negative evidence for the acceptance of scientific theories.[21] Consequently, he writes that "contrary to common belief, it can be rational to raise philosophical and religious objections against a particular theory or research tradition, if the latter runs counter to a well-established part of our general *Weltbild*—even if that *Weltbild* is not 'scientific' (in the usual sense of the word)."[22]

An external conceptual problem occurs when a scientific theory implies or asserts something that we have good reason to believe from another area of knowledge may be false. Moreland provides an example:

> Philosophers . . . [have] raised problems with the concept of action at a distance. Newton postulated two kinds of forces: the force of impact, when two bodies contact each other, and gravitational force, which can operate at a distance without two bodies being in contact. Philosophers such as Rene Descartes . . . pointed out that it would be a simpler theory if the latter force could be reduced to some type of force involving contact and that there was no clear conception of causation that did not involve such contact. This conceptual problem did not go away, and it led to further study of gravity. Today many scientists deny action at a distance and see the gravitational force between spatially separated bodies as due to an intermediate field or transmitted by an exchange of particles (called gravitons) between the bodies.[23]

Consider another example. Suppose someone claims that evolutionary science tells us that our moral intuitions are really the result of natural selection and thus only have survival value. And suppose, for example, that we are told, based on that theory of morality, that mothers who kill their newborns do so because of the forces of evolutionary biology and thus should not be too vigorously condemned by society for committing these homicides.[24] What if, however, I have good philosophical reasons to reject this moral theory and the repugnant conclusions that apparently flow from it?

Here's one such argument. Evolution is concerned only with the sorts of *behavior* that are conducive to the preservation of the species. But morality is more than just behavior, for it includes, among other things, motive and intent. In fact, a moral judgment is incomplete without taking these into consideration. For one can be immoral without any behavior, simply on the basis of motive and intent. For example, I can intend to carry out a murder and never do it. On the other hand, one can be immoral simply on the basis of motive and intent even if the behavior has "good" results. For example, if I intend to trip someone in order to harm him, but it results in the person not being hit by a car and thus saving his life, the results are good even though what I did was immoral. However, "bad" results may be part of a morally good act simply on the basis of motive and intent. For example, if a surgeon operates on a terminal patient with the intent to remove a cancer, but during the operation the patient dies of cardiac arrest, the surgeon has not acted immorally. Since evolution, at best, can only *describe* what behaviors are conducive to the preservation of the species and does not address the role of motive and intent in evaluating those behaviors, evolution is an inadequate explanation for the existence of moral norms.

Second, because the evolutionary explanation of morality is only *descriptive,* it merely tells us what behaviors in the past may have been conducive to the survival of the species and why I may have on occasion moral feelings to act consistently with those behaviors. But evolution cannot tell me whether I ought to act on those feelings in the present and in the future. Granted, I am grateful that people in the past behaved in ways that made my existence possible. But why should I emulate only those behaviors that many people today say are "good"? After all, some people in the past raped, stole, and murdered. And I know of many people today who have feelings to rape, steal, and murder. Perhaps these behaviors were just as important for my existence and the preservation of the species as were the "good" behaviors. Unless there is a morality above the morality of evolution, it is difficult to see how one can distinguish between morally good and bad actions if both types may have been conducive to the preservation of the species.[25] It seems then that it is at least rational to believe that there is a morality above the morality of evolution that cannot be reduced to the nonmoral and nonrational flux of matter and the organisms that survive and thus arise from that matter.

Therefore, the moral theory some believe is entailed by naturalistic evolution[26] can be critiqued, and perhaps rejected, because of this external conceptual problem. But if one were to reject a moral theory *entailed by* naturalistic evolution, then naturalistic evolution has an external conceptual problem with which its proponents must deal.

As Kekes noted above, not every conceptual issue in science whose proper domain may be another discipline, such as philosophy, is a *problem,* though it makes Laudan's point that conceptual issues apparently external to science may count for or against scientific claims, theories, or hypotheses, and/or may provide a conceptual resource by which one may assess rival theories, hypotheses, or apparently contrary evidence. For example, Del Ratzsch asks us to "consider the principle of the uniformity of nature . . . [,] as nearly scientifically essential a principle as one can find." However, this principle, according to Ratzsch, is "metaphysically rooted, nonnegotiable, normative, systemically protected, immune to empirical challenge, untestable, non-predictive, and unlimitedly flexible."[27] Nevertheless, "it has been a deep background part of a guiding conceptual framework within which attempts to understand the cosmos have met with significantly more systemic success than was achieved within alternative conceptual frameworks of irregularity and arbitrariness." For example, when confronted with an apparent change in nature that seems to have occurred for no reason, scientists do not entertain abandoning the principle of the uniformity of nature. Rather, "[t]he nearly invariable approach is to retain unquestioned the commitment to uniformity" and "to refocus the search for the relevant uniformity at some deeper level."[28]

The point of the above examples is to show that knowledge from other areas of study, such as ethics and metaphysics, have provided and may provide an important conceptual resource for the practice of empirical science as well as assessing the presuppositions and inferences that seem to be preconditions for, and entailments of, this practice.

According to ID proponents, external conceptual problems, if they are grounded in at least plausible arguments, provide more reasons to call MN (as well as ontological materialism) into question. We go over some of these problems under four general categories: (a) Naturalism and Cosmology, (b) Souls, Minds, and Essences, (c) Moral Claims and Properties, and (d) Materialism, Naturalism, and Self-Refutation.

a. Naturalism and Cosmology

ID proponents have revived classical "first cause" arguments by employing highly sophisticated philosophical arguments, some of which have premises derived from the natural sciences.[29] These arguments attempt to show that there exists, or at least it is reasonable to believe that there exists, a nonmaterial personal agent who brought the universe into existence. Probably the most influential of these arguments is the *kalam* cosmological argument, a Medieval product of Islamic philosophy rehabilitated by William Lane Craig in his 1977 Ph.D. dissertation at the University of Birmingham (England) under John Hick.[30] The influence of this argument is so far-reaching that it is difficult to find a textbook in philosophy of religion or religion and science that does not mention it or republish one of the many versions of it defended by Craig or others. It is a formidable argument that has garnered serious attention by philosophers of all stripes.[31] Because my purpose is to show how the kalam argument may serve as an external conceptual problem for naturalism, my review of it is brief.

The argument can be presented as a series of exhaustive dilemmas. Craig offers the following diagram:[32]

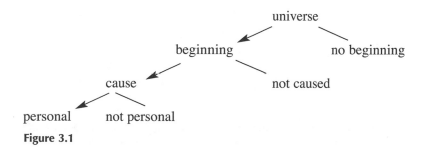

Figure 3.1

First, it is asserted that the universe either had a beginning or it did not. Second, if the universe in fact had a beginning, then it was either caused or uncaused. And third, if the beginning of the universe was caused, then this cause was either personal or impersonal. In showing one part of each alternative to be more reasonable than the other, this argument intends to show the reasonableness of believing that a timeless, unchanging, immaterial and all-powerful agent is the cause of the universe's coming into existence.

Concerning the first dilemma, Craig employs four arguments to show that the universe had a beginning. The first two arguments are philosophical, the last two are scientific. The first "is based upon the impossibility of the existence of an actual infinite." The second is an "argument from the impossibility of the formation of an actual infinite by successive addition."[33] If either one of the first two arguments works, it would entail that the past cannot consist of a beginningless series of events. The third is an "argument from the expansion of the universe,"[34] an argument from the Big Bang, that the universe began "from a state of affairs that has been described by some as nothingness."[35] And the fourth is an "argument from thermodynamics."[36] We look at the second and fourth arguments.

In order to support his second argument, Craig first points out that an *infinite set* of numbers is one that is complete and cannot be added to, e.g., the infinite set of natural numbers $\{1, 2 \ldots 10 \ldots 1,000,000 \ldots\}$. This set contains an *unlimited* number of members from 1 to infinity. But since an actual infinite is a *complete* set with an infinite amount of members, the series of events in time cannot be actually infinite. This is because the series of events in time is always increasing (being added to) and one can never arrive at infinity by adding one member after another. Consider the following example.

If you were on Interstate 95 driving from New York City to Princeton, New Jersey, with forty-eight miles to traverse, there is no doubt that you will eventually arrive in Princeton. However, if you were to drive on 95 from New York to Princeton with an infinite number of miles to traverse, you would never arrive in Princeton. But if you did arrive in Princeton, it would only prove that the distance was not infinite. Since an infinite number is unlimited, one can never complete an infinite number of miles.[37]

Applying this to a universe with no beginning, a certain absurdity develops: if the universe had no beginning, then every event has been preceded by an infinite number of events. But if one can never arrive at infinity by adding one member after another, one could never arrive at the present day, because to do so one would have to traverse (or complete) an infinite number of moments to arrive at the present moment. Moreland, in his defense of the kalam argument, explains:

> [S]uppose a person were to think backward through the events in the past. In reality, time and the events within it move in the other direction. But mentally he

can reverse that movement and count backward farther and farther into the past. Now he will either come to a beginning or he will not. If he comes to a beginning, then the universe obviously had a beginning. But if he never could, even in principle, reach a first moment, then this means that it would be impossible to start with the present and run backward through all of the events in the history of the cosmos. Remember, if he did run through all of them, he would reach a first member of the series, and the finiteness of the past would be established. In order to avoid this conclusion, one must hold that, starting from the present, it is *impossible* to go backward through all of the events in history.

But since events really move in the other direction, this is equivalent to admitting that if there was no beginning, the past could have never been exhaustively traversed to reach the present.[38]

In his fourth argument Craig maintains that the second law of thermodynamics reveals the impossibility of an infinite past. The second law can be defined in the following way: "The whole universe must eventually reach a state of thermodynamic equilibrium; everywhere the situation will be exactly the same, with the same temperature, the same pressure, etc., etc."[39] To use an illustration, when one puts ice cubes in a glass with warm soda, both the soda and the ice cubes tend toward the same temperature: the ice cubes begin to melt and the soda gets a bit cooler. Just think of this on a cosmic scale: the universe is running down and will inevitably reach heat death, a point at which there is thermodynamic equilibrium.

Applying this to the question of the beginning of the universe, Craig makes the inquiry: If the universe is moving toward a point when everything will be the same temperature, why has it not occurred if the universe has had no beginning? If the universe has always existed, there certainly has been enough time (infinite time) for thermodynamic equilibrium to have occurred. But since it has not occurred, the universe began at some point in the finite past.

For the second dilemma, Craig appeals to the well-grounded intuition that whatever begins to exist must do so through a cause. Although some philosophers have mused that "[w]e have no good ground for an *a priori* certainty that there could not have been a sheer unexplained beginning of things,"[40] and although "something coming from nothing" is logically possible,[41] its counterintuitiveness means that there is a strong presumption against it. And for that reason, merely citing its sheer logical possibility to counter the strong presumption against it, in the words of philosopher R. Douglas Geivett, "does not have the makings of a principle of explanation."[42]

Assuming the universe has a beginning and a cause, the third dilemma inquires about the nature of that cause. Craig concludes that it is a personal agent. For if all the conditions for the existence of the universe were present from all eternity, then the universe would be as eternal as its cause. But if the universe began to exist, then some condition for its coming into existence was present at that moment which was not present for all eternity prior. Moreland explains that the most plausible way to resolve this problem is to think of the first cause as a personal agent:

> If the necessary and sufficient conditions for a match to light are present, the match lights spontaneously. There is no deliberation, no waiting. In such situations, when *A* is the efficient cause of *B,* spontaneous change or mutability is built into the situation itself.
>
> The only way for the first event to arise spontaneously from a timeless, changeless, spaceless state of affairs, and at the same time be caused, is this—the event resulted from the free act of a person or agent. In the world, persons or agents spontaneously act to bring about events. I myself raise my arm when it is done deliberately. There may be necessary conditions for me to do this (e.g., I have a normal arm, I am not tied down), but these are not sufficient. The event is realized only when I freely act. Similarly, the first event came about when an agent freely chose to bring it about, and this choice was not the result of other conditions which were sufficient for that event to come about.[43]

In an essay published in 2000, Craig explores the nature of this cause in greater detail:

> [A]s the cause of space and time, this entity must transcend space and time and therefore exist atemporally and nonspatially, at least sans the universe. This transcendent cause must therefore be changeless and immaterial, since timelessness entails changelessness, and changelessness implies immateriality. Such a cause must be beginningless and uncaused, at least in the sense of lacking any antecedent causal conditions. Ockham's Razor will shave away further causes, since we should not multiply causes beyond necessity. This entity must be unimaginably powerful, since it created the universe out of nothing.
>
> Finally, and most strikingly, such a transcendent cause is plausibly regarded as personal. As [Richard] Swinburne points out, there are two types of causal explanations: scientific explanations in terms of laws and initial conditions and personal explanations in terms of agents and their volitions. A first state of the universe cannot have a scientific explanation, since there is nothing before it, and therefore it can be accounted for only in terms of a personal explanation. Moreover, the personhood of the cause of the universe is implied by its timelessness and immateriality, since the only entities we know of which can possess such properties are either minds or abstract objects, and abstract objects do not stand in causal relations. Therefore, the transcendent cause of the origin of the universe must be of the order of mind.[44]

Therefore, Craig concludes that a timeless, unchanging, immaterial, and all-powerful agent is the cause of the universe coming into existence.

The kalam argument, of course, has its critics, who do not believe that it succeeds,[45] and Craig and his supporters have responded to and interacted with those critics.[46] Nevertheless, even if the premises of the kalam argument are not certain, they are not obviously unreasonable. In fact, its scientific premises have a good deal of support in the scientific community, even though many in that community reject the conclusion Craig and others draw from those premises. In any event, if the kalam's premises are not obviously unreasonable, then any theory of cosmological origins that affirms a wholly material and beginningless universe, i.e., a materialist ontology, must account for the external conceptual problems raised by the kalam or other arguments.[47] Moreover, the reasonableness of the kalam argument means that an argument based on empirical and scientific premises whose conclusion is inconsistent with philosophical naturalism is in principle possible. Thus, ID cannot be dismissed a priori by its critics merely because its conclusions, inferred from empirical data, are inconsistent with some stipulated and controversial definition of "science."

b. Souls, Minds, and Essences

If MN is a necessary precondition of science, then nonmaterial entities, such as souls, minds, and essences, either do not exist (if MN entails ontological materialism),[48] or if they do, they cannot be the proper object of knowledge and thus cannot be employed as a check to the apparent deliverances of natural science. Thus, naturalistic evolution and its commitment to MN and ontological materialism entails the view that the human person is an exclusively material being whose functions are either reducible to matter or realized by matter. In the words of William Lycan, "If materialism is true, then human beings are large collections of small physical objects and nothing more, ontologically. It follows that any human being could be described, and described completely, in purely scientific terms."[49]

Those who maintain a metaphysical commitment to materialism typically affirm one of two views of the human person: mind-body physicalism or property-dualism. The first is the view that the human person is merely a physical brain with no mental properties as well as no underlying nonphysical substance or human nature. "The only things that exist are physical substances, properties, and events. When it comes to humans, the physical substance is the body or brain and central nervous system. The physical substance called the brain has physical properties, such as weight, volume, size, electrical activity, chemical composition, and so forth."[50]

Proponents of the second position, property-dualism, assert that "there are some physical substances that have only physical properties. A billiard ball is hard and round. In addition, there are no mental substances. But there is one material substance that has both physical *and* mental properties—the brain. . . . The brain is the possessor of all mental properties. I am not a mental self that *has* my thoughts and experiences. Rather, I am a brain and a series or bundle of successive experiences themselves."[51] Although mind-body physicalism and property dualism are widely held viewpoints in the intellectual community,[52] they are disputed with rigorous argumentation by both ID proponents and others.[53]

These critics argue that materialist construals of human personhood are seriously flawed in many ways,[54] including: (1) they are self-refuting,[55] (2) they cannot adequately account for personal identity through change,[56] (3) they are inconsistent with libertarian free will and moral responsibility,[57] and (4) they do not make sense of our basic awareness of the self.[58] These critics typically defend some version of substance dualism,[59] which is inconsistent with materialism as a metaphysical position as well as inconsistent with physicalist and property-dualist views of the human person.

Substance dualism is the view that the human being is an immaterial substance that is not identical to the physical body to which it is related. The immaterial substance, sometimes called "the soul," is the locus of the self. It maintains absolute identity through physical change, is the place from which thought arises (and thus, it has mental properties not reducible to matter), and because souls have natures (or essences) they have the teleological function that internally directs the growth and development of the human being. That is, "human being" is a natural kind whose members all instantiate the same nature (or essence).

However, if the human being is merely a collection of physical parts with no intrinsic purpose—as the Darwinian story tells us—then she is a property thing, like a car or computer, an entity that has "no underlying bearer of properties existing ontologically prior to the whole, and no internal, defining essence that diffuses, informs and unites its parts and properties. It is merely a collection of parts, standing in external, spacial-temporal relations which, in turn, gives rise to a bundle of properties determined by those parts."[60]

According to substance dualism, a human being develops certain functions, organs, and attributes as a result of what it is, what it is internally directed to do by its nature, while a car or a computer will be built only when its parts are put together and ordered by an outside force, and even then it will just sit there unless manipulated by something external to itself. A human being, unlike a computer or car, is prior to its parts, for its parts function as a result of the nature of the human organism itself. A human being *has* parts while a car or computer *is* parts. This is why a human being maintains absolute identity through change while a computer or car does not. In addition, because the human being has an immaterial soul that maintains absolute identity through change, its mental properties are not the result of undirected physical laws (and thus the deliverances of the mind may be the deliverances of reason), libertarian free will is possible, and basic awareness of the self makes sense.

Consequently, substance dualism, if it is at least a plausible alternative to materialist construals of human personhood, poses an external conceptual problem with which the evolutionary naturalist must deal.

c. Moral Claims and Properties

Some ID theorists, and other critics of naturalism, argue that moral claims, and moral properties in particular, cannot be reduced to material properties.[61] And if that is the case, then the existence of moral properties is an external conceptual problem that *counts against* MN (as well as ontological materialism). For if moral properties are real and are irreducibly nonmaterial, then the presence of moral properties in the universe, in the words of atheist philosopher J. L. Mackie, "constitute such an odd cluster of properties and relations that they are most unlikely to have arisen in the ordinary course of events without an all-powerful god to create them."[62]

Thus, if we have good independent philosophical reasons for believing that there are such immaterial entities, i.e., moral properties, that are a proper object of knowledge, then moral realism is likely true. Consequently, any moral theory, such as Michael Ruse's or Steven Pinker's,[63] that is based on a Darwinian paradigm, is suspect. Of course, the Darwinian may reject moral realism because of his commitment to MN (and ontological materialism), but that plays right into the hands of design theorists, for the Darwinian is implicitly conceding that his rejection of moral realism is based solely on his *philosophical commitment* rather than what appears to be prima facie the nature of moral properties. Perhaps this is why some moral philosophers, such as Kai Nielsen and John Rawls,[64] put the question of morality's ontological status aside. Writes Nielsen, "[Rawls and I] are concerned with the justification of moral beliefs, practices, and principles, so we don't try to say what truth is, whether there's moral truth or anything. We say here's a bunch of moral judgments that a culture shares and that I may or may not share. And we see whether those fit together with everything else we know and match with our considered convictions."[65]

d. Materialism, Naturalism, and Self-Refutation

Some ID theorists argue that materialism is self-refuting.[66] Ironically, a variation on this external conceptual problem was recognized by Charles Darwin in a letter to William Graham. "With me," Darwin writes, "the horrid doubt always arises whether the convictions of man's mind, which has been developed from the mind of the lower animals, are of any value or at all trustworthy. Would any one trust in the convictions of a monkey's mind, if there are any convictions in such a mind?"[67] Alvin Plantinga calls this "Darwin's Doubt," and based on it employs an argument against naturalism. Here is a summary of his argument.[68]

If the evolutionary naturalist provides reasons for her belief that her cognitive faculties function properly, she must rely on those very cognitive functions in order to arrive at those reasons. However, her cognitive functions, we are told by the evolutionary naturalist, arrived in their present state as a result of blind nonrational forces combined with natural selection and/or perhaps other material causes. But, as Plantinga points out, "[e]volution is interested, not in true belief, but in survival or fitness." Thus, "[i]t is . . . unlikely that our cognitive faculties have the production of true belief as a proximate or any other function, and the probability of our faculties' being reliable (given naturalistic evolution) would be fairly low."[69] Thus, "any argument" the naturalist "offers" for the reliability of her cognitive faculties "is in this context delicately circular or question-begging."[70] Although it is not *formally* circular in the sense that the conclusion appears in the argument's premises, it is, writes Plantinga, "*pragmatically* circular in that it purports to give a reason for trusting our cognitive faculties, but is itself trustworthy only if those faculties (at least the ones involved in its production) are indeed trustworthy." Thus, she "subtly assumes the very proposition" she "proposes to argue for." In other words, "[o]nce I come to doubt the reliability of my cognitive faculties, I can't properly try to allay that doubt by producing an *argument;* for in doing so I rely on the very faculties I am doubting."[71] Thus, if the proper function of our cognitive faculties makes more conceptual sense if they were designed rather than the result of naturalistic evolution,[72] Plantinga's self-refuting charge against naturalism is an external conceptual problem with which the supporters of MN and philosophical naturalism must deal.[73]

B. THE CASE FOR INTELLIGENT DESIGN

In addition to challenging methodological naturalism, design theorists present a positive case for their position. We cover four aspects of this case. First we review the most widely held theoretical grounding of the ID project, *specified complexity* (SC).[74] Then we review three applications of SC: the irreducible complexity of some biological systems, the information content found in deoxyribonucleic acid (DNA), and the fine-tuning of the universe for the existence of life. I conclude this section with a brief review of other concerns and arguments as well as a summary of the legal difference between ID and Creationism.

1. Specified Complexity

At the core of the ID research program is its criteria by which its proponents can detect or falsify design. One such criterion is proposed by William A. Dembski. He proposes an explanatory filter in order to detect *specified complexity* (SC), something that we recognize in many fields as evidence of intelligent agency, e.g., "forensic science, intellectual property law, insurance claims investigation, cryptography, and random number generation."[75] Thus, what Dembski is suggesting is not something unknown to the world of science. Rather, what he and his colleagues in the ID movement are proposing is that we extend these insights, which have proved so fruitful in other fields, to the world of the natural sciences.

Why specified complexity? According to Dembski, "[w]henever we infer design, we must establish three things—*contingency, complexity* and *specification*. Contingency, by which we mean that an event was one of several possibilities, ensures that the object is not the result of an automatic and hence unintelligent process." In other words, an event that is not contingent is one that can be completely accounted for by natural law (or an algorithm). To cite an example, a salt crystal "results from forces of chemical necessity that can be described by the laws of chemistry. A setting of silverware is not."[76] The place setting is contingent, for there are no laws of chemistry or physics that direct the knife and spoon to the right side of the plate and the fork to the left. In other words, a contingent event cannot be reduced to natural law.

"Complexity," writes Dembski, "ensures that the object in question is not so simple that it can readily be explained by chance." For Dembski, "complexity . . . is a form of probability."[77] For example, the improbability of opening a combination lock by chance depends on the complexity of the mechanism. The more complex the mechanism, the greater the improbability that one will be able to open the lock by chance. Therefore, "the greater the complexity, the smaller the probability. Thus to determine whether something is sufficiently complex to warrant a design inference is to determine whether it has sufficiently small probability."[78] Nevertheless, complexity by itself may not be design. For example, a random selection of 1,000 symbols (rtvwix%*<3q498d. . . .) and the result of 1,000 coin flips are complex and improbable, but can be explained by randomness or chance. This is why specification is essential.

"Specification ensures that this object exhibits the type of pattern that is the trademark of intelligence."[79] Specificity by itself may not be design. For example, redundant order, such as the beating of a pulsar or the earth's orbiting of the sun every 365 days, can be explained by law and necessity. However, if specification is combined with complexity, a design inference may be warranted. Dembski offers an example of how from one area of science, the Search for Extra-Terrestrial Intelligence (SETI). SETI researchers, in their attempt to detect intelligence outside earth, have developed a filter that has certain preset patterns so that it may discard radio waves that do not exhibit specified complexity. In the novel (authored by Carl Sagan) and movie versions of *Contact,* SETI researchers detect extraterrestrial intelligence when they discover a sequence of beats and pauses that correspond to the prime numbers from 2 to 101.[80]

Dembski makes a distinction between *specification* and *fabrication*. The latter occurs when one infers a pattern ad hoc after the fact even though chance and necessity may account for the pattern. For example,[81] suppose a hurricane moves through my neighborhood, destroying four out of the seven homes on my street, and the three homes not destroyed are owned by me and my two brothers. Moreover, my brothers and I own the second, fourth, and sixth homes on the block, which means that the hurricane destroyed only the odd-numbered homes. Suppose I were to infer from this pattern either that the hurricane intentionally spared the property of the Beckwith boys and/or that the hurricane did not like odd-numbered homes on my block. This design inference would not be warranted since the "pattern" may be adequately accounted for by chance and necessity and thus is ad hoc. On the other hand, the pattern detected by the SETI researchers in *Contact* is not a fabrication. It is an instance of SC because it is not only highly complex and improbable, but it has specification, a pattern that is *independent* of, or *detachable* from, the event it explains. That is to say, the pattern is one that is not derived exclusively from the event—as is the ad hoc pattern read back into the hurricane example—but one we could construct even if we did not know which one of the possible events would occur. Thus, my winning the lottery with eight randomly selected numbers, though the outcome of a highly complex process with a result that is antecedently improbable, is not detachable, for it does not exhibit a pattern one could have constructed if one did not know which numbers would have been chosen. On the other hand, the pattern of the message from space in *Contact* is detachable, for our background knowledge (or side information, as Dembski calls it[82]) about binary arithmetic provides us the resources by which we can construct this pattern independent of the message itself. As a researcher in the movie *Contact* exclaimed, "This isn't noise, this has structure."[83] In other words, the message is not merely complex with an improbable random pattern, but has "structure," a pattern that one could have constructed independent of the message itself (as the SETI researchers evidently assumed when they constructed their preset patterns in a way that would not discard patterns that exhibited specified complexity). According to Dembski, "[t]his distinction between specifications and fabrications can be made with full statistical rigor."[84]

The U.S. Supreme Court, in at least one case, has applied a similar type of filter in order to detect intentional racial discrimination. *Yick Wo v. Hopkins*[85] concerned an ordinance in San Francisco that required the approval of the Board of Supervisors for operating a laundry in a wooden building. (A permit was not necessary if the laundry was in a brick or stone building.) According to Gerald Gunther and Kathleen Sullivan, "[t]he Board granted permits to operate laundries in wooden buildings to all but one of the non-Chinese applicants, but to none of about 200 Chinese applicants. A Chinese alien who had operated a laundry for many years was refused a permit and imprisoned for illegally operating a laundry."[86] Even though the ordinance was facially neutral, its administration was discriminatory, for, according to the Court, intentional discrimination was the best explanation of the pattern of the board's granting of permits. To employ Dembski's language, chance and necessity could not account for the specified complexity found in the pattern of excluding every single Chinese applicant. It is contingent (i.e., it is one of many possibilities), complex (i.e., it involves numerous applicants from different racial groups with buildings made of different materials), and specified (i.e., a pattern that one would construct if one had the goal of discriminating against Chinese applicants).

Las Vegas pit bosses, though they likely do not use the term *specified complexity,* understand the concept quite well. For example, if a casino patron wins ten games in a row at a blackjack table, and does so every day for two weeks, the pit boss will likely entertain the possibility that the patron is a card counter, someone who has mastered a skill that involves good memory and a knowledge of probability theory sufficient to beat the house. The patron's apparent gambling success is contingent (i.e., it is one of many possibilities), complex (i.e., it involves numerous games of blackjack and different card combinations), and specified (i.e., card combinations that a patron would construct if she wanted her blackjack playing to result in financial gain). Her intelligent intervention alters the games in which she plays from largely ones of chance and necessity to ones that tip the scales significantly in her favor. This is why card counters are banned from virtually every Las Vegas casino.

Detecting plagiarism in books and academic papers is another way in which Dembski's filter may be applied. In 2001 and 2002 the plagiarisms of three writers—Stephen Ambrose, Doris Kearns Goodwin, and Winston Frost[87]—made national news. For our purposes here, the Frost case is the most illustrative, since, unlike Ambrose and Kearns Goodwin, Frost has consistently denied that he plagiarized. Frost was the dean of Trinity Law School (Santa Ana), a small California Bar accredited school affiliated with Trinity International University, a Christian institution of higher learning whose main campus is in Deerfield, Illinois.[88] In mid-July 2001, an anonymous member of the Trinity community discovered, by accident,[89] that substantial portions of the first part of Mr. Frost's Fall 2000 *Trinity Law Review* article (about eight out of the first ten pages) appeared nearly word for word in a 1986 *Encyclopedia Britannica* piece authored by internationally renowned human rights expert Burns Weston.[90] Frost replied to the charge of plagiarism by blaming it on poor editing by student editors; he claimed early on that it could all be accounted for by a "missing footnote"[91] and later by footnotes that "are off."[92] To employ the language of Dembski's filter, Frost attributed the alleged plagiarism to "chance." Even though Frost's theory was implausible, some students[93] at the school seemed to entertain it as a real option.[94]

Frost's chance hypothesis could not withstand the strain of the obvious earmarks of specified complexity: no missing footnote or student editing errors—no chance occurrence—could reasonably account for the detailed and surgical lifting, and slight altering, of Weston's text as it appeared in Frost's article; there were over 200 lines of Frost's article that were nearly word for word from Weston's. Frost's plagiarism is contingent (i.e., it is one of many possibilities), complex (i.e., it involves thousands of words and hundreds of sentences), and specified (i.e., patterns of word and sentence combinations that one would have constructed if one were to imagine an article in which a writer takes another's work and tries to pass it off as his own). Consequently, only an intelligent agent (though not a moral or wise one) could account for such specified complexity.[95]

There are at least three ways in which design theorists employ Dembski's filter in order to detect design in nature: the irreducible complexity of certain biological systems, the information content found in DNA, and the fine-tuning of the universe for the existence of life.

2. Irreducible Complexity of Certain Biological Systems

In his groundbreaking book *Darwin's Black Box,*[96] Michael Behe, a Lehigh University biochemist, takes seriously Darwin's claim that "[i]f it could be demonstrated that any complex organ existed which could not possibly have been formed by numerous, successive, slight modifications, my theory would absolutely break down."[97] The contemporary popularizer of Darwinism, Richard Dawkins, agrees:

> Evolution is very possibly not, in actual fact, always gradual. But it must be gradual when it is being used to explain the coming into existence of compli-

cated, apparently designed objects, like eyes. For if it is not gradual in these cases, it ceases to have any explanatory power at all.[98]

Thus, a system that is *irreducibly complex* (IC) is a serious challenge to the explanatory power of the Darwinian paradigm. Behe defines an IC system as "a single system of several well-matched, interacting parts that contribute to the basic function, wherein the removal of any one of the parts causes the system to effectively cease functioning."[99] A mechanical mousetrap is an example of such a system. Writes Behe:

> The mousetraps my family uses consist of a number of parts . . . : (1) a flat wooden platform to act as a base; (2) a metal hammer, which does the actual job of crushing the mouse; (3) a wire spring with extended ends to press against the platform and the hammer when the trap is charged; (4) a sensitive catch which releases when slight pressure is applied; and (5) a metal bar that connects to the catch and holds the hammer back when the trap is charged. (There are also assorted staples to hold the system together.)[100]

The trap will not function if any one of its components (the base, hammer, spring, catch, or holding bar) is removed. Because an IC system has no function until all its parts are in place, it cannot be accounted for by gradual changes over time, for according to natural selection a biological entity must have some function so that it may exist, change, and pass that change on to its progeny. But with IC systems, there can be no functioning intermediate forms that have yet to acquire the requisite parts, for IC systems are *irreducible* and cannot be the legacy of intermediate forms. Thus, as Behe points out, "If there is no function, selection has nothing to work on, and Darwinian evolution is thwarted."[101]

Behe cites a number of examples of irreducibly complex biological systems including those contained within the cell. One of the cell's molecular machines is the cilium.[102] Behe explains that in order for the cilium to work a number of components are needed. Writes Behe:

> Ciliary motion certainly requires microtubles; otherwise, there would be no strands to slide. Additionally, it requires a motor, or else microtubles of the cilium would lie stiff and motionless. Furthermore, it requires linkers to tug on neighboring strands, converting the sliding motion into a bending motion, and preventing the structure from falling apart. All of these parts are required to perform one function: ciliary motion. Just as the mousetrap does not work unless all of its constituent parts are present, ciliary motion simply does not exist in the absence of microtubles, connectors, and motors. Therefore we can conclude that the cilium is irreducibly complex—an enormous monkey wrench thrown into its presumed gradual, Darwinian evolution.[103]

Behe notes that among the more than one thousand essays on the cilium that have appeared in the major journals in biochemistry published between 1975 and 1995 "only two articles even attempted to suggest a model for the evolution of the cilium that takes into account real mechanical considerations. Worse, the two papers disagree with each other even about the general route such an evolution might take. Neither paper discusses crucial quantitative details, or possible problems that would quickly cause a mechanical device such as a cilium or mousetrap to be useless."[104] Consequently, reviewers of *Darwin's Black Box* "admit[ted] the current lack of Darwinian explanations," even though most "expressed confidence that in the future such explanations will be found."[105]

Behe does not share this optimism. Rather, he argues that the data are more consistent with an ID explanation. He suggests this explanation, not from ignorance, but because he maintains that we do have legitimate criteria by which to detect design (e.g., SC), and that an IC system exhibits the characteristics these criteria are meant to detect. It is contingent (i.e., it is one of many possibilities; Darwinian algorithms cannot account for it), complex (i.e., it involves numerous systems, subsystems, and parts), and specified (i.e., patterns of biological systems and subsystems a capable intelligence would have constructed if it intended to bring about certain functions in an organism).

3. The Information Content Found in DNA

Stephen C. Meyer provides another case for design: an argument from the information content of DNA.[106] Since the arrival of Darwin's *Origin of Species,* a number of theories have been proposed, and experiments conducted, in order to provide a wholly naturalistic account of the initial conditions that gave rise to life.[107] Meyer argues that none of these theories or experiments has succeeded.[108] But even if they did succeed in accounting for the chemistry of life, Meyer maintains that a wholly naturalistic explanation cannot account for the information content of DNA or the increase of information that is supposed to have occurred over time through natural selection resulting in the highly complex organisms with which the earth is teeming.

According to Meyer, "[m]odern molecular biology has revealed that living cells—the fundamental units of life—possess the ability to store, edit, and transmit information and to use information to regulate their fundamental metabolic processes."[109] Unlike physical structures that are the result of scientific laws and/or chance—e.g., crystals, snowflakes, a home destroyed by a hurricane—DNA has information content that has the earmarks of specified complexity, intelligent design. An ice crystal, in contrast, is highly ordered with no information content, for it is the result of the redundant order of the chemical composition of its constituent parts. Concerning DNA, Meyer writes:

> As in the case of protein, the sequence specificity of the DNA molecule strongly resembles the sequence specificity of human codes or languages. Just as the letters in the alphabet of a written language may convey a particular message depending on their sequence, so too do the sequences of nucleotides or bases in the DNA molecule convey precise biochemical messages that direct protein synthesis within the cell. . . . Thus the sequence specificity in DNA begets sequence specificity in proteins. Or put differently, the sequence specificity of proteins depends upon a prior specificity—upon information—encoded in DNA.[110]

Meyer critiques naturalistic attempts to account for this. He argues that self-organization scenarios (theories based on necessity) and chance hypotheses (theories based on randomness) are simply incapable of accounting for the specified complexity of the information content of DNA. Both types of theories might account for either order or complexity, but they cannot account for the specified complexity of information.[111] To employ an example,[112] the laws of physics can account for the constituent parts of the tiles that contain the letters in a Scrabble game. Chance in combination with the law of gravity can account for the random arrangement of the tiles after they hit the floor following an earthquake that knocks them off the dining room table. But only an intelligent agent can account for some of the letters appearing together as a coherent message on my computer: "Go to the store and buy some chicken."

Meyer concludes that the best explanation for the specified complexity, the information content, of DNA is intelligent design. After all,

> [w]e know from experience that intelligent agents create information all the time. Indeed, experience teaches that whenever high information content is present in an artifact or entity whose causal story is known, invariably creative intelligence—design—has played a causal role in the origin of the entity. Moreover, citing the activity of an intelligent agent really does explain the origin of certain features such as, for example, the faces on Mount Rushmore or the inscriptions on the Rosetta Stone. (Imagine the absurdity of an archaeologist who refused to infer an intelligent cause for the inscriptions on the Rosetta Stone because such an inference would constitute a scribe-of-the-gaps fallacy.) Inferences to design need not depend upon our ignorance, but instead are often justified by our knowledge of the demonstrated causal powers of nature and agency, respectively. Recent developments in the information sciences formalize this knowledge, helping us to make inferences about the causal histories of various artifacts, entities or events based upon the information-theoretic

signatures they exhibit. . . . Thus knowledge (albeit provisional) of established
cause-effect relationships, not ignorance, justifies the design inference as the
best explanation for the origin of biological information in a prebiotic context.[113]

Consequently, according to Meyer, it is virtually impossible that unguided
chemistry could produce the information-rich DNA molecule, which functions like a written text or machine code. Like the communication sent by the
aliens in the book and movie versions of *Contact,* and like the signals the real-
life SETI's preset filter is programmed not to exclude, the information content of DNA exhibits specified complexity and thus cannot be accounted for
by either chance or necessity. It is contingent (i.e., it is one of many possibilities; Darwinian algorithms cannot account for it), complex (i.e., it has the
characteristics of a written text or machine code), and specified (i.e., it is a
pattern a capable intelligence could have constructed if it intended to store,
edit, and pass on information in living organisms). In the words of Darwinian
Richard Dawkins, "The machine code of the genes is uncannily computer
like."[114] And, as computer software mogul Bill Gates puts it, "DNA is like a
computer program, but far, far more advanced than any software we've ever
created."[115]

4. The Fine-Tuning of the Universe for
the Existence of Human Life

In the 1960s some physicists began making the observation that our universe
appears to have been fine-tuned for the existence of human life.[116] During the
1980s and 1990s a number of works, authored by scientists, have assessed
this "anthropic coincidence" in differing ways.[117] According to Meyer, these
scientists "discovered that the existence of life in the universe depends upon
a highly improbable but precise balance of physical factors. The constants of
physics, the initial conditions of the universe, and many other of its features
appear delicately balanced to allow for the possibility of life."[118] Any slight
alteration in these constants would have made human life impossible. For example, there would have been no life in the universe if the rate of the universe's expansion had been faster or slower, the strength of gravitational at-
traction had been stronger or weaker, or Planck's constant had had a different
value.[119] These, of course, are not the only characteristics of the universe that
had to be in place to make life possible. In 1998 astrophysicist and design advocate Hugh Ross estimated that there are "twenty-nine characteristics of the
universe that must be fine-tuned for any kind of physical life to be possible"
and that our solar system has forty-five characteristics that are necessary for
human life to arise in it. Given the individual and collective probabilities for
these characteristics to all arise by chance with precisely the correct values to

make human life possible, Ross estimates that there is "[m]uch less than 1 chance in one hundred billion trillion trillion trillion [that there] exists . . . even one" planet on which life "would occur anywhere in the universe."[120] This is why Nobel laureate in physics Arno Penzias writes that "astronomy leads us to a unique event, a universe which was created out of nothing, and delicately balanced to provide exactly the conditions required to support life. In the absence of an absurdly-improbable accident, the observations of modern science seem to suggest an underlying, one might say, supernatural plan."[121]

ID advocates have applied Dembski's explanatory filter to this phenomenon.[122] That is, because there is a conjunction of small probabilities and independent specificity, one has warrant to infer that the emergence of human life is best explained by an intelligent designer.[123] However, as Meyer points out, other interpretations, consistent with philosophical naturalism, have been proposed as alternatives to the ID hypothesis: "(1) the so-called weak anthropic principle, which denies that the fine tuning needs explanation; (2) explanations based on natural law; and (3) explanations based on chance [including the multiple-universes hypothesis]."[124] ID advocates have responded to these alternatives.[125]

Supporters of the weak anthropic principle (WAP) argue that "if the universe were not fine-tuned to allow for life, then humans would not be here to observe it." Therefore, they maintain, "the fine tuning requires no explanation."[126] Calling WAP the "selection effect argument," Dembski explains it in the following way:

> According to this argument, just as the winner of a lottery is shocked at winning it, so we are shocked to have evolved. But the lottery was bound to have a winner, and so too something was bound to have evolved. The appeal here is to a selection effect: Something vastly improbable was bound to happen, so the fact that it happened to us (i.e., that we were selected—hence the name *selection effect*) does not preclude chance.[127]

In my judgment, this argument and ones similar to it have been refuted by a number of philosophers and scientists.[128] Dembski points out that the problem with this argument is that "it confuses a necessary condition (i.e., our being selected) with an explanation (i.e., why us)."[129] To employ an example used by John Leslie, imagine that a person is sentenced to death before a firing squad consisting of one hundred outstanding marksmen. The marksmen fire at the blindfolded prisoner, and they all miss their target. The fact that the prisoner is alive to appreciate his good fortune—that his survival is a necessary condition for his gratitude—does not mean that the event is not in need of an explanation.[130] Winning the California lottery is one thing; winning it every day for a year with a completely different arrangement of numbers each time is quite another.

According to Meyer, explanations based on natural law "have proven to be the least popular for one simple reason. The precise 'dial settings' of the different constants in physics are specific features *of the laws of nature themselves*."[131] In other words, the laws themselves and the delicate balance of their values, i.e., the features of these laws that make human life possible are the things that need explaining. Thus, one cannot appeal to scientific laws to explain the features of those same laws. In addition, because laws are employed to describe phenomena that are repetitive and regular, it seems unlikely that the fine-tuning of the universe and all the values of the constants necessary for that fine-tuning could be accounted for by any scientific law, "for the idiosyncratic values of the physical constants and initial conditions of the universe constitute a highly irregular and nonrepetitive ensemble."[132] That is, "as a group," this collection of constants does "not seem to exhibit a regular pattern that could in principle be subsumed or explained by natural law."[133] Like the information content of DNA, the fine-tuning of the universe exhibits specified complexity.

Chance explanations, according to design theorists, also cannot account for the fine-tuning of the universe. For, as Ross noted above, the improbability of human life arising by chance in this universe is practically infinitesimal. Roger Penrose, the Rouse Ball Professor of Mathematics at Oxford, citing *just one* parameter, points out:

> How big was the original phase-space volume . . . that the Creator had to aim for in order to provide a universe compatible with the second law of thermodynamics and with what we now observe? . . . The Creator's aim must have been [precise] to an accuracy of one part in $10^{10^{123}}$. This is an extraordinary figure. One could not possibly even *write the number down* in full, in ordinary denary notation: it would be "1" followed by 10^{123} successive "0"s! Even if we were to write a "0" on each separate proton and on each separate neutron in the entire universe—and we could throw in all the other particles as well for good measure—we should fall far short of writing down the figure needed. [Such is] the precision needed to set the universe on its course.[134]

In order to rescue the chance hypothesis from this insurmountable improbability, some thinkers have proposed that multiple universes, including ours, exist. Although the existence of human life resulting from chance in this universe seems virtually impossible given its probabilistic resources, given the existence of multiple parallel universes, the probability of human life arising from chance increases since the existence of other universes dramatically enlarges the probabilistic resources from which chance can produce human life while appearing to be the result of fine-tuning.[135]

Design theorists and others have replied to this hypothesis (MUH) in a number of ways[136] including the fact that there is no evidence for the existence of multiple universes,[137] that the ID hypothesis is far more consistent with what we already know about the causal powers of agents and nonagents,[138] that MUH is unparsimoniously ad hoc and less simple in comparison to the ID hypothesis,[139] that MUH is motivated by a dogmatic commitment to methodological naturalism and ontological materialism rather than based on a fair assessment of the evidence,[140] and that MUH is itself contingent upon a mechanism for generating universes whose laws and characteristics, if slightly different, could not produce any universe capable of producing human life (and thus relies on fine-tuning in order to try to refute it).[141]

Thus, according to some design theorists, the fine-tuning of the universe for the possibility of human life exhibits the characteristics of specified complexity, and thus can be attributed to an intelligent agent. For it is contingent (i.e., it is one of many possibilities), complex (i.e., it is a highly improbable arrangement of independent variables), and specified (i.e., it is a cosmological pattern a capable intelligence could have constructed if it intended to make the universe conducive to the arising of human life).

5. Other Concerns and Arguments

Both proponents and opponents of design theory have raised nonlegal concerns about ID and its use in the practice of science, some of which may be raised by teachers, school board members, school administrators, scientists, and/or legislators who are assessing whether their schools ought to permit or require the teaching of ID. Because of the detail required to address these concerns adequately, and because of the modest goal of this chapter given the purpose of this book, I briefly mention these concerns and refer the reader to works that address them. Some of these concerns include the problem of dysteleology,[142] the practical payoffs and/or fruitfulness of design,[143] whether ID will be a "science stopper,"[144] the "God-of-the-gaps" objection,[145] design theory's invoking of unobservables,[146] its lack of appeal to natural law and mechanism,[147] and the testability of design theory,[148] all of which have been replied to by design advocates. Although I have not directly addressed in this book all of these concerns by name, most of them have been addressed implicitly and/or in a cursory fashion in much of what has been covered concerning the arguments for ID (chapter 3, section B), the nature of science (chapter 1, section B, part 4; chapter 3, section A), and the problems with methodological naturalism (chapter 3, section A).

The four areas that we covered in presenting the case for design—specified complexity, irreducible complexity of biological systems, the information content of DNA, and the fine-tuning of the universe for life—are not the only areas in which or by which design theorists have made their case.[149] For example, some design theorists have argued that the fossil record fits better with a design hypothesis than with a Darwinian one. For evolutionists admit that the record does not reveal gradual development from simple to more complex species,[150] as predicted by Darwin (see chapter 1, section A, part 2). Rather, in what is called the "Cambrian explosion,"[151] the record reveals the sudden appearance at differing times of information-rich organisms within a hierarchical diversity of species with apparently no precursors. Their body plans with their improbable arrangement of parts including the information content of their DNA and the irreducible complexity of their biological systems and subsystems exhibit the characteristics of specified complexity, intelligent design. Hence, some design theorists employ the facts of the Cambrian explosion in their arguments for ID and against both Darwinism as well as its leading naturalistic competitor, "punctuated equilibrium."[152]

6. Difference between Intelligent Design and Creationism

As we saw in chapters 1 and 2, the Supreme Court as well as other courts have ruled that creation science (or creationism) is a religious belief transparently derived from a fundamentalist interpretation of the Book of Genesis. Thus, the Establishment Clause of the First Amendment is violated when the government requires that creationism be taught in public school science classes. Therefore, if there are no essential differences between ID and creation science, the teaching of ID in public schools, whether permitted or required by the state or voluntarily imparted by an ambitious teacher, would not pass constitutional muster. In light of what we have covered thus far in this chapter, ID can be summarized in the following way (with the appropriate section of this chapter in parentheses):

(A) If an apparently designed entity exhibits specified complexity (SC), one is warranted in inferring that the entity is the result of an intelligent agent (section B, part 1).[153]

(B) SC can be reliably detected by an explanatory filter (section B, part 1).

(C) The information content of DNA (section B, part 3), the fine-tuning of the universe for the existence of life (section B, part 4), and the irreducible complexity of some biological systems (section B, part 2) are instances of specified complexity.

(D) Presupposing methodological naturalism and relying exclusively on the resources of ontological materialism (i.e., chance and necessity) cannot account for SC in the instances listed in (C) (section B).

(E) One cannot exclude ID from serious consideration because it is inconsistent with a particular demarcation theory (section A, part 2).

(F) Therefore, given (A) through (E), ID best accounts for the irreducible complexity of some biological systems, the information content of DNA, and the fine-tuning of the universe for life.

(G) Methodological naturalism and ontological materialism have been challenged in other significant ways including their apparent inability to provide the epistemological and metaphysical resources to account for the existence of the universe (section A, part 3.a), mind (section A, part 3.b), morality (section A, part 3.c), and rationality (section A, part 3.d).

(H) Therefore, given (F) and (G), we have good reason to reject both the epistemological presupposition of evolution (methodological naturalism) as well as its entailment (ontological materialism).

As I noted in the summaries of chapters 1 and 2, the courts in *Epperson, McLean,* and *Edwards* rejected the teaching of creationism and/or the prohibition of teaching evolution in public schools on four grounds, one of which concerned the content of the creationism to be taught as well as the creationism that motivated the prohibition of evolution: How closely does the curricular content required by the statute parallel the creation story in Genesis, and/or is the curricular content prohibited by the statute proscribed because it is inconsistent with the creation story in Genesis?

No doubt ID has implications for the veracity of naturalistic evolution: if its arguments work, then ID is a defeater to naturalistic evolution (as defined in chapter 1). But such arguments propose conclusions whose premises do not contain the Book of Genesis and its tenets as explicit or implicit propositions. These premises and their propositions, unlike the ones of creation science, are not derived from, nor are they grounded in, any particular religion's interpretation of its special revelation. They are, rather, the result of empirical facts (e.g., the information content of DNA, the structure of the cell), well-grounded conceptual notions (e.g., SC, IC), and critical reflection. These subsequently serve as the basis from which one may infer that an intelligent agent is likely responsible for the existence of certain apparently natural phenomena. Granted, the conclusions inferred by these premises may be consistent with, and lend support to, a tenet or tenets of a particular belief system. Dembski, for example, claims that the inference to a disembodied intelligence that can account for specified complexity in nature "is compatible with pantheism, panentheism, Stoicism, Neoplatonism, deism, and theism. It is incompatible with naturalism."[154] But that, in itself, would not make ID ipso facto creationism or even constitutionally suspect. After all, the Big Bang theory (see section A, part 3.a of this chapter), the most widely accepted theory of the universe's origin, is more consistent with, and lends support to, theism in comparison to other metaphysical rivals such as atheism. Yet, no one is suggesting that the Big Bang theory ought not to be taught in public schools because it has metaphysical implications friendly to theism and may serve as an impetus for some students to abandon naturalism as a worldview.[155]

Given the courts' understanding of creation science, ID clearly *is not* creation science. In fact, no less an authority than Henry M. Morris, one of the founders of the modern creationist movement,[156] writes that Intelligent Design "won't work . . . because it is not the Biblical method."[157] Therefore, if ID is to be declared unconstitutional, it cannot be on the grounds that it is the creationism repudiated by the courts.

C. THE CASE FOR THE ILLIBERALITY OF TEACHING NATURALISTIC EVOLUTION IN PUBLIC SCHOOLS

In this section we take a look at a philosophical argument proposed by Alvin Plantinga that addresses the question of whether it is politically just for public schools to teach only one theory of origins. It is an argument that relies heavily on a notion of political liberalism found in the writings of John Rawls. What makes Plantinga's argument germane to this book's purpose is that it addresses two issues—religious neutrality and the nature of public education—that were important in the Supreme Court's assessment of the statute it struck down in *Edwards*.[158] However, unlike the Court, Plantinga seems to really understand the deep philosophical questions—both politically and epistemologically—that percolate beneath the surface of this volatile debate. There is much that partisans on all sides can learn from Plantinga's work.

1. Political Liberalism and State Neutrality

According to most versions of political liberalism (PL), the government ought to be neutral on metaphysical questions over which there is deep and impassioned disagreement. This view has had a tremendous impact on the law and the way in which courts, especially the Supreme Court, have dealt with "social issues" including the debate over teaching origins.[159]

Because Rawls is probably the most influential contemporary philosopher of liberal political thought, and because Plantinga's use of PL in his essay relies heavily on Rawls, a brief presentation of Rawls's view is in order.[160]

According to Rawls, a state (or government) is just if it is the result of principles people would have arrived at if they knew nothing about what they are or what they will become (i.e., whether they are rich or poor, black or white, homosexual or heterosexual, short or tall, male or female, etc.).[161] To employ

Rawls's terminology, the principles of justice are those agreed to by parties in "the original position" (an imaginary time and place where there is no government) behind "a veil of ignorance" (an imaginary situation in which nobody has any personal knowledge of themselves or their futures). In other words, the principles of justice are those arrived at by means of a social contract that all the "unbiased" parties would agree on so that they can receive full political and social freedom and a minimum standard of financial entitlement just in case it turns out one is, for example, not well-off, not naturally gifted, or holds unpopular political, religious, and/or philosophical opinions. This means that Rawls's principles of justice have little or nothing to do with the good, the true, or the beautiful. They are principles for ensuring economic entitlement as well as for preventing conflict between individuals each pursuing his or her own vision of the good life. They are rules for protecting one's interests as well as refereeing the conflicts that result from individuals exercising their autonomy.[162]

According to Rawls, "no comprehensive doctrine is appropriate as a political conception." A doctrine is comprehensive for Rawls "when it includes conceptions of what is of value in human life, and ideals of personal character, as well as ideals of friendship and familial and associational relationships, and much else that is to inform our conduct, and in the limit to our life as a whole."[163] Rawls maintains that both religious and philosophical perspectives can be comprehensive doctrines. Although he claims that his view of state neutrality does not prevent proponents of comprehensive doctrines from influencing public policy, their proposals must not be in conflict with the principles of justice (which are the basis, according to Rawls, of constitutional rights) and they must provide publicly accessible reasons (i.e., secular reasons) for their positions.[164] According to Rawls, "Political liberalism sees its form of political philosophy as having its own subject matter: how is a just and free society possible under conditions of deep doctrinal conflict with no prospect of resolution?" His answer is state neutrality: "To maintain impartiality between comprehensive doctrines, [political liberalism] does not specifically address the moral topics on which those doctrines divide."[165]

This is where Rawls's book *Political Liberalism* departs from his *Theory of Justice*. Rawls concedes that the thesis of the latter depended on a premise that, he now maintains, his present views rule out: "[I]n the well-ordered society of justice as fairness [as defended in *A Theory of Justice*], citizens hold to the same comprehensive doctrine, and this includes aspects of Kant's comprehensive liberalism, to which the principles of justice as fairness might belong."[166] Explaining Rawls's changing view, Robert P. George writes:

> The problem with this idea is that neither liberalism, considered as a "comprehensive doctrine," nor any other comprehensive view is held by citizens generally in pluralistic societies such as ours. Nor is it reasonable under the

circumstances of political freedom that characterize modern constitutional democratic regimes to expect that "comprehensive liberalism," or any other competing comprehensive view, ever would be adopted by citizens generally. Rawls refers to this state of affairs as "the fact of reasonable pluralism," and it is the starting point of his revised argument for an antiperfectionist resolution to the problem of moral disagreement.[167]

Although Rawls believes the philosophical case for his principles of justice succeed, he understands that for political liberalism to be the ground of a stable and enduring society of competing comprehensive doctrines each proponent must conclude that Rawls's principles of political liberalism are reasonable from her perspective. This is what Rawls calls an "overlapping consensus." "Thus," according to Rawls, "political liberalism looks for a political conception of justice that we hope can gain the support of an overlapping consensus of reasonable religious, philosophical, and moral doctrines in a society regulated by it."[168]

Rawls writes that it is permissible for one to support a policy proposal based on the beliefs one holds as part of one's comprehensive doctrine. Nevertheless, in the public square one ought to provide reasons that are publicly accessible to fellow citizens who have contrary comprehensive doctrines so that they may be able to understand and appreciate one's views and perhaps be persuaded of their correctness.

Paul J. Weithman, in a slightly different reading of Rawls's argument, states that "Rawls did not say that citizens may not appeal to religious doctrines when constitutional essentials or matters of basic justice are at stake or that appealing to public reason is preferable." Rather, according to Weithman, Rawls is arguing that "what virtuous citizenship—the virtue of civility—requires is that citizens be *ready* and *able* to show that their views can be supported by public reason."[169]

No matter which way one may interpret Rawls, it is clear that he maintains that at some point in one's political argument for a particular policy one must be prepared to present a secular or public reason if one wants to advance one's views in a society whose diverse citizenry arrive at the public square armed with contrary comprehensive doctrines. Reasons that are not publicly accessible—that is, reasons inexorably linked to, and cannot in principle be detached from, a comprehensive doctrine—cannot be the basis of a fair and just public policy.

2. Plantinga's Argument

Plantinga, in a paper presented at the 1998 Eastern Division meeting of the American Philosophical Association (and published in 2001), takes a Rawlsian version of PL and applies it to the creation/evolution debate in public education.[170] Plantinga's analysis can be easily extended to include the question of whether it is permissible to teach ID in public schools. His argument goes something like this: since naturalistic evolution presupposes a controversial epistemological position (methodological naturalism) that entails a controversial metaphysical position (ontological materialism or philosophical naturalism), a comprehensive doctrine over which rational citizens disagree, therefore, naturalistic evolution should not be taught in public schools unless students are told that naturalistic evolution is likely the best explanation of origins *only if* one accepts methodological naturalism. Consequently, those who seek to institutionalize naturalistic evolution by employing the coercive power of the state to indoctrinate citizens who reject naturalism, violate PL.

In order to make his case, Plantinga makes a number of points. First, we live in a pluralistic society, one in which its citizens believe a diversity of comprehensive doctrines including philosophical naturalism.[171] Second, citizens typically believe that their children ought to be taught the correct and true comprehensive doctrine; "they think it is a matter of great importance which comprehensive beliefs their children adopt, some even thinking that one's eternal welfare depends on accepting the true comprehensive beliefs."[172] This is why some parents who cannot afford private religious schools enroll their children in after-hours or weekend church, synagogue, or mosque education programs, so that these children may be taught the fundamental beliefs of their family's religious tradition. Third, public schools, which are supported by the tax dollars of a diverse citizenry, cannot teach every comprehensive belief as true or even pick one as true and exclude all others. According to Plantinga, "fairness dictates that no belief be taught as settled truth that conflicts with the comprehensive beliefs of some group of citizens party to the [social] contract." He calls this "the basic right" (BR). Consequently, "[e]ach of the citizens party to the contract has the right not to have comprehensive beliefs taught to her children that contradict her own comprehensive beliefs."[173] Plantinga draws the conclusion:

> So there is therefore a clear prima facie question of justice here: these citizens are party to the implicit contract; they pay their taxes; they support these public schools, and send their children to them. But then they have a prima facie right to have their children taught, as settled fact, only what is consistent with their comprehensive beliefs. And this means that it is unfair or unjust to teach evolution—universal common ancestry, for example—in the public schools, at any rate where there is a substantial segment of the population whose comprehensive beliefs are incompatible with evolution. In the very same way, of course, it would be unjust to teach creationism as the settled truth. Both doctrines conflict with the comprehensive beliefs of some of the parties of the contract.[174]

Plantinga presents an objection to his view:[175] although BR may be a prima facie right, it should be trumped by requirements of truth. After all, is not science education's primary goal to provide students a true description of the natural world? And if naturalistic evolution is the view a vast majority of scientists believe is true and grounded in empirical fact, would it not be unfair and unjust not to teach such a theory in the public schools? Plantinga believes that the reasoning behind these questions is "deeply flawed." He explains: "Suppose Christianity is in fact true, as indeed I believe it is: would that mean that it is fair to teach it in public schools where most of the citizens, citizens who support those schools, are not Christians and reject Christian comprehensive beliefs?"[176] He does not think so. For the unfairness of teaching the comprehensive beliefs override their truth. After all, the other parties, the non-Christians, "also believe that their comprehensive beliefs are true: that is why they hold them."[177]

Plantinga deals with a variation on the previous objection:[178] since science deals with "facts," and since religion deals with "values," it is not unfair to teach in the public schools what apparently contradicts another's comprehensive beliefs, for such beliefs are either outside the realm of "fact" or they should be disbelieved if they contradict the "facts" or the overwhelming consensus of the scientific community.

Plantinga first replies that it is mistaken to believe that religion does not deal with factual claims. For example, Muslims believe that there was such a person as Mohammed and that there is such a person as God; so, if there is no historical evidence for Mohammed and philosophical naturalism is the case, Islam has some external factual issues with which its theologians must deal.

Second, "why should we think scientific consensus overrides (BR)?" Maybe it is "because we think science is our best bet with respect to the discovery of the truth or the approximate truth on the subjects on which it speaks."[179] However, if it is the truth with which we are concerned, then current science may not be the best place to look. Plantinga points out that "[w]e all know how often scientific opinion has changed over the years; there is little reason to think that now it has finally arrived at the unrevisable truth."[180] He then goes on to cite a number of historical examples including Newtonian physics, caloric theories of heat, vital forces in physiology, and the luminiferous ether.

Plantinga deals with one more objection to his argument:[181]

[T]he way to approach questions of empirical fact is by way of science, not by way of religion; thus scientific consensus trumps religious or comprehensive belief in such a way that prima facie requirements of (BR) are overridden; and hence, it is fair to teach evolution as settled fact, even if it does conflict with the religious beliefs of some of the citizens party to that implicit contract.[182]

This objection, Plantinga says, is grounded in a more primitive claim, (PC), which he defines in the following way: "the right way to answer questions of empirical fact—for example, questions about the origin of life, the age of the earth, whether human beings have evolved from earlier life forms—is by way of science, or scientific method." Plantinga first points out "that (PC) is not, of course, itself a question of empirical fact."[183] It is a question of philosophy, for (PC) is not a claim *of* science, but a claim *about* science. This is something we saw earlier in our analysis of Judge Overton's opinion in *McLean*[184] and our evaluation of methodological naturalism (MN) and demarcation theories in this chapter.[185] Thus, this objection concerns the philosophical question of whether a certain epistemology (methodological naturalism) and metaphysics (philosophical naturalism) are able to settle ultimate questions about the nature and order of things. Consequently, this dispute, according to Plantinga, "is philosophical or religious rather than scientific."[186]

Second, (PC) is part of the comprehensive beliefs of many people, such as philosophical naturalists; but its denial is part of the comprehensive doctrines embraced by others who are also part of the social contract, such as orthodox Christians, Jews, and Muslims.

Thus, according to Plantinga, one's acceptance of any theory of origins is contingent upon the epistemic base—a part of one's comprehensive doctrine—with which one grounds his or her knowledge claims. Therefore, if one embraces MN as part of one's epistemic base, then naturalistic evolution is more likely true than not. However, if one believes that one has epistemic warrant in believing all sorts of claims that are inconsistent with philosophical naturalism, then one may rationally reject MN. But if one were to do that, one would think that naturalistic evolution is unlikely to be true; in fact, one might think that its truth is highly improbable. This is why Plantinga suggests the following should occur in the public schools.

First, naturalistic evolution should be taught as "the best hypothesis (the one most likely to be true), or even that it is much more likely than not with respect to" the naturalist's epistemic base (EBp).[187] That claim would be consistent with everyone's comprehensive doctrines, for even the creationist and the ID proponent would agree that given EBp naturalistic evolution is probably true. And second, "the same would go for Creationism: with respect to certain widely shared epistemic bases, the most likely or satisfactory hypothesis will be the claim that God created human beings specially."[188] This too would not be inconsistent with anyone's comprehensive doctrine, for even the philosophical naturalist would agree that given the falsity of EBp as well as the truth of other epistemic bases, some form of creationism (broadly defined) is more likely true than not. Plantinga concludes: "should Creationism be taught in the public schools? Should evolution? The answer is in each case the same: no, neither should be taught unconditionally; but yes, each should be taught conditionally."[189] In other words, if one were to teach in public schools any theory of origins without these conditions, one would violate PL, for one would be basing a public policy on a comprehensive doctrine rather than on publicly accessible reasons.[190]

D. SUMMARY OF CHAPTER 3

In this chapter we covered the topic of Intelligent Design by going over three general areas: (A) The Case against Methodological Naturalism, (B) The Case for Intelligent Design, and (C) The Case for the Illiberality of Teaching Naturalistic Evolution in Public Schools. In A we went over three topics: (1) Methodological Naturalism Is Not A Claim *Of* Science, (2) The Failure of Demarcation Theories, and (3) Science and External Conceptual Problems, in which we reviewed (a) Naturalism and Cosmology, (b) Souls, Minds, and Essences, (c) Moral Claims and Properties, and (d) Materialism, Naturalism, and Self-Refutation. In my presentation of B, we reviewed the notion of specified complexity, the filter by which many design theorists maintain that one can detect design. We then reviewed its application in three areas: Michael Behe's argument for the irreducible complexity of certain biological systems, Stephen Meyer's analysis of the information content of DNA, and the case for the fine-tuning of the universe for the existence of human life. Design theorists maintain that an intelligent designer best accounts for each phenomenon. We also dealt with other concerns and arguments as well as the differences between ID and what the courts recognize as creationism. Finally, in section C we briefly reviewed John Rawls's view of the liberal state and then presented Plantinga's application of Rawlsian liberalism to the debate over the teaching of origins in public schools.

Of course, the ID movement is highly controversial and, as we have seen, has its share of critics.[191] Nevertheless, the arguments of its advocates are serious and sophisticated,[192] and thus they pose an important challenge to the constitutional jurisprudence that is found in *Epperson, McLean,* and *Edwards*.[193]

The ID movement is making what should be considered an uncontroversial claim: science is fundamentally about arguments and their soundness. It is not, and should not be, about legislating epistemology and metaphysics. Thus, as we saw in our analysis of methodological naturalism and political liberalism,[194] science is a subdiscipline of philosophy and, therefore, its practitioners should follow the evidence and arguments wherever they lead, even if they lead to conclusions inconsistent with materialist metaphysics. To use a legal metaphor, when it comes to arguments about the order and nature of things there should not be an exclusionary rule that forbids the collection of evidence without a materialist warrant.

NOTES

1. As I noted in note 5 in the introduction, for the purposes of this book the terms "naturalism" and "materialism," when describing a metaphysical point of view, are employed here interchangeably, but they are not necessarily synonymous when used elsewhere. As Moreland points out, "[O]ne could be a naturalist without being a physicalist [or materialist], say be embracing Platonic forms, possibilia or abstract objects like sets, and one can be a physicalist [or materialist] and not a naturalist (e.g., if one held that God is a physical object)" (J. P. Moreland, "Theistic Science and Methodological Naturalism," *The Creation Hypothesis: Scientific Evidence for an Intelligent Designer,* ed. J. P. Moreland [Downers Grove, IL: InterVarsity Press, 1994], 50). However, in the context of this book, materialism and naturalism (or philosophical naturalism) are treated as synonymous terms.

2. *See* introduction, section A of this book.

3. *See* introduction, section A of this book.

4. This is precisely the position taken by Larry Arnhart, an opponent of ID, who nevertheless believes it should be taught in public schools. *See* Larry Arnhart, "Evolution and the New Creationism: A Proposal for Compromise," *Skeptic,* 8, 4 (2001).

5. This third point is supported by the second. That is, if ID proponents have made a reasonable and intellectually respectable case, then the state has a legitimate interest in exposing its students and faculty to these insights. For education is a legitimate state interest. *See Board of Education, Island Trees Union Free School Dist. No. 26 v. Pico,* 457 U.S. 853, 893 (1982) (Powell, J., dissenting) ("States and locally elected school boards should have the responsibility of determining the educational policy of the public school"); and *Edwards v. Aguillard,* 482 U.S. 578, 583 (1987) ("State and local school boards are generally afforded considerable discretion in operating public schools").

6. If ID does not unconstitutionally advance religion, then there are no Establishment Clause concerns and the state just needs a rational basis to justify its legislation, assuming that no fundamental rights are at stake.

7. William A. Dembski, *Intelligent Design: The Bridge between Science and Theology* (Downers Grove, IL: InterVarsity Press, 1999), 119.

8. Phillip E. Johnson, *Reason in the Balance: The Case against Naturalism in Science, Law, and Education* (Downers Grove, IL: InterVarsity Press, 1986), 208.

9. Dembski, *Intelligent Design,* 119.

10. Richard Lewontin, "Billions and Billions of Demons," in *New York Review of Books* (January 9, 1997), 31.

11. *See* note 29 in chapter 1 of this book.

12. I originally used this term, *naturalism-of-the-gaps* in my Ph.D. dissertation (Fordham University, November 1988), which was published as a book, Francis J. Beckwith, *David Hume's Argument against Miracles: A Critical Analysis* (Lanham, MD: University Press of America, 1989), 76. I describe Hume's a priori rejection of miracle claims as an *"ad hoc naturalism-of-the-gaps."*

13. *See,* for example, Moreland, "Theistic Science and Methodological Naturalism"; Johnson, *Reason in the Balance*, 205–218; Phillip E. Johnson, "Dogmatic Materialism," *Boston Review* (February/March 1997), *available at* http://www.polisci.mit. edu/bostonreview/br22.1/ johnson.html (January 14, 2001); Dembski, *Intelligent Design*, 97–183; Alvin Plantinga, "Methodological Naturalism?" *Origins & Design*, 18, 1 (1997), *available at* http://www.arn.org/docs/odesign/od181/methnat181.htm (February 16, 2001); Alvin Plantinga, "Methodological Naturalism?: Part 2," *Origins & Design*, 18, 2 (1997), *available at* http://www.arn.org/docs/odesign/od182/methnat182. htm (February 16, 2001); Jonathan Wells, "Unseating Naturalism: Recent Insights from Developmental Biology," in *Mere Creation: Science, Faith and Intelligent Design,* ed. William A. Dembski (Downers Grove, IL: InterVarsity Press, 1998).

14. Moreland, "Theistic Science and Methodological Naturalism," 43.

15. John Kekes, *The Nature of Philosophy* (Totowa, NJ: Rowman & Littlefield, 1980), 156–157.

16. Although he is writing about creationism, Ruse makes a claim—that can only be described as a bizarre concession—that is applicable to ID as well: "Even if Scientific Creationism were totally successful in making its case as science, it would not yield a *scientific* explanation of origins. Rather, at most, it could prove that science shows that there can be *no* scientific explanation of origins." However, "the Creationists believe that the world started miraculously. But miracles lie outside of science, which by definition deals only with the natural, repeatable, that which is governed by law" (Michael Ruse, *Darwinism Defended: A Guide to the Evolution Controversies* [Reading, MA: Addison-Wesley, 1982], 322) (emphasis added). As we have seen, this definition of science is highly problematic (see chapter 1, section B, part 4 of this book) and an example of one of the many failed demarcation theories (*see* section A, part 2 of this chapter).

17. Stephen C. Meyer, "The Methodological Equivalence of Design and Descent," in *The Creation Hypothesis*, 87.

18. Meyer's work ("The Methodological Equivalence of Design and Descent") is an outstanding analysis, as well as a rich source of information, on this topic. *See also,* Larry Laudan, "The Demise of the Demarcation Problem," in *But Is It Science?: The Philosophical Question in the Creation/Evolution Controversy,* ed. Michael Ruse (Buffalo, NY: Prometheus Books, 1988); and Phillip Quinn, "The Philosopher of Science as Expert Witness," in *But Is It Science?*

19. Dembski writes: "Science is . . . testable if by testable one means sensitive to new evidence and to further theoretical insight. Indeed it was in this sense that Darwin tested William Paley's account of design and found it wanting. But testability is a double-edged sword. If it is possible for evidence to count against a claim, it must also be possible for evidence to confirm a claim. Testability is a symmetric notion.

One cannot say, 'Design isn't testable,' and then turn around and say, 'Darwin tested design and refuted it.' Intelligent design is indeed testable, and it has been confirmed across a wide range of disciplines, spanning everything from natural history to molecular biology to information theory" (Dembski, *Intelligent Design,* 258) (note omitted).

20. Laudan, "The Demise of the Demarcation Problem," 349.

21. Larry Laudan, *Progress and Its Problems: Towards a Theory of Scientific Growth* (Berkeley: University of California Press, 1977), 45–69.

22. Laudan, *Progress and Its Problems,* 124. Moreland cites a number of examples of external conceptual problems shaping scientific theories. See J. P. Moreland, *Christianity and the Nature of Science* (Grand Rapids, MI: Baker Book House, 1989), 52–56.

23. Moreland, *Christianity and the Nature of Science,* 54.

24. This is an argument made by Steven Pinker, professor of psychology, Massachusetts Institute of Technology. *See* Michael Kelly's critique of Pinker: "Arguing for Infanticide," *Washington Post* (November 6, 1997). *See also* Pinker's response to Kelly, in which Pinker argues that understanding why infanticide occurs (which Pinker claims he is doing) is not the same as condoning it: "Arguing against Infanticide," *Washington Post* (November 21, 1997). If, however, human action is reducible to nonrational material causes, as Pinker admits in his writings, it is difficult to know how Pinker can *condemn* maternal infanticide in a morally robust way. Pinker writes: "Ethical theory requires idealizations like free, sentient, rational, equivalent agents whose behavior is uncaused, and its conclusions can be sound and useful even though the world, as seen by science, does not really have uncaused events. . . . A human being is simultaneously a machine and a sentient free agent, depending on the purpose of the discussion" (Steven Pinker, *How the Mind Works* [New York: Norton, 1997], 55–56). To see how Pinker's mind works, the following comments are instructive:

> If you believe the right to life inheres in being sentient, you must conclude that a hamburger-eater is a party to murder. If you believe it inheres in being a member of Homo sapiens, you are just a species bigot. If you think it begins at conception, you should prosecute IUD users for murder and divert medical research from preventing cancer and heart disease to preventing the spontaneous miscarriages of vast numbers of microscopic conceptuses. If you think it begins at birth, you should allow abortion minutes before birth, despite the lack of any significant difference between a late-term fetus and a neonate. (Steven Pinker, "A Matter of the Soul," Letter to the Editor, in *The Weekly Standard* [February 2, 1998], *available at* http://www.mit.edu/~pinker/standard.html [May 15, 2002].)

Pinker's letter was in reply to Andrew Ferguson, "How Steven Pinker's Mind Works," *The Weekly Standard* (January 12, 1998).

25. *See* Jeffrey P. Schloss, "Evolutionary Accounts of Altruism and the Problem of Goodness by Design," in *Mere Creation: Science, Faith & Intelligent Design,* ed. William A. Dembski (Downers Grove, IL: InterVarsity Press, 1998); and Gregory P. Koukl in Francis J. Beckwith and Gregory P. Koukl, eds., *Relativism: Feet Firmly Planted in Mid-Air* (Grand Rapids, MI: Baker Book House, 1998), 156–170.

26. *See,* e.g., Pinker, *How the Mind Works,* 55–56; E. O. Wilson, *Sociobiology: The New Synthesis* (Cambridge, MA: Harvard University Press,1975); E. O. Wilson, *On Human Nature* (Cambridge, MA: Harvard University Press, 1978); Richard A. Posner, "The Problematics of Moral and Legal Theory," *Harvard Law Review,* 111 (1998); and Michael Ruse, "The New Evolutionary Ethics," in *Evolutionary Ethics,* ed. Matthew H. Nitecki and Doris V. Nitecki (Albany: State University of New York Press, 1993), 133–162. Ruse writes:

> Considered as a rationally justifiable set of claims about an objective something, [moral- ity] is illusory. I appreciate that when somebody says, "Love thy neighbor as thyself," they think they are referring above and beyond themselves. . . . Nevertheless, to a Darwinian evolutionist it can be seen that such reference is truly without foundation. Morality is just an aid to survival and reproduction, and has no being beyond or without this. . . . [A]ny deeper meaning is illusory. (Michael Ruse, *The Darwinian Paradigm: Essays on Its His- tory, Philosophy, and Religious Implications* [New York: Routledge, 1989], 268–269)

Of course, not all Darwinists agree with this assessment of morality. *See,* e.g., James Q. Wilson, *The Moral Sense* (New York: The Free Press, 1993); and Ronald Dworkin, "Darwin's New Bulldog," *Harvard Law Review,* 111 (1998).

27. Del Ratzsch, *Nature, Design, and Science: The Status of Design in Natural Sci- ence,* SUNY Series in Philosophy and Biology (Albany: State University of New York Press, 2001), 138.

28. Ratzsch, *Nature, Design, and Science,* 139, 138.

29. *See,* e.g., William Lane Craig, "Naturalism and Cosmology," in *Naturalism: A Critical Analysis,* ed. William Lane Craig and J. P. Moreland (New York: Routledge, 2000); William Lane Craig in William Lane Craig and Quentin Smith, *Theism, Athe- ism, and Big Bang Cosmology* (New York: Oxford University Press, 1993); William Lane Craig, *The Kalam Cosmological Argument* (New York: Macmillan, 1979); William Lane Craig, "Design and the Cosmological Argument," in *Mere Creation;* Hugh Ross, *The Fingerprint of God: Recent Scientific Discoveries Reveal the Unmis- takable Identity of the Creator,* 2nd ed. (Orange, CA: Promise, 1991); Hugh Ross, *The Creator and the Cosmos* (Colorado Springs: NavPress, 1993); Hugh Ross, "Astro- nomical Evidences for a Personal Transcendent God," in *The Creation Hypothesis;* and Hugh Ross, "Big Bang Refined by Fire," in *Mere Creation,* 363–384.

30. It was published as a book in 1979 by Macmillan Publishing. *See* Craig, *The Kalam Cosmological Argument.*

31. *See,* e.g., Michael Martin, *Atheism: A Philosophical Justification* (Philadel- phia: Temple University Press, 1990), 101–106; Smith's criticisms and Craig's replies in Craig and Smith, *Theism, Atheism, and Big Bang Cosmology;* G. Oppy, "Craig, Mackie, and the *Kalam* Cosmological Argument," *Religious Studies,* 27 (1991); William J. Wainwright, review of William Lane Craig, *The Kalam Cosmo- logical Argument, Nous,* 16 (1982); J. L. Mackie, *The Miracle of Theism* (New York: Oxford University Press, 1982), 92–95; Richard Sorabji, *Time, Creation, and the Continuum* (1983), 221–222; and James Sadowsky, review of William Lane Craig, *The Kalam Cosmological Argument, International Philosophical Quarterly,* 21 (June 1981).

32. William Lane Craig, "Philosophical and Scientific Pointers to Creation ex Nihilo," *Journal of the American Scientific Affiliation,* 32 (March 1980), 5.

33. Craig, *The Kalam Cosmological Argument,* 69, 102–103.

34. Craig, *The Kalam Cosmological Argument,* 111.

35. J. P. Moreland in J. P. Moreland and Kai Nielsen, *Does God Exist?: The Debate between Theists and Atheists* (Amherst, NY: Prometheus Books, 1993), 38. Moreland quotes, among others, Cambridge astronomer Fred Hoyle, "The universe was shrunk down to nothing" (Fred Hoyle, *Astronomy and Cosmology* [San Francisco: W.H. Freeman & Co., 1975], 658, quoted in Moreland in *Does God Exist,* 38). According to four of the world's most prominent astronomers, the Big Bang theory points toward a beginning of the universe at which time and space had their origin:

> The universe began from a state of infinite density. Space and time were created in that event and so was all the matter in the universe. It is not meaningful to ask what happened before the big bang; it is somewhat like asking what is north of the north pole. Similarly, it is not sensible to ask where the big bang took place. The point-universe was not an object isolated in space; it was the entire universe, and so the only answer can be that the big bang happened everywhere. (J. Richard Gott III, James E. Gunn, David N. Schramm, Beatrice M. Tinsley, "Will the Universe Expand Forever?" *Scientific American* [March 1976], 65)

36. Craig, *The Kalam Cosmological Argument,* 130.

37. This is my example, not Craig's.

38. J. P. Moreland, *Scaling the Secular City* (Grand Rapids, MI: Baker Book House, 1987), 29.

39. P. J. Zwart, *About Time* (Amsterdam: North Holland Publishing, 1976), 136.

40. Mackie, *The Miracle of Theism,* 94.

41. When a philosopher says something is *logically possible* she is merely saying that it does not entail a logical contradiction, such as "Frank is 15 feet tall and can flap his arms and fly to Anaheim Hills from Princeton, New Jersey, by his own power." However, to say "Frank is both married and a bachelor" is to assert the logically impossible. It seems to me that appealing to the bare logical possibility of a position is the last refuge of someone without a good argument.

42. R. Douglas Geivett, *Evil and the Evidence of God: The Challenge of John Hick's Theodicy* (Philadelphia: Temple University Press, 1993), 111.

43. Moreland, *Scaling,* 42.

44. Craig, "Naturalism and Cosmology," 234–235 (note omitted), citing Richard Swinburne, *The Existence of God,* 2nd ed. (New York: Oxford University Press, 1991), 32–48. Someone may raise the objection that if the first cause is itself beginningless, would not it, like the universe, fall prey to the impossibility of an infinite regress? The answer would appear to be no, for the first cause is timeless and changeless and, therefore, would not be the sort of entity whose existence would consist of a series of events.

45. *See,* for example, Martin, *Atheism,* 101–106; Smith's criticisms in Craig and Smith, *Theism, Atheism, and Big Bang Cosmology;* G. Oppy, "Craig, Mackie, and the *Kalam* Cosmological Argument"; Wainwright, review of Craig, *The Kalam Cosmological Argument;* Mackie, *The Miracle of Theism,* 92–95; Sorabji, *Time, Creation,*

and the Continuum, 221–222; and Adolf Grunbaum, "The Pseudo-Problem of Creation in Physical Cosmology," *Philosophy of Science,* 56 (1989).

46. *See,* for example, Craig's replies in Craig and Smith, *Theism, Atheism, and Big Bang Cosmology;* Craig, "Naturalism and Cosmology"; Craig, "Design and the Cosmological Argument"; William Lane Craig, "The Origin and Creation of the Universe: A Reply to Adolf Grunbaum," *British Journal for the Philosophy of Science,* 43 (1992); Geivett, *Evil and the Evidence for God,* 99–112; Moreland, *Scaling,* 18–42; Paul Copan and William Lane Craig, "Craftsman or Creator?: An Examination of the Mormon Doctrine of Creation and a Defense of Creatio ex Nihilo," *The New Mormon Challenge: Responding to the Latest Defenses of a Fast-Growing Movement,* ed. Francis J. Beckwith, Carl Mosser, and Paul Owen (Grand Rapids, MI: Zondervan, 2002).

47. For example, some ID advocates argue for a designer based on the fine-tuning of the universe for the possibility of human life and the vast improbability of the large number of independent cosmic characteristics that would have had to occur to bring this about without a designer. See section B, part 4 of this chapter.

48. David Hull points out that the existence of nonmaterial essences and natures is not logically inconsistent with a Darwinian model of origins, but their existence is highly unlikely. See David L. Hull, *The Metaphysics of Evolution* (Albany: State University of New York Press, 1989), 74–75.

49. William Lycan, *Consciousness and Experience* (Cambridge, MA: M.I.T. Press, 1996), 45.

50. J. P. Moreland, "A Defense of the Substance Dualist View of the Soul," in *Christian Perspectives on Being Human: A Multidisciplinary Approach,* eds. J. P. Moreland and David M. Ciocchi (Grand Rapids, MI: Baker Book House, 1993), 58–59.

51. Moreland, "A Defense of the Substance Dualist View of the Soul," 60.

52. *See,* for example, Francis Crick, *The Astonishing Hypothesis: The Scientific Search for the Soul* (New York: C. Scribner's Sons, 1994); Paul Churchland, *Matter and Consciousness: A Contemporary Introduction to the Philosophy of Mind* (Cambridge, MA: M.I.T. Press, 1984); and David Hull, *Philosophy of Biological Science* (1974), 125–141.

53. *See,* for example, Moreland, "A Defense of the Substance Dualist View of the Soul"; J. P. Moreland and Scott B. Rae, *Body and Soul: Human Nature and the Crisis in Ethics* (Downers Grove, IL: InterVarsity Press, 2000); Charles Taliaferro, "Naturalism and the Mind," in *Naturalism;* and Richard Swinburne, *The Evolution of the Soul,* 2nd ed. (New York: Oxford University Press, 1997).

54. *See,* for example, works cited in note 53 and note 57.

55. Although similar, the self-refutation charge against materialist construals of the self is slightly different than the self-refutation charge against naturalism in general, which is covered in section A, part 3.d of this chapter. Moreland explains the charge as it applies to the issue here:

[I]t is self-refuting to *argue* that one *ought* to *choose* physicalism *because* he should *see* that the *evidence* is *good* for physicalism. Physicalism cannot be offered as a rational theory because physicalism does away with the necessary preconditions for there to be such a thing as rationality. Physicalism usually denies intentionality by reducing it to a physical relation of input/output, thereby denying that the mind is genuinely capable of having thoughts *about* the world. Physicalism denies the existence of propositions and nonphysical laws of logic and evidence which can be in minds and influence thinking. Physicalism denies the existence of a faculty capable of rational insight into these nonphysical laws and propositions, and it denies the existence of an enduring "I" which is present through the process of reflection. Finally, it denies the existence of a genuine agent who deliberates and chooses positions because they are rational, an act possible only if physical factors are not sufficient for determining future behavior. (Moreland, *Scaling,* 96) (emphasis in original)

Although Moreland is referring in this quote to mind-body physicalism, the self-refuting charge may also be leveled against property-dualism, for the emergent mental properties stand in a rigid causal relation to the physical events of the brain. Thus, "[t]here is no room for a rational agent to intervene in this causal sequence. Mental agents do not act here. The physical level determines all the action. Mental states are mere byproducts of their physical states as smoke is a byproduct of fire" (99).

56. Moreland, for example, argues that substance dualism, in comparison to materialist construals of the self, best accounts for personal identity through change. *See* Moreland and Rae, *Body and Soul,* 157–196.

57. On this matter, John A. Mitchell and Scott B. Rae write that "a necessary condition for libertarian free will is the existence of an agent (e.g., agent-causation or noncausal agent theory); and a substance ontology of the agent is arguably a necessary condition for agency theory" (John A. Mitchell and Scott B. Rae, "The Moral Status of Fetuses and Embryos," in *The Silent Subject: Reflections on the Unborn in American Culture,* ed. Brad Stetson [Westport, CT: Praeger, 1996], 22). *See also* Stewart Goetz, "Naturalism and Libertarian Agency," in *Naturalism.*

58. Moreland argues that first-person awareness counts against materialist construals of the self. *See* Moreland and Rae, *Body and Soul,* 182–187.

59. Substance dualism, as presented in this book, refers to Thomistic not Cartesian dualism (though good arguments for the latter also count against materialist construals of the self). For Descartes, the soul is reducible to consciousness and merely occupies the body, a physical machine, as a driver occupies an automobile. In contrast, for Thomas Aquinas, the soul is the underlying unity that is the metaphysical grounding of the living organism. That is, there is a deep, almost mysterious, connection between body and soul so that even though one undergoes bodily change one still remains the same organism over time. In addition, as Moreland points out, "the body develops and matures as a teleological development in which the soul's internal structure for a body is progressively realized in a lawlike way, grounded in the human essence in the soul, toward the end of realizing a mature, human body. The various biological operations of the body have their roots in the internal structure of the soul, which forms a body to facilitate those operations" (Moreland in *Body and Soul,* 206) (note omitted). Thus, consciousness is only one aspect of the soul. For more on this, *see* Moreland in *Body and Soul,* 199–228.

60. Mitchell and Rae, "The Moral Status of Fetuses and Embryos," 20.

61. *See,* for example, Moreland in Moreland and Nielsen, *Does God Exist?,* 111–135; Moreland, *Scaling,* 105–132; and Koukl in Koukl and Beckwith, *Relativism,* 156–170. And *see,* for example, John E. Hare, "Naturalism and Morality," in *Naturalism;* and J. L. A. Garcia, "*Dues sive Natura':* Must Natural Lawyers Choose?" in *Natural Law, Liberalism, and Morality,* ed. Robert P. George (New York: Oxford University Press, 1996).

62. Mackie, *The Miracle of Theism,* 115. *See* Francis J. Beckwith, "Moral Law, the Mormon Universe, and the Nature of the Right We Choose," in *The New Mormon Challenge.*

63. *See* chapter 1, notes 21–23 of this book; *see* note 24 in this chapter.

64. This is not to say that Nielsen and Rawls are in agreement with Ruse and Pinker, or even with each other, on the question of what ethical theory is correct.

65. Nielsen in Moreland and Nielsen, *Does God Exist?,* 128 (note omitted).

66. *See,* for example, Moreland, *Scaling,* 77–103; Alvin Plantinga, *Warrant and Proper Function* (New York: Oxford University Press, 1993), 216–237; and Alvin Plantinga, "An Evolutionary Argument against Naturalism," in *Faith in Theory and Practice: Essays on Justifying Religious Belief,* ed. Carol White and Elizabeth Radcliffe (Chicago: Open Court Publishing, 1993).

67. Letter to William Graham from Charles Darwin, July 3, 1881, in *The Life and Letters of Charles Darwin Including an Autobiographical Chapter,* ed. Francis Darwin (London: J. Murray, 1887), 1: 315–316.

68. Plantinga, *Warrant and Proper Function,* 216–237.

69. Plantinga, *Warrant and Proper Function,* 219. Philosopher Anthony O'Hear, who is not part of the ID movement, makes a similar observation:

In the Darwinian view, even our reason is simply an instrument of survival. It was not given to us to unearth the ultimate truth about things but simply to find our way around the savannah well enough to survive and reproduce. That we have a disinterested power to seek and the ability to find the truth for its own sake is as much of an illusion as our faith that our moral sense is truly altruistic and other-regarding. It may be, like our moral faith, a useful illusion, for purposes of survival and reproduction, in that having the illusion may encourage us to uncover facts that aid survival. But it is an illusion none the less, foisted on us by our genes, that we are really engineered by nature to discover ultimate, universally valid truth. Neither our sense nor evolution in general provides any guarantee that what our investigations reveal is the real truth, as opposed to a set of notions useful for a time in the struggle for existence, which of course, leaves a question over the Darwinian notion itself that we are basically survival machines. Is that real truth or merely a notion useful in the struggle for survival? The Darwinian account, seeing our knowledge, as everything else about us, in terms simply of selective advantage, gives us no hope for deciding. (Anthony O'Hare, *After Progress: Finding the Old Way Forward* [London: Bloomsbury, 1999], 68)

70. Plantinga, *Warrant and Proper Function,* 234.

71. Plantinga, *Warrant and Proper Function,* 234.

72. Plantinga suggests that the idea of properly functioning cognitive faculties makes the most sense if they were designed by a being for that purpose. That is, "nat-

uralistic epistemology flourishes best in the garden of supernaturalistic metaphysics. Naturalistic epistemology conjoined with naturalistic metaphysics leads *via* evolution to skepticism or to violation of canons of rationality; conjoined with theism it does not. The naturalistic epistemologist should therefore prefer theism to metaphysical naturalism" (Plantinga, *Warrant and Proper Function,* 237).

73. For a response to Plantinga's case, see Branden Fitelson and Elliot Sober, "Plantinga's Probability Arguments against Evolutionary Naturalism," in *Intelligent Design Creationism and Its Critics: Philosophical, Theological, and Scientific Perspectives,* ed. Robert T. Pennock (Cambridge, MA: M.I.T. Press, 2001). This article was originally published in *Pacific Philosophical Quarterly,* 79 (1998).

74. I say "widely held," because there are some thinkers associated with the ID movement who have expressed doubts and concerns about Dembski's "explanatory filter." *See,* for example, Ratzsch's critique of Dembski's filter in the appendix of a book in which he defends the legitimacy of the design inference in science: *Nature, Design, and Science.*

75. William A. Dembski, "Reinstating Design within Science," *Rhetoric & Public Affairs,* 1, 4 (1998), 506. For more sophisticated defenses of the explanatory filter, *see* William A. Dembski, *The Design Inference: Eliminating Chance through Small Probabilities,* Cambridge Studies in Probability, Induction, and Decision Theory (New York: Cambridge University Press, 1998); William A. Dembski in *Science and Evidence for Design in the Universe* by Michael J. Behe, William A. Dembski, and Stephen C. Meyer, The Proceedings of the Wethersfield Institute, vol. 9 (San Francisco: Ignatius Press, 2000), 17–51; and Dembski, *No Free Lunch,* chapter 1.

76. Dembski in *Science and Evidence for Design in the Universe,* 25, 26.

77. Dembski in *Science and Evidence for Design in the Universe,* 25–26, 27.

78. Dembski in *Science and Evidence for Design in the Universe,* 27.

79. Dembski, "Reinstating Design," 508.

80. Dembski, "Reinstating Design," 507–509.

81. This is my example, not Dembski's.

82. See Dembski in *Science and Evidence for Design in the Universe,* 47–51 n. 17.

83. Quoted in Dembski, "Reinstating Design," 509.

84. Dembski, "Reinstating Design," 510 (note omitted, citing Dembski, *The Design Inference,* ch. 5). See William A. Dembski, *No Free Lunch: Why Specified Complexity Cannot Be Purchased without Intelligence* (Lanham, MD: Rowman & Littlefield, 2002), ch. 2.

85. *Yick Wo v. Hopkins,* 118 U.S. 356 (1886).

86. Gerald Gunther and Kathleen Sullivan, *Constitutional Law,* 13th ed. (Westbury, NY: Foundation Press, 1997), 750.

87. *See* David D. Kirkpatrick, "2 Accuse Stephen Ambrose, Popular Historian, of Plagiarism," *New York Times* (January 5, 2002) and David D. Kirkpatrick, "Author Admits He Lifted Lines from '95 Book," *New York Times* (January 6, 2002), both *available at* http://www.research.umbc.edu/~lindenme/hist201/Ambrose.htm (May 15, 2002); *See* Mark Lewis, "Doris Kearns Goodwin and the Credibility Gap," in *Forbes.Com* (February 27, 2002), *at* http://www.forbes.com/ 2002/02/27/0227goodwin.html (May 15, 2002); *See* Richard Monastersky, "Trinity International University Fires Its Law

Dean Amid Charges That He Plagiarized," *Chronicle of Higher Education* (August 20, 2001), *available at* http://www.gmu.edu/ departments/provost/integrity/trinity.html (October 27, 2001); and Dennis McLellan and H. G. Reza, "O.C. School Dean Accused of Plagiarism," *Los Angeles Times* (July 28, 2001), *available at* 2001 Westlaw 2506410.

88. *See* http://www.tiu.edu (May 14, 2002).

89. Valaria Godines, "Professor Says Internet Search Sparked Plagiarism Allegation," *Orange County Register* (August 17, 2001), *available at* 2001 Westlaw 9681245. Since mid-October 2001 I have told several people, including students and colleagues, that I am the person who discovered Frost's plagiarism of Weston's work (on the evening of July 11, 2001) and subsequently reported it to the university president (on the morning of July 12, 2001). Over the course of several months after this initial find, I discovered other instances of plagiarism by Frost in other venues, including his lifting from his alma mater's (Regent University School of Law) law review and a student's master's thesis (Simon Greenleaf University). *See* note 95.

90. Burns H. Weston, "Human Rights," *Encyclopedia Britannica,* vol. 20 (15th edition, 1986 printing), reprinted in 133 Cong.Rec. S8613-02 (daily ed. June 24, 1987) (submitted by Senator Thomas Harkin).

91. "[Frost's] attorney, Tom Borchard, said he and Frost are trying to determine what happened, but said the portions in question appear to involve a missing footnote and perhaps editing mistakes by the law review staff" (Valaria Godines, "Trinity Dean Steps Down Temporarily," *Orange County Register* [August 1, 2001], *available at* 2001 Westlaw 9679828).

92. "Frost blames students and editing mistakes, saying that his academic papers with incorrect footnotes have become the basis for the series of allegations. 'The issue is whether footnotes are off,' said Frost. 'If they are off in one version, then they will be off in another version'" (Valaria Godines, "Frost Says He's Being Treated Unfairly," *Orange County Register* [August 15, 2001], *available at* 2001 Westlaw 9681123). *See* H. G. Reza and Thuy-Doan Le, "Disputing Charges of Plagiarism, Attorney for Winston Frost Says Sloppy Editing on Article Is to Blame," *Los Angeles Times* (July 31, 2001), *available at* 2001 Westlaw 2507070.

93. "[David] Hiersekorn, 32, who worked on the Law Review 2000 edition, said he worked on an article that was published with mistakes. 'When I was presented with the final version of the . . . article after editing by the Law Review staff, I was shocked to see that none of the footnotes I had prepared were included in the article. . . . It was as if my work was completely wasted and unnecessary and none of it included in the article,' he stated in a declaration that was part of Frost's response" (Tiffany Montgomery and Valaria Godines, "Plagiarism Case Shines Spotlight on Tiny Trinity," *Orange County Register* [August 16, 2001], *available at* 2001 Westlaw 9681214). Hiersekorn, an outstanding student (J.D. cum laude, 2002), was unaware when he spoke to the press that Frost's plagiarism was more vast and diverse than anyone suspected.

94. After being removed as dean, Frost suggested a stunningly audacious theory, offered by his attorney, Tom Borchard: "Frost never attempted to pass off this article as wholly his own work" (H. G. Reza, "O.C. Law School Fires Dean in Plagiarism Case," *Los Angeles Times* [August 18, 2001], *available at* 2001 Westlaw 2511416).

Thus, Frost denied that he had ever claimed to have authored the essay on which he placed his name, submitted to the law review, and included on his curriculum vitae as an authored work. Consequently, according to Frost, law review editors, university regents, students, faculty, alumni, and other law review readers all held the same mistaken belief that he actually wrote the article on which he placed his name and submitted to the periodical that published it with his approval.

95. As it turned out, virtually all the remaining portions of Frost's article were nearly word for word from another document, one authored by former American Bar Association President Jerome Shestack, "The Jurisprudence of Human Rights," in *Human Rights in International Law: Legal and Policy Issues,* ed. Theodor Meron (New York: Oxford University Press, 1984). *See* H. G. Reza, "Second Source Calls Law School Dean Plagiarist," *Los Angeles Times* (August 11, 2001), *available at* Westlaw 2510009. Thus, between 85 and 90 percent of Frost's article was nearly verbatim from two other authors. In addition, a different version of Frost's law review article appeared months later in the journal *Fides et Historia:* Winston L. Frost, "Human Rights and Justice: A Historical and Philosophical Perspective," *Fides et Historia,* 33, 1 (Winter/Spring 2001). According to the journal's editor, Frost agreed to and incorporated editorial suggestions over the months following Frost's submission of the article. Frost also approved of the final version that was eventually published. *See* H. G. Reza, "School to Kick Alleged Plagiarist Off Faculty," *Los Angeles Times* (August 24, 2001), *available at* 2001 Westlaw 2512993; and Council on Faith and History Board, "Statement on *Fides et Historia* and Plagiarism Charges" (August 29, 2001), *at* http://www.huntcol.edu /cfh/plagiarism.htm (October 27, 2001).

It was also discovered that Frost's articles had their origin in his 1996 M.A. thesis (approved in 1998) in International Human Rights, untouched by the student editors of the 2000 law review: Winston L. Frost, "God, Justice, and Human Rights" (M.A. thesis, Simon Greenleaf University, 1996) (on file with author). In addition to containing much of the material taken from Weston and Shestack that is also found in the published articles, this thesis also seems to have sections that were lifted from a book and an article by Gary T. Amos: *Defending the Declaration* (Nashville, TN: Wolgemuth & Hyatt, 1989) and "Unalienable Rights: The Biblical Heritage," *Journal of Christian Jurisprudence* (1990). The latter work is significant because it is a law review once published by Frost's law school alma mater, Regent University. To make matters worse for Frost, about 30 to 35 percent of a paper he delivered at a University Faculty for Life conference in 1998 (Winston L. Frost, "Is Abortion an International Human Right?" *Life and Learning VIII: Proceedings of the Eighth Annual University Faculty for Life Conference,* ed. Joseph W. Koterski, S.J. [Washington, DC: University Faculty for Life, 1999]) was taken nearly word for word from a student thesis: Jeffrey Le Pere, "The Convention on the Rights of the Child: A Familial Perspective" (M.A. thesis, Simon Greenleaf University, 1994)) (on file with author).

Needless to say, Frost was fired as dean for plagiarism. *See* Reza, "O.C. Law School Fires Dean in Plagiarism Case"; H. G. Reza, "School: Disgraced Law Dean Must Go," *Los Angeles Times* (August 24, 2001), *available at* 2001 Westlaw 2512961. Soon afterward he resigned his tenured faculty position in disgrace. *See* Release Statement, Trinity International University (October 16, 2001) (on file with author) ("Winston Frost has informed Trinity International University of his decision to resign his position with Trinity Law School as a tenured faculty member"). Nevertheless, he still maintains his innocence. As of the completion of this manuscript (June 1, 2002), the California Bar is conducting an investigation of Frost.

96. Michael Behe, *Darwin's Black Box: The Biochemical Challenge to Evolution* (New York: The Free Press, 1996).

97. Charles Darwin, *The Origin of Species* (6th ed., 1872), 154, as quoted in Michael Behe, "Intelligent Design as an Alternative Explanation for the Existence of Biomolecular Machines," *Rhetoric & Public Affairs,* 1, 4 (1998), 566.

98. Richard Dawkins, *River Out of Eden* (New York: Basic Books, 1995), 83.

99. Behe, *Darwin's Black Box,* 39.

100. Behe, *Darwin's Black Box,* 42.

101. Behe, "Intelligent Design," 567. There is controversy surrounding Behe's mousetrap example. *See*, for example, H. Allen Orr, "Darwin v. Intelligent Design (Again)," *Boston Review* (December 1996/January 1997), *available at* http://bostonreview.mit.edu/br21.6/orr.html (March 25, 2002); and John H. McDonald, "A Reducibly Complex Mousetrap," *at* http://udel.edu/~mcdonald/mousetrap.html (May 14, 2002). However, I do not believe that these critiques of Behe's illustration fundamentally undercut his argument for the irreducible complexity of actual biological systems. For a response to these critiques as well as a fine-tuning of Behe's case, see Dembski, *No Free Lunch,* 256–267, 279–289.

102. In addition to the cilium, Behe includes the bacterial flagellum, the mechanism of blood clotting, vesicular transport, and immune systems as examples of irreducibly complex biological systems.

103. Behe, *Darwin's Black Box,* 64–65.

104. Behe, *Darwin's Black Box,* 68.

105. Behe, "Intelligent Design," 569.

106. Stephen C. Meyer, "DNA By Design: An Inference to the Best Explanation for the Origin of Biological Information," *Rhetoric & Public Affairs,* 1, 4 (1998), 519–556; Stephen C. Meyer, "The Explanatory Power of Design: DNA and the Origin of Information," in *Mere Creation,* 113–147; and Stephen C. Meyer, "DNA and the Origin of Life: Information, Specification and Explanation," in both *Debating Design: From Darwin to DNA,* ed. William A. Dembski and Michael Ruse (New York: Cambridge University Press, forthcoming 2004) and *Darwinism, Design, and Public Education,* ed. John A. Campbell and Stephen C. Meyer (East Lansing, MI: Michigan State University Press, forthcoming 2003).

107. Meyer, "The Explanatory Power of Design," 113–119, 122–134.

108. Meyer, "The Explanatory Power of Design," 113–119, 122–134.

109. Meyer, "The Explanatory Power of Design," 113–114.

110. Meyer, "The Explanatory Power of Design," 121–122.

111. Meyer, "The Explanatory Power of Design," 126–134.

112. This is my example, not Meyer's.

113. Meyer, "The Explanatory Power of Design," 139 (citation omitted).

114. Dawkins, *River Out of Eden,* 17.

115. Bill Gates, *The Road Ahead,* rev. ed. (New York: Penguin, 1996), 228.

116. K. Giberson, "The Anthropic Principle," *Journal of Interdisciplinary Studies,* 9 (1997).

117. John Barrow and Frank Tipler, *The Anthropic Cosmological Principle* (Oxford: Clarendon Press, 1988); John Leslie, *Universes* (New York: Routledge, 1989); Paul Davies, *The Accidental Universe* (Cambridge: Cambridge University Press, 1982); Paul Davies, *Superforce* (Portsmouth, NH: Heinemann, 1984); John Gribbin and Martin Rees, *Cosmic Coincidences* (New York: Bantam, 1989); Reinhard Breuer, *The Anthropic Principle,* trans. Harry Newman and Mark Lowery (Boston: Birkhauser, 1991); Gilles Cohen-Tannoudji, *Universal Constants in Physics,* trans. Patricia Thickstun (New York: McGraw-Hill, 1993); Ross, *The Fingerprint of God;* Ross, *The Creator and the Cosmos;* Ross, "Astronomical Evidences for a Personal Transcendent God"; Ross, "Big Bang Refined by Fire"; and Walter L. Bradley, "The 'Just So' Universe: The Fine-Tuning of Constants and Conditions in the Cosmos," in *Signs of Intelligence: Understanding Intelligent Design,* ed. William A. Dembski and James M. Kushiner (Grand Rapids, MI: Brazos Press, 2001).

118. Stephen C. Meyer in *Science and Evidence for Design,* 56–57 (notes omitted).

119. Meyer in *Science and Evidence for Design,* 57.

120. Ross, "Big Bang Refined by Fire," 372, 381.

121. Quoted in Walter L. Bradley, "Designed or Designoid," in *Mere Creation,* 40, quoting from D. L. Brock, *Our Universe: Accident or Design?* (Wits, South Africa: Star Watch, 1992), n. p.

122. *See,* for example, Meyer in *Science and Evidence for Design,* 56–66.

123. Meyer in *Science and Evidence for Design,* 58.

124. Meyer in *Science and Evidence for Design,* 58.

125. *See,* for example, Meyer in *Science and Evidence for Design,* 58–66; Dembski, *Intelligent Design,* 264–268; and Robert Kaita, "Design in Physics and Biology: Cosmological Principle and Cosmic Imperative?" in *Mere Creation,* 385–401.

126. Meyer in *Science and Evidence for Design,* 59.

127. Dembski, *Intelligent Design,* 267.

128. *See,* for example, Dembski, *Intelligent Design,* 267–268; Meyer in *Science and Evidence for Design,* 59; William Lane Craig, "Cosmos and Creator," *Origins & Design,* 20, 2 (Spring 1996), 23; Francis Crick, *Life Itself: Its Origin and Nature* (New York: Simon & Schuster, 1981), ch. 7; John Earman, "The Sap Also Rises: A Critical Examination of the Anthropic Principle," *American Philosophical Quarterly,* 24, 4 (1987): 307–316; Bernd-Olaf Kuppers, *Information and the Origin of Life* (Cambridge, MA: M.I.T. Press, 1990), ch. 6; John Leslie, "Anthropic Principle, World Ensemble, Design," *American Philosophical Quarterly,* 19, 2 (1982), 150; John Leslie, *Universes* (London: Routledge, 1989); and Richard Swinburne, *The Existence of God* (Oxford: Oxford University Press, 1979), 133–151.

129. Dembski, *Intelligent Design,* 267.

130. Leslie, "Anthropic Principle, World Ensemble, Design," 150.

131. Meyer in *Science and Evidence for Design,* 59.

132. Meyer in *Science and Evidence for Design,* 59.

133. Meyer in *Science and Evidence for Design,* 59.

134. Robert Penrose, *The Emperor's New Mind* (New York: Oxford, 1989), 344, as quoted in Dembski, *Intelligent Design,* 266 (parenthetical insertions are Dembski's).

135. For a defense of the multiple universes hypothesis, see Martin Rees, *Just Six Numbers: The Deep Forces That Shape the Universe* (New York: Basic Books, 1999).

136. For a nice overview of some responses, *see* Meyer in *Science and Evidence for Design,* 62–66. *See also* Jay Wesley Richards, "Many Worlds Hypotheses: A Naturalistic Alternative to Design," *Perspectives on Science and Christian Belief,* 49, 4 (1997), 218–227; and William Lane Craig, "Barrow and Tipler on the Anthropic Principle v. Divine Design," *British Journal for the Philosophy of Science,* 38 (1988), 389–395.

137. "Though clearly ingenious, the many-worlds hypothesis suffers from an overriding difficulty: we have no evidence for any universes other than our own" (Meyer in *Science and Evidence for Design,* 62).

138. *See,* for example, Robin Collins, "The Fine-Tuning Design Argument: A Scientific Argument for the Existence of God," in *Reason for the Hope Within,* ed. Michael Murray (Grand Rapids, MI: Eerdmans, 1999), 60–61.

139. *See,* for example, Richard Swinburne, "Argument from the Fine-Tuning of the Universe," in *Physical Cosmology and Philosophy,* ed. John Leslie (New York: Macmillan, 1990), 154–173.

140. For example, Clifford Longley writes in the *London Times:* "The [anthropic-design argument] and what it points to is of such an order of certainty that in any other sphere of science, it would be regarded as settled. To insist otherwise is like insisting that Shakespeare was not written by Shakespeare because it might have been written by a billion monkeys sitting at a billion keyboards typing for a billion years. So it might. But the sight of scientific atheists clutching at such desperate straws has put new spring in the step of theists" (Clifford Longley, "Focusing on Theism," *London Times* [January 21, 1989], 10, as quoted in Meyer in *Science and Evidence for Design,* 65) (parenthetical insertion is Meyer's).

141. *See,* for example, Collins, "The Fine-Tuning Design Argument," 61.

142. *See* Dembski, *Intelligent Design,* 261–264.

143. *See* Ratzsch, *Design, Nature, and Science,* 137–147; Dembski, *No Free Lunch,* 311–371; Moreland, "Theistic Science and Methodological Naturalism," 62–64; and Bruce L. Gordon, "Is Intelligent Design Science?: The Scientific Status and Future of Design-Theoretic Explanations," in *Signs of Design,* 207–216.

144. *See* Dembski, *Intelligent Design,* 150–152.

145. *See* Dembski, *Intelligent Design,* 238–245; Ratzsch, *Design, Nature, and Science,* 143–147; Moreland, "Theistic Science and Methodological Naturalism," 59–60; and John Mark Reynolds, "God of the Gaps," in *Mere Creation,* 313–331.

146. *See* Moreland, "Theistic Science and Methodological Naturalism," 60–62.

147. *See* Dembski, *No Free Lunch,* 325–333.

148. *See* Behe in *Science and Evidence for Design,* 144–147; and Dembski, *No Free Lunch,* 355–365.

149. *See,* for example, Ratzsch, *Design, Nature, and Science;* Cornelius G. Hunter, *Darwin's God: Evolution and the Problem of Evil* (Grand Rapids, MI: Brazos Press, 2001); and the essays in the following anthologies: ed. Dembski, *Mere Creation, The Creation Hypothesis,* ed. Moreland; ed. Dembski and Ruse, *Debating Design,* and ed. Campbell and Meyer, *Darwinism, Design, and Public Education.*

150. *See,* for example, Niles Eldridge and Stephen Jay Gould, "Punctuated Equilibria: An Alternative of Phyletic Gradualism," in *Models in Paleobiology,* ed. T. J. Schopf (San Francisco: Freeman Cooper, 1972), 82–115; and Stephen J. Gould and Niles Eldridge, "Punctuated Equlibrium Comes of Age," *Nature,* 223 (1993).

151. The Cambrian explosion refers "to the geologically sudden appearance of at least twenty animal body plans 530 million years ago" (Stephen C. Meyer, Paul A. Nelson, and Paul Chien, "The Cambrian Explosion: Biology's Big Bang," in *Darwinism, Design, and Public Education*) (no pagination; from prepublication manuscript).

152. *See* Stephen Jay Gould, "Darwinism and the Expansion of Evolutionary Theory," in *Philosophy of Biology,* ed. Michael Ruse (Amherst, NY: Prometheus, 1998). For a critical examination of Gould's theory, see Michael Ruse, *The Darwinian Paradigm: Essays on Its History, Philosophy, and Religious Implications* (New York: Routledge, 1989), 118–145; and Meyer, Nelson, and Chien, "The Cambrian Explosion: Biology's Big Bang" (no pagination; from prepublication manuscript).

153. However, as Dembski points out in *No Free Lunch* (23–24), an entity may be "designed" by an agent in order for the entity to appear to not be designed. Hence, an entity may be designed, but if it does not exhibit specified complexity—that is, its maker has adequately made it undetectable—one is not warranted in inferring that it is designed unless one has other evidence.

154. Dembski, *No Free Lunch,* 334.

155. See David K. DeWolf, "Academic Freedom after *Edwards,*" *Regent University Law Review,* 13, 2 (2000–2001), 480–481.

156. See Ronald L. Numbers, *The Creationists* (New York: Alfred A. Knopf, 1992), chapters 10–12, 14; and Raymond A. Eve and Francis B. Harrold, *The Creationist Movement in America,* Twayne's Social Movements Series (Boston: Twayne Publishers, 1991), 52–53, 121–126.

157. Henry M. Morris, "Design Is Not Enough!" *Back to Genesis,* 127 (July 1999), a.

158. *See* chapter 2 of this book.

159. For example, the Court writes in *Epperson* that "government . . . must be neutral in matters of religious theory, doctrine, and practice. It may not be hostile to any religion or to the advocacy of nonreligion; and it may not aid, foster, or promote one religion or religious theory against another or even against the militant opposite. The First Amendment mandates governmental neutrality between religion and religion, and between religion and nonreligion" (*Epperson v. Arkansas,* 393 U.S. 97, 103–104 [1968]).

160. See John Rawls, *Political Liberalism* (New York: Columbia University Press, 1993); and John Rawls, *A Theory of Justice* (Cambridge, MA: Harvard University Press, 1971).

161. See Rawls, *Political Liberalism,* 22–28. Rawls's two principles of justice are:

a. Each person has an equal claim to a fully adequate scheme of equal basic rights and liberties, which scheme is compatible with the same scheme for all; and in this scheme the equal political liberties, and only those liberties, are to be guaranteed their fair value.

b. Social and economic inequalities are to satisfy two conditions: first, they are to be attached to positions and offices open to all under conditions of fair equality of opportunity; and second, they are to be to the greatest benefit of the least advantaged members of society. (Rawls, *Political Liberalism,* 5–6)

162. Rawls probably would not agree with my depiction of his view, for he considers his theory of justice to be deontological and not utilitarian or egoistic. He denies that his view is merely a modus vivendi. He writes in one place that his principles of justice, like Immanuel Kant's, are categorical imperatives. *See* Rawls, *A Theory of Justice,* 253. However, some scholars have made assessments of Rawls's theory that are similar to mine. *See,* for example, Michael Sandel, *Liberalism and the Limits of Justice* (New York: Cambridge University Press, 1983), 66–132; J. P. Moreland, "Rawls and the Kantian Interpretation," in *Simon Greenleaf Review of Law and Religion: A Scholarly Forum Interrelating Law, Theology and Human Rights,* 8 (1988–1989); and Keith Pavlischek, *John Courtney Murray and the Dilemma of Religious Toleration* (Kirksville, MO: Thomas Jefferson University Press, 1994), 208–212.

163. Rawls, *Political Liberalism,* 115, 13.

164. Rawls, *Political Liberalism,* 195–211. There are those to Rawls's political right, such as secular libertarians, who espouse state "neutrality" when it comes to such questions. For example, libertarian social philosopher Murray Rothbard writes:

[W]hile the behavior of plants and at least the lower animals is determined by their biological nature or perhaps by their "instincts," the nature of man is such that *each individual person must, in order to act, choose his own ends and employ his own means in order to attain them.* Possessing no automatic instincts, each man must learn about himself and the world, *use his mind to select values,* learn about cause and effect, and act purposively to maintain himself and advance his life. . . . Since each individual must think, learn, value, and choose his or her ends and means in order to survive and flourish, the right of self-ownership gives man the right to perform these vital activities without being hampered and restricted by coercive molestation. (Murray N. Rothbard, *For a New Liberty: A Libertarian Manifesto,* rev. ed. [San Francisco: Fox & Wilkes, 1978], 28–29) (emphasis added)

165. Rawls, *Political Liberalism,* xxviii.

166. John Rawls, *Political Liberalism,* 2nd ed. (New York: Columbia University Press, 1996), xiii.

167. Robert P. George, "Public Reason and Political Conflict: Abortion and Homosexuality," *Yale Law Journal,* 106 (Summer 1997), 2477–2478 (note omitted).

168. Rawls, *Political Liberalism,* 2nd ed., 10 (note omitted).

169. Paul J. Weithman, "Introduction: Religion and the Liberalism of Reasoned Respect," in *Religion and Contemporary Liberalism,* ed. Paul J. Weithman (Notre Dame, IN: University of Notre Dame Press, 1997), 12–13. To support this interpreta-

tion of Rawls, Weithman cites Rawls, *Political Liberalism,* 2nd ed., 217, 218, 243. This seems to be consistent with one of Rawls's subsequent works: John Rawls, "The Idea of Public Reason Revisited," *University of Chicago Law Review,* 64 (1997). For critiques of Rawls's view of public reason, *see* George, "Public Reason and Political Conflict"; and John Finnis, "Public Reason, Abortion, and Cloning," *Valparaiso University Law Review,* 32, 2 (Spring 1998).

170. Alvin Plantinga, "Creation and Evolution: A Modest Proposal," paper presented at the Eastern Division Meeting of the American Philosophical Association, Washington, DC (December 27–30, 1998). This paper was subsequently published under the same title in *Intelligent Design Creationism*, 779–792. Citations of this essay are to the published version.

171. Plantinga defines philosophical naturalism as "the idea that there is no such person as God or anything or anyone at all like him; on this use, naturalism is or can be a quasi-religious view" (Plantinga, "Creation and Evolution," 780).

172. Plantinga, "Creation and Evolution," 781.

173. Plantinga, "Creation and Evolution," 781.

174. Plantinga, "Creation and Evolution," 783.

175. Plantinga, "Creation and Evolution," 783, citing, and responding to, a paper presented by Robert Pennock at the same meeting at which Plantinga delivered his paper, the 1998 annual meeting of the Eastern Division of the American Philosophical Association. Pennock's paper was subsequently published under the title "Why Creationism Should Not Be Taught in Public Schools" in *Intelligent Design Creationism,* 755–778.

176. Plantinga, "Creation and Evolution," 784.

177. Plantinga, "Creation and Evolution," 784 (note omitted).

178. Plantinga, "Creation and Evolution," 784, attributing this objection to Stephen J. Gould. Gould suggests what he calls the NOMA principle, "non-overlapping magisteria": "Each subject [science and religion] has a legitimate magesterium, or domain of teaching authority—and these magesteria do not overlap. . . . The net of science covers the empirical universe; what it is made of (fact) and why does it work this way (theory). The net of religion extends over questions of moral meaning and value" (Stephen Jay Gould, "Nonoverlapping Magisteria," *Natural History,* 106 [March 1997], 16).

179. Plantinga, "Creation and Evolution," 785.

180. Plantinga, "Creation and Evolution," 785.

181. Plantinga, "Creation and Evolution," 785, attributing this objection to Pennock, "Why Creationism Should Not Be Taught in Public Schools."

182. Plantinga, "Creation and Evolution," 785.

183. Plantinga, "Creation and Evolution," 786.

184. *See* chapter 1, section B, part 4 of this book.

185. *See* chapter 3, section A.

186. Plantinga, "Creation and Evolution," 789.

187. Plantinga, "Creation and Evolution," 789.

188. Plantinga, "Creation and Evolution," 790.

189. Plantinga, "Creation and Evolution," 790.

190. See Pennock's response to Plantinga: Robert T. Pennock, "Reply to Plantinga's 'Modest Proposal,'" in *Intelligent Design Creationism and Its Critics.*

191. *See* introduction of this book.

192. It should be kept in mind that the case for ID is far more multifaceted and sophisticated than I could possibly convey in this brief chapter. For representative defenses of ID, see David K. DeWolf, Stephen C. Meyer, and Mark Edward DeForrest, "Teaching the Origins Controversy: Science, Religion, or Speech?" *Utah Law Review* (2000), 49–66; Dembski, ed., *Mere Creation;* Moreland, ed., *The Creation Hypothesis;* Dembski, *The Design Inference;* Dembski, *No Free Lunch;* Behe, Dembski, and Meyer, *Science and the Evidence for Design in the Universe;* Dembski and Ruse, eds. *Debating Design*; and eds. Campbell and Meyer, *Darwinism, Design, and Public Education.*

193. *See* chapter 1, section B, parts 2, 4; and chapter 2 of this book.

194. *See* chapter 3, section A and section C in this book.

Chapter Four

Would Teaching Intelligent Design in Public Schools Violate the Establishment Clause?

Given the Supreme Court's holding in *Edwards,* current Establishment Clause jurisprudence, and the nature of ID,[1] would ID pass constitutional muster if it were permitted or required by a government entity to be part of a public school's curriculum? In order to answer this question, we must answer two other questions: (A) What is religion? and (B) Is ID a religion? In the process of answering both questions, I reply to several concerns that may be raised. I do not deal with the question of a teacher's right to voluntarily instruct her students in design theory. That was addressed in my analysis of *LeVake v. Independent School District* (2001)[2] in chapter 2, section B, part 4.

A. WHAT IS RELIGION?

Throughout the history of our republic courts have proposed or implied different definitions of religion, broadening their definitions as the country increased in religious diversity and the judiciary began to face new types of cases. Since the literature on "defining religion" constitutionally is vast,[3] it is not possible to conduct a thorough study in this book. For this reason, I focus on a few important cases and theoretical insights that I believe will be helpful in assessing ID.

Although it is true that "the Supreme Court has been reluctant to elaborate an authoritative definition of religion, it has addressed the issue in a number of cases stretching back to the nineteenth century."[4] Religion was defined in early decisions "as an organized body of believers employing religious ceremony and having a faith in and commitment to a supernatural Supreme Being."[5] In an 1890 case, *Davis v. Beason,* the Supreme Court first attempted to give content to the constitutional meaning of religion: "The term 'religion' has reference to one's view of his relations to his Creator, and to the obligations they impose of reverence for his being and character, and of obedience to his will."[6]

The modern trend in the courts toward a broader and more global view of religion began in a Second Circuit Court case.[7] The court denied an atheist status as a conscientious objector because his refusal to serve in the military was based exclusively on political grounds. However, in writing for the court, Judge Augustus Hand, in dictum, denied that belief in God was a necessary condition of "religious training and belief" under the congressional statute in question. That is to say, he held that conscientious objection prodded by conscience and grounded in firmly held beliefs that are not conventionally religious could nonetheless be considered "religious," even though Hand believed "it is unnecessary to attempt a definition of religion; the content of the term is found in the history of the human race and is incapable of compression into a few words":[8]

Religious belief arises from a sense of the inadequacy of reason as a means of relating the individual to his fellow-men and to his universe—a sense common to men in the most primitive and in the most highly civilized societies. It accepts the aid of logic but refuses to be limited by it. . . . [A] conscientious objection to participation in any war . . . may justly be regarded as a response of the individual to an inward mentor, call it conscience or God, that is for many persons at the present time the equivalent of what has always been thought a religious impulse.[9]

The courts continued to broaden their definition of religion, accepting as religious many belief systems and practices that may not initially strike one as religious. For instance, in *Torcaso v. Watkins* the Supreme Court held that it was unconstitutional for the commonwealth of Maryland to make belief in God a requirement for becoming a notary public. The Court affirmed that a belief system can be religious without being theistic: "Among religions in this country which do not teach what would generally be considered a belief in God are Buddhism, Taoism, Ethical Culture, Secular Humanism and others."[10] In *United States v. Seeger* the Court ruled that a belief is religious if it is a "sincere and meaningful belief which occupies in the life of its possessor a place parallel to that filled by" traditional belief in God.[11]

In *Seeger* the Court cited as an authority the work of theologian Paul Tillich[12] who has argued that all human beings, including atheists, have an ultimate commitment of one sort or another, something that serves as a unifying center for their personality and consciousness. This ultimate concern is "religious."[13] It is evident, therefore, why the Court defined religion as a sincere belief "based upon a power or being or upon a faith, to which all else is subordinate or upon which all else is ultimately dependent."[14] Perhaps the same sort of reasoning was behind the Court's comments in *School District of Abington Township v. Schempp* (1963), in which it asserted that "the State may not establish a 'religion of secularism' . . . thus preferring those who believe in no religion over those who do believe."[15]

This type of reasoning is sometimes called the *parallel position test* (PPT), a type of definition by analogy:[16] does the disputed belief function in the life of the individual in a way parallel to the way in which conventional religion functions in the life of the believer? This has been typically applied in Free Exercise cases in which the designation of "religion" is a benefit (such as in *Torcaso* and *Seeger*). The few Establishment Clause cases in which plaintiffs have suggested that the PPT be applied to beliefs that are not prima facie religious, the courts have largely ruled in favor of defendants.[17] An exception to this general rule is the *Malnak I* and *II* cases in which a district court and the Third Circuit concluded, by applying PPT, that the Science of Creative Intelligence/Transcendental Meditation (SCI/TM) is religion, and thus offering nonrequired classes in it in New Jersey public schools violated the Establishment Clause. But in these cases, the plaintiffs provided reams of evidence that made it clear and convincing to the courts that SCI/TM is a religion.[18] In the Ninth Circuit cases, cited in note 17, in which the Court rejected claims of Establishment, these claims were rejected, not because the Court did not apply PPT, but rather *because* the Court applied the test and concluded that the policy in question did not advance a religion.[19] Granted, it is fair to ask whether the Courts' opinions in those two cases—*Peloza* and *Alvarado*—were well-reasoned and/or rightly decided. It is clear, however, that courts apply the same test in both Free Exercise and Establishment cases.

This is why commentators are mistaken when they claim that there are two different definitions of religion, one for the Free Exercise Clause and another for the Establishment Clause.[20] In fact, "the Supreme Court never has accepted this position."[21] In *Everson v. Board of Education (1947)*, Justice Wiley B. Rutledge unequivocally rejected the notion of a dual definition of religion: "'Religion' appears only once in the Amendment. But the word governs two prohibitions and governs them alike. It does not have two meanings, one narrow to forbid 'an establishment' and another, much broader, for 'securing the free exercise thereof.'"[22]

In order to better understand how modern courts have come to their conclusions about what constitutes a religion, let us engage in a brief thought experiment by trying to answer the philosophical question "What is a religion?" This question has been given many answers. For instance, some have said that a religion is some sort of belief system that necessarily includes a belief in a god and/or life after death. But, as the courts have come to appreciate, one problem with this definition is that it excludes beliefs, such as Taoism and Theravada Buddhism, that are generally thought of as religions but do not include a belief in God or gods.[23] Other religions do not have a full-fledged belief in life after death, as in the cases of early Greek religion and Unitarianism,[24] though no one doubts that they are religions. There are other belief systems, such as Humanism, whose creeds put forth answers to most of the questions traditional religions try to answer.[25] This is why the Supreme Court has said that forms of nontheism can be religion for both Free Exercise[26] and Establishment purposes.[27] Although no courts, to my knowledge, have made this point, it is worth mentioning that some philosophers have argued that belief in God may not even be a sufficient condition for a belief to be religious if "God" is employed as an explanatory postulate rather than worshiped as an object of devotion.[28] Admittedly, Judge Overton, in *McLean,* rejects this notion,[29] but it is certainly not because he tried and failed to extend his philosophical imagination; he just did not even try.[30]

In sum, one thing is clear about the courts and religion: they have provided us with no clear definition of religion. Nevertheless, they have provided us with some general guidelines that we can extract from the above analysis:

Conventional religions—e.g., Christianity, Judaism, Buddhism—are paradigm cases of religion.
Whether other belief systems are religious ought to be evaluated by the parallel position test (PPT): Does the disputed belief function in the life of the individual in a way parallel to the way in which conventional religion functions in the life of the believer?
The parallel position test is applied in both Free Exercise and Establishment Clause cases.

If we combine these guidelines with the standard for teaching origins set down in *Edwards,* we are prepared to answer the question of whether ID is religion.

B. IS ID A RELIGION?

We first apply the above guidelines to ID, then we apply the standard put forth by the Supreme Court in *Edwards,* and then we conclude with one final objection to the teaching of ID in public schools.

1. Applying the General Guidelines

a. Is ID a Conventional Religion?

ID is not a conventional religion and thus is not a paradigm case of a religion.

Rather, it is a point of view based on philosophical and empirical arguments. The purpose of ID is to provide answers to the same questions for which the evolutionary paradigm is said to provide answers. That is, design theory and naturalistic evolution are two conflicting perspectives about the same subject. Admittedly, if the ID arguments are plausible, they do lend support to the metaphysical claims of some conventional religions such as Christianity, Judaism, and Islam. However, as Justice Powell wrote in his *Edwards* concurrence, "a decision respecting the subject matter to be taught in public schools does not violate the Establishment Clause simply because the material to be taught 'happens to coincide or harmonize with the tenets of some or all religions.'"[31] After all, as I pointed out in chapter 3, the Big Bang theory (see section A, part 3.a of that chapter), the most widely accepted theory of the universe's origin is more consistent with, and lends support to, theism in comparison to other metaphysical rivals such as atheism. Yet, no one is suggesting that the Big Bang theory ought not to be taught in public schools because it has metaphysical implications friendly to theism and may serve as an impetus for some students to abandon naturalism as a worldview.[32] In addition, design advocate William A. Dembski claims that the inference to a disembodied intelligence that can account for specified complexity in nature "is compatible with" an array of metaphysical points of view such as "pantheism, panentheism, Stoicism, Neoplatonism, deism, and theism. It is incompatible with naturalism."[33] Consequently, if a point of view is religious because its plausibility lends support to a religion or a religious point of view, then we would have to conclude that naturalistic evolution is as much a religion as ID, for it lends support[34] to some nontheistic and antireligious perspectives recognized as religions by the Court.[35] Perhaps this is why atheist and skeptic groups are the most vociferous opponents of ID, for they see ID as a possible defeater to evolution, a viewpoint whose truth is essential to the veracity of their worldview, philosophical naturalism.[36]

Thus, forbidding the teaching of ID (or legitimate criticisms of evolution) in public schools because it lends support to a religion, while exclusively permitting or requiring the teaching of naturalistic evolution unconditionally, might be construed by a court as viewpoint discrimination,[37] a violation of state neutrality on matters of religion,[38] and/or the institutionalizing of a metaphysical orthodoxy,[39] for ID and naturalistic evolution are *not* two different subjects (the first religion, the second science) but two different answers about the same subject.

Jay Wexler disagrees with this analysis, asserting that "evolution in pure form addresses only the question of how living creatures change over time." He writes, "It does not address the question of origins nor does it postulate the meaning of life. It deals only with proximate causes, not ultimate ones."[40] Thus,

evolution and design are not two answers to the same question, but two different subjects. Ironically, in defense of these assertions Wexler cites several
works including ones by Monroe Strickberger and Douglas J. Futuyama.[41] But
Wexler takes these citations out of context. For both authors, as we saw above,[42]
in fact claim that naturalistic evolution and design are different and incompatible answers to the same subject and that ID is mistaken. Consider first the following claims made by Strickberger in the same text cited by Wexler:

> The presently accepted view . . . suggests that at a distant time in the past the
> whole universe was a small sphere of concentrated energy/matter. This sub-
> stance then exploded in a big bang to form hydrogen first and then eventually
> all the galaxies and stars. . . .

> The variability on which selection depends may be random, but adaptions are
> not; they arise because selection chooses and perfects only what is adaptive. In
> this scheme a God of design and purpose is not necessary.[43]

The following are claims made by Futuyama in the book cited by Wexler:

> The implications [in arguing that life came from inorganic matter] are so daunting
> that Darwin himself was reluctant to commit his beliefs to paper. In *The Origin of
> Species* he limited himself to saying that "probably all organic beings which have
> ever lived on earth, have descended from one primordial form, into which life was
> first breathed" — a phrase which is certainly open to theological interpretation. . . .

> We will almost certainly never have direct fossil evidence that living molecular
> structures evolved from nonliving precursors. Such molecules surely could not
> have been preserved without degradation. *But a combination of geochemical ev-
> idence and laboratory experiment shows that such evolution is not only plausi-
> ble but almost undeniable.* . . .

> By providing materialistic, mechanistic explanations, instead of miraculous
> ones, for the characteristics of plants and animals, Darwin brought biology out
> of the realm of theology and into the realm of science. For miraculous spiritual
> forces fall outside the province of science; *all of science* is the study of material
> causation. . . .

> [O]rder *in nature* is no evidence of design.[44]

If one takes these quotes and combines them with what we covered in the
section of this book in which I define evolution,[45] it is crystal clear that
Wexler is wide of the mark. Naturalistic evolution in fact provides an answer
to the *very same* question ID provides an answer: What is the origin of apparent design in biological organisms and/or other aspects of the natural universe? Evolution answers the question by appealing to the forces of unguided
matter, the latter to intelligent agency. Same question, different answers.

Wexler makes another point that's worth addressing, since it has been employed in a few court cases:[46] "belief in evolution and belief in religion are not mutually exclusive, as evidenced by the many generations of devout religious believers who have also believed in evolution."[47] This is hardly persuasive, for at least two reasons.

(1) The fact that people claim that beliefs they hold are consistent with one another is not the same as providing an argument that they are in fact consistent. By appealing to people's subjective perceptions of their own beliefs rather than to the content of the beliefs themselves, Wexler commits a category mistake, for internal consistency is a property had by systems of belief that contain numerous propositional claims. Those *claims* and not those *who believe* those claims are the appropriate objects of analysis. After all, if Wexler were a criminal defense attorney confronted with an apparently friendly witness who testified in deposition that Wexler's client was not at the scene of the crime but at trial testified that the defendant was at the scene of the crime, Wexler would not get very far with the jury by claiming that the witness's inconsistent testimonies are in fact consistent because *she believes* they are consistent.

(2) If Wexler is talking about belief in an intelligent designer and belief in naturalistic evolution, they are not compatible beliefs but two answers to the *same* question. This is what one continually finds in the literature published by leading evolutionists.[48] For if all that is meant by evolution is that biological species adapt over time to changing environments and pass on those adaptations genetically to their offspring, not even most creationists would disagree with that modest definition of evolution. Thus, what Wexler proposes as a definition of evolution is vague enough to refer to either microevolution, macroevolution, or both. But, as we have seen, that is not what many citizens find objectionable about evolution, and it is not what is actually defended by proponents of evolutionary theory. What these citizens find objectionable, and what is actually affirmed in the literature, is the methodological naturalism that evolution presupposes and the ontological materialism it entails. As I noted in my criticisms of Judge Overton's similar argument in *McLean*,[49] *belief* in the existence of God is not *logically* inconsistent with materialism, but the *existence* of God—if God is defined as the immaterial self-existent Creator of all that contingently exists—is *inconsistent* with materialism, the view that the natural universe is all that exists and all the entities in it can be accounted for by strictly material processes without resorting to any designer, Creator, or nonmaterial entity as an explanation for either any aspect of the natural universe or the universe as a whole. Given the fact that materialist explanations, according to

the naturalists who dominate the academy, are the only ones accorded the privilege of being called "knowledge" (the others are pejoratively called "supernatural" or "miraculous" and are never permitted to count against materialist explanations), to say that belief in God's existence is not inconsistent with naturalistic evolution is to imply that God is not really an object of knowledge. For if it were, the existence of a God (and/or any other nonmaterial reality, e.g., mind, moral properties, numbers), if one had good reasons to believe in it, would be allowed to count against methodological naturalism and ontological materialism and not provoke the ridicule and derision[50] and/or the intellectual segregation suggested by the newest "friends" of God who nevertheless do not believe in him.[51] The question then is whether nonmaterialist claims to knowledge really can be knowledge. If they cannot, then ID and naturalistic evolution are consistent, since the first is a *belief* (in the popular sense of unproven opinion) and the latter is knowledge. However, if they both can be claims of knowledge—that is, contrary answers to the same question—then they are inconsistent claims. Thus, Wexler, like Judge Overton, can coherently claim that the existence of God (if this is what Wexler means by "belief in religion"),[52] a nonmaterial reality, is consistent with the truth of evolution only if (1) he defines evolution in such a modest fashion that it is unobjectionable to even hardline creationists or (2) he takes evolution to entail materialist metaphysics and defines belief in God in such a subjective fashion that God is not a proper object of knowledge.

b. Applying the Parallel Position Test to ID

Because ID is not a conventional religion, could someone challenge the teaching of it in public schools on establishment grounds[53] and legitimately argue that it is a "religion" on the basis of the parallel position test (PPT)? Does ID function in the life of its proponents in a way parallel to the way in which conventional religion functions in the life of the believer? In order to assess whether a purported belief is constitutionally a religion, the Ninth Circuit developed a tripartite application of PPT, which it extracted from prior opinions in the Third Circuit:[54]

> First, a religion addresses fundamental and ultimate questions having to do with deep and imponderable matters. Second, a religion is comprehensive in nature; it consists of a belief-system as opposed to an isolated teaching. Third, a religion often can be recognized by the presence of certain formal and external signs.[55]

(1) ID does not "address fundamental and ultimate questions having to do with deep and imponderable matters."[56] Rather, it addresses the same question raised by Darwinists: What is the origin of apparent design in bi-

ological organisms and/or other aspects of the natural universe? Of course, as I pointed out above, design theory lends plausibility and support to theism, but that is not enough for it to meet this test. For naturalistic evolution lends plausibility and support to some nontheisms and thus addresses the same questions as ID but provides different answers. In other words, if one claims that ID meets this test, then one must claim that naturalistic evolution does as well. In addition, to cite Justice Powell yet again, a public school curriculum "does not violate the Establishment Clause simply because the material to be taught 'happens to coincide or harmonize with the tenets of some or all religions.'"[57] Federal Court interference with the policy decisions of local and state educational authorities is warranted "only when the purpose for their decisions is *clearly* religious."[58]

(2) ID is not "comprehensive in nature" and it is not a "belief-system." Rather it is an example of "an isolated teaching,"[59] something that is consistent with certain religious belief systems but is itself not a "religion," for one can logically hold to ID without accepting the comprehensive belief system of any conventional religion. In this sense ID is similar to a moral claim. For example, believing that human beings have intrinsic dignity by nature (a moral claim) is a rationally defensible belief that is consistent with many religious belief systems even though one may logically hold to the position while denying the truth of every religious belief system.

Moreover, design theorists do not defend their position by appealing to esoteric knowledge, special revelation, or religious authority. They make philosophical and scientific arguments whose merits should be assessed by their soundness rather than because their conclusions are inconsistent with philosophical naturalism.

(3) ID does not have the "presence of certain formal and external signs" such as "formal services, ceremonial functions, the existence of clergy, structure and organization, efforts at propagation, observance of holidays and other similar manifestations associated with traditional religions."[60] Although ID proponents "have formed organizations and institutes, . . . these resemble other academic or professional associations rather than churches or religious institutions."[61]

Thus, according to the general guidelines laid down by the courts, ID is not a religion, and thus to teach it in public schools would not violate the Establishment Clause.

2. The Edwards Standard

Suppose someone agrees that according to the above guidelines ID is not a religion, but contends that those guidelines are not the appropriate standard by which to evaluate ID. Rather, the proper test is found in *Edwards,* the case that set the standard by which public school curricula on origins should be evaluated.

As we saw earlier,[62] the statute assessed in *Edwards* was struck down for four reasons: (1) its historical continuity with *Scopes,* (2) its textual connection to the Genesis-inspired statutes struck down in *Epperson* and *McLean,* (3) the religious motivation of its supporters, and (4) its illegitimate means (i.e., advancing religion, limiting what teachers may teach) to achieve appropriate state ends (i.e., academic freedom), though the Court concluded that the statute's purported purpose (or end) was "a sham,"[63] and so the statute had no real secular purpose. Therefore, the Court concluded that the Louisiana statute advanced religion and thus violated the first prong of the Lemon test.

a. Reasons 1 and 2

Concerning reasons (1) and (2), ID is neither historically connected to *Scopes* nor is its literature replete, as is creationist literature, with "science" and recommended curricula that are transparently derived directly from the Book of Genesis. ID's intellectual pedigree is of a different order than the creation science the Court repudiated in *Edwards.* The works of ID scholars have been published by prestigious academic presses and respected academic journals, attracting the attention of the wider academic and research community.[64] Although most design theorists are theists, there is a wide range of opinion within the ID camp.[65]

Wexler argues that because ID has *some* historical connection to the creation/evolution controversy, it would not pass the *Edwards* standard.[66] But that seems patently unreasonable. It would make the genetic fallacy[67] a principle of constitutional jurisprudence. It is hard to imagine why anyone would find that acceptable. After all, if a historical connection of any sort, no matter how distant or loose, is sufficient to prohibit the teaching of a subject, then perhaps astronomy and chemistry ought to be prohibited from public school classrooms since they have their historical origin in the religiously oriented practices of astrology and alchemy. As we saw earlier,[68] the Court's historical problem with the creation science curriculum required in the statute struck down in *Edwards* was its transparent connection to the Book of Genesis and the contents of previously repudiated statutes in *Epperson* and *McLean.* As I noted in chapter 3 (section B, part 6), ID simply does not have these attributes. For the arguments of ID advocates include conclusions whose premises do not contain the Book of Genesis and its tenets as explicit or implicit propositions. These premises and their propositions, unlike the ones of creation science, are not derived from, nor are they grounded in, any particular religion's interpretation of its special revelation. They are, rather, the result of empirical facts (e.g., the information content of DNA, the structure of the cell), well-grounded conceptual notions (e.g., specified complexity, irreducible complexity), and critical reflection. These subsequently serve as the basis from which one may infer that an intelligent agent is likely responsible for the existence of certain apparently natural phenomena. Although the conclusions inferred from these premises may be consistent with, and lend support to, a tenet or tenets of a particular belief system, that, in itself, would not make ID ipso facto Creationism or even constitutionally suspect.

After all, consider what we would think if the shoe were on the other foot. Suppose we lived in a society in which the scientific establishment is dominated by ID (as it had been prior to Darwin). That is, design theory is generally regarded by the scientific community as the only legitimate paradigm for assessing the origin of the universe, irreducible complexity and information in nature. However, there is a small but growing group of young scholars, whose parents and communities have embraced for decades, and whose schools tutor them on, the writings of Democritus, an ancient Greek philosopher who embraced materialism. Suppose that Democritus's views, though the object of religious devotion by some, are considered anachronistic by the scientific establishment and that those who believe these views are pejoratively labeled "nonmentalists." However, four young scholars — Kevin Marx, Freddie Nietzsche, Sid Freud, and Chuck Darwin — develop sophisticated theories of economics, human institutions, human nature, the human mind, and the origin of life that, if plausible, count against ID, for each theory entails materialism, the metaphysical ground of the religion of Democritus. Imagine, however, that Marx, Nietzsche, Freud, and Darwin are forbidden from voicing their views and presenting their best arguments in public school curricula and academic journals. Also, they are called names (e.g., "nonmentalist"), denied prestigious academic appointments, advised by sympathetic colleagues not to publish on the subject, and told that their views are "unscientific" and "religious" for no other reason than that they have a loose connection to nonmentalism and, if plausible, entail a metaphysical position that supports the religion of Democritus. What would we think about such a state of affairs? I imagine that most serious scholars would find it offensive, because the scientific establishment would be employing an a priori commitment to design theory, guilt by association, social barriers, and professional marginalization, rather than actual arguments, to discard the views of the renegade opposition. Suppose, however, we replace the names and views of Marx, Nietzsche, Freud, and Darwin with the names and views of leading ID supporters: Johnson, Behe, Dembski, and Meyer. With this change in the cast of characters, most scholars, who are otherwise circumspect, would not be able to detect the wrong, even though only the names and views have been changed. And yet the problem would remain: an a priori commitment (in this case, to materialism rather than design), guilt by association, social barriers, and professional marginalization, rather than actual arguments, would be doing virtually all the intellectual work in dismissing the views of the ID opposition. This is why Wexler's reliance on the "history" of the creation/evolution controversy, and ID's loose connection to that history, is logically fallacious and thus philosophically irrelevant.

b. *Reasons 3 and 4*

If an ID statute, law, or policy, such as the one proposed in Ohio in 2002 (see introduction, section B), is to pass constitutional muster, it is judicially assessed in light of reasons (3) and (4), as well as reasons (1) and (2), of the Edwards Standard. Because, as of the completion of this book the Ohio policy had not been challenged in court, (3) and (4) are analyzed with a bit of speculation and critique. We cover two general areas: (1) secular reasons, and (2) religious motivation and the statute's means-end relationship.

Secular reasons.   Any government body that sought to require or permit ID to be taught in its public schools would have to justify it by appealing to secular reasons. Although having a religious motivation or reason would not invalidate the statute, the absence of a secular reason would.[69] The following are four possible secular reasons such a body could employ.

The Endorsement Test. It could offer an endorsement test justification of the statute. As we saw earlier,[70] in *Lynch* Justice O'Connor proposed an "endorsement test" as an alternative to the Lemon test, and some recent opinions seem to have either explicitly or implicitly embraced it as well.[71] According to this test, if a government action creates a *perception* that it is either endorsing or disfavoring a religion, the action is unconstitutional. The concern of this test is whether the disputed activity suggests "a message to nonadherents that they are outsiders, not full members of the political community, and an accompanying message to adherents that they are insiders, favored members of the political community."[72] (O'Connor, however, has presented differing definitions of what counts as a nonadherent.[73])

Although each of the cases cited in note 71 does *not* involve public school curricula, but rather the providing of public funds to, and/or the use of public facilities and forums by, individuals and/or institutions that propagate religious-oriented speech, it would take little imagination to extend the principle that grounds the endorsement test and apply it to curricula as well. That is, if a particular curriculum gives the impression that a certain disputed, irreligious point of view is favored—in this case, naturalistic evolution and ontological materialism—the state can argue that in order to erase that perception, a statute requiring or permitting the teaching of ID is necessary.

The Neutrality Test. In order to accommodate jurists who reject the endorsement test and believe that the state should be "neutral" when it comes to religion and irreligion, an ID statute and its proponents could appeal to basic fairness, relying on two different types of arguments: (1) the Court's continuing emphasis on state neutrality concerning religion and irreligion, and (2) Alvin Plantinga's argument combined with the Court's opinions on the importance of parents' control over their children's education. Let us briefly look at each argument.

The Supreme Court, in a series of decisions going back to *Everson*,[74] has held that the government should remain neutral between religions and between religion and irreligion. The Court in *Epperson* writes that the "government . . . must be neutral in matters of religious theory, doctrine, and practice. It may not be hostile to any religion or to the advocacy of nonreligion; and it may not aid, foster, or promote one religion or religious theory against another or even against the militant opposite. The First Amendment mandates governmental neutrality between religion and religion, and between religion and nonreligion."[75] Thus, an ID statute could be justified on the basis of neutrality by arguing that to teach only one theory of origins (naturalistic evolution)—that presupposes a controversial epistemology (methodological naturalism), entails a controversial metaphysics (ontological materialism), and is antithetical to traditional religious belief—the state is in fact advocating, aiding, fostering, and promoting irreligion, which it is constitutionally forbidden from doing. The state is not *merely* teaching what some religious people find antagonistic or offensive to their faith, which would not be unconstitutional.[76] Rather, it is promoting a point of view—a metaphysical perspective—"that occupies in the life of its possessor a place parallel to that filled by" traditional belief in God.[77]

Perhaps this is why Justice Black, in his *Epperson* concurrence, raised the question: "If the theory [of evolution] is considered anti-religious, as the Court indicates, how can the State be bound by the Federal Constitution to permit its teachers to advocate such an 'anti-religious' doctrine to schoolchildren?" According to Justice Black, "this issue presents problems under the Establishment Clause far more troublesome than are discussed in the Court's opinion," for "[t]he very cases cited by the Court as supporting its conclusion that the State must be neutral" assert that the State should not favor "one religious or anti-religious view over another."[78] As Michael McConnell points out:

> In the marketplace of ideas, secular viewpoints and ideologies are in competition with religious viewpoints and ideologies. It is no more neutral to favor the secular over the religious than it is to favor the religious over the secular. It is time for a reorientation of constitutional law: *away* from the false neutrality of the secular state, *toward* a genuine equality of rights.[79]

According to the Court in *Planned Parenthood v. Casey,* "[a]t the heart of liberty is the right to define one's own concept of existence, of meaning, of the universe, and of the mystery of human life. Beliefs about these matters could not define the attributes of personhood were they formed under compulsion by the State."[80] Thus, when government schools, whose attendance is generally compulsory, delve into matters epistemological and metaphysical— matters that touch on the scope of human knowledge, the ultimate nature of things, and who and what we are—and imply or affirm an "orthodox" position on such matters,[81] they define the attributes of personhood in a particular sectarian way, and consequently, violate what the Court maintains is a fundamental liberty.[82]

In this regard, one may employ Justice Kennedy's no coercion test, which he applied in *Lee v. Weisman,* a case in which the Court ruled as unconstitutional a public middle school's invitation to a local clergyman to perform an invocation and benediction at its graduation ceremony.[83] According to Justice Kennedy, "[t]he Establishment Clause was inspired by the lesson that in the hands of government what might begin as a tolerant expression of religious views may end in a policy to indoctrinate and coerce. Prayer exercises in elementary and secondary schools carry a particular risk of indirect coercion."[84] Even though a student who objects to such prayers is technically free to opt out of her graduation ceremony, according to Justice Kennedy, it does not mean that she is not being coerced to attend, for the student's absence from her graduation "would require forfeiture of those tangible benefits which have motivated the student through youth and all her high school years." Thus, "a school rule which excuses attendance is beside the point."[85]

The no coercion test is important to the legal case for permitting or requiring the teaching of ID in public schools, for it rests on the same principle from which Justice Kennedy reasoned in *Lee*: the state may not use the coercive power of government to enforce a particular religious or antireligious orthodoxy. This principle applies to the curricular case for ID for the following two reasons (combined, not separate).

First, school attendance—in virtually every jurisdiction—is mandatory, an act of government coercion. Although parents may choose to send their children to private secular or religious schools, they may only do so if they are financially able, for public schools do not charge tuition to their students. Thus, public school attendance—though not formally or directly coercive—is practically and indirectly coercive, for families are financially burdened if they choose to send their children to private secular or religious schools. Therefore, to paraphrase Justice Kennedy, absence from the public school would require a student's family to forfeit those tangible resources that could go to the purchase of other important familial benefits that the student will not have the opportunity to enjoy (e.g., a larger home, better computers, better foods, better vacations, better health care).

Second, if a public school curriculum teaches students one point of view on origins—naturalistic evolution—"it may appear to the nonbeliever or dissenter," i.e., the believer in ID, "to be an attempt to employ the machinery of the State to enforce a religious [or antireligious] orthodoxy."[86] Thus, both of the components the Court found troubling in *Lee* are present here: mandatory attendance (i.e., coercion) and instruction in an orthodoxy.

Although *Lee* dealt with a graduation prayer and not a curriculum, its guiding principle is clearly applicable to the case for teaching ID in public schools: the state may not use the coercive power of government to enforce a particular religious or antireligious orthodoxy. Therefore, permitting or requiring public schools to teach the alternative to naturalistic evolution—Intelligent Design—would be a way to ensure that the Establishment Clause is not violated via the no coercion test.

One objection to this analysis is that the no coercion test was applied by the Court to a formal religious exercise, e.g., a benediction or invocation prayer, and thus may not apply to a curriculum.[87] This objection, however, misses the point of principle that Justice Kennedy was trying to convey. His point, it seems to me, does not depend on the particular type of activity for which government coercion is employed, but rather whether that activity is a case in which the state is employing its coercive powers to enforce a particular orthodoxy. After all, if a public school, as part of a new relaxation and meditation curriculum, were teaching its students, who were forbidden from opting out of the class, how to pray to the Christian God—though never actually requiring its teachers to lead their students in prayer—it is difficult to see why this required curriculum would not violate the no coercion test. Admittedly, the Court may not want to extend the no coercion test in this direction, for it has other tests at its disposal that have worked just as well when applied to school curriculum. However, it seems to me that applying the no coercion test to public school curricula is defensible and its case persuasive, especially given the principle on which the test is based.

Like the courts,[88] Plantinga understands that public education is special and that parents in a liberal democracy have certain expectations of religious neutrality and fairness when they send their children to public schools.[89] Parents also have a prepolitical right to educate their children, reflected in the First Amendment and the Fourteenth Amendment's due process clause.[90] Moreover, given the purpose of the Establishment Clause—to ensure that religious conflict is not fomented by government bias[91]—public school science curricula should teach origins conditionally (if they teach it all), acknowledging that ID and naturalistic evolution are more or less plausible *given* certain epistemological assumptions and metaphysical entailments. I hash out Plantinga's argument in greater detail in chapter 3, section C.

Exposing Students to New and Important Scholarship. A state could appeal to the importance of exposing students to reputable scholarship that critiques the methodological naturalism behind naturalistic evolution and the ontological materialism entailed by it. Remember that the *Edwards* Court maintains that its holding does "not imply that the legislature could never require that scientific critiques of prevailing scientific theories be taught." The Court asserts that "teaching a variety of scientific theories about the origins of humankind to schoolchildren might be validly done with the clear secular intent of enhancing the effectiveness of science instruction."[92] In addition, the Court points out, with apparent approval, that the unconstitutional Balanced-Treatment Act was unnecessary because the state of Louisiana already did not prohibit teachers from introducing students to alternative points of view.[93]

Furthering and Protecting Academic Freedom. A state could also make the argument that an ID statute enhances and protects the academic freedom of teachers and students who may suffer marginalization, hostility, and public ridicule because of their support of ID and/or doubts about the veracity of the evolutionary paradigm.[94] This is not as far-fetched as one may think. Consider just the following examples.

(1) Historian Ronald L. Numbers relates how "one annoyed critic no doubt captured the feelings of many when he described [ID] as 'the same old creationist bullshit dressed up in new clothes.'"[95] Numbers cites a few more examples:

> When the Jewish magazine *Commentary* in 1996 published a version of ID theory by the mathematician and novelist David Berlinski, letters of protest poured onto the editor's desk. [Daniel] Dennett ridiculed Berlinski's stylish essay as "another hilarious demonstration that you can publish bull[shi]t at will—just as long as you say what an editorial board wants to hear in a style it favors." Another reader characterized Berlinski's "intuitions about the Design of the World as neither more nor less reliable than those of flat-earthers, goat entrail-readers, or believers in the Oedipus complex."[96]

(2) As I mentioned in the introduction, in 1999 the state board of education in Kansas revised its standards for the teaching of evolution in its public schools.[97] The revisions included the modest, and defensible, claims that natural selection adds no new genetic information[98] and that science is defined as the "human activity of seeking *logical explanations* for what we observe in the world around us."[99] The standards also implied that mi-

croevolution does not entail macroevolution.[100] The board did not require the teaching of creationism or Intelligent Design. As I noted, it merely *suggested* that science teachers present the deliverances of their disciplines, on the matter of evolution, with tentativeness and modesty. It did not, for example, mandate that the state's teachers instruct their students that microevolution entails macroevolution, though teachers were free to do so if they wanted to. Moreover, these standards were "explicitly not binding on local school boards as an official curriculum," but were "designed to assist in the development of local curriculum by presenting the 'benchmarks' by which students will ultimately be evaluated on mandatory standardized tests."[101] But the board's suggestion did not sit well with many who saw the revisions as the first step in a slippery slope back to the Dayton, Tennessee, of 1925. The following are a few of the comments made about and to the Kansas school board as well as the state's citizens.[102]

The editor of *Scientific American,* John Rennie, sounding like Tony Soprano giving orders to his lieutenants, instructed members of college or university admission boards to "please contact the Kansas State Board of Education or the office of [the] Governor . . . [and] [m]ake it clear that in light of the newly lowered education standards in Kansas, the qualifications of any students applying from that state in the future will have to be considered very carefully. Send a clear message to the parents in Kansas that this bad decision carries consequences for their children."[103]

Washington Post columnist Gene Weingarten depicted God saying to the Kansas school board, "[t]hank you for your support" and then instructing them "to go forth and multiply. Beget many children. And yea, your children shall beget children. And their children shall beget children, and their children's children after them. And in time the genes that have made you such pinheads will be eliminated through natural selection. Because that is how it works."[104] The British writer A. N. Wilson called the entire U.S. Midwest the "land of born again bone heads." "[N]early all" of the reasonable people in America are "living on the eastern seaboard and in the big cities," Wilson opines. But in places like Kansas "the stupidity and insularity of the people is quite literally boundless. . . . These are people who believe that Elvis Presley has risen from the dead or that President Clinton repented of his sins and never looked at another bimbo since Monica. Their simple, idiotic credulity as a populace would have been the envy of Lenin."[105]

Phillip Johnson relates the time when he read Wilson's comments to an audience he was addressing in Kansas City, "and they laughed heartily with me at the stupidity and insularity of a London intellectual who thinks that it is characteristic of conservative Midwestern Christians to worship Elvis or to put their faith in the promises of Bill Clinton."[106]

(3) In 1999, a Burlington, Washington, high school biology teacher, Roger DeHart, was instructed by his superiors, as a result of a student complaint filed by the American Civil Liberties Union (ACLU), to "drop references to design and stick to the textbook."[107] In 2001, "DeHart was told he could not even introduce materials questioning Darwin's theories," something he had been doing for over nine years until the 1999 incident.[108] Although no one disputes that Mr. DeHart taught the required curriculum correctly, and although he never mentioned God, he nevertheless was accused of the Socratic transgression of encouraging his pupils to think deeply and thoughtfully about the philosophical implications that flow from the Darwinian paradigm. According to a report in the *Los Angeles Times,* DeHart "dissected such scientific topics as bacterial flagella, fossil records and embryonic development. Examine the evidence, he told the students, and ponder the Big Question: Is life the result of random, meaningless events? Or was it designed by an intelligent force?"[109]

Mr. DeHart's story may be just the beginning of a political and legal melee about the nature of academic freedom in public schools and whether that liberty extends to those who embrace what a majority of their peers are convinced is metaphysical heresy. For instance, the 2001 Kansas science standards define science as "[t]he human activity of seeking *natural explanations* for what we observe in the world around us," in contrast to the 1999 standards that define science as the "human activity of seeking *logical explanations.*"[110] Of course, in the debate over origins, dem are fightin' words. Hence, in a press release issued by the Discovery Institute, Mark Edwards, an Intelligent Design spokesperson, replies that "[t]he [2001] Kansas decision to impose naturalism on students in the name of science will not end the new debate over life's origins. . . . What is heralded as the triumph of science is instead a victory for censorship and viewpoint discrimination. This is not what science, or America, is about; discussion of the dissenting scientific opinion on Darwinism should be allowed in science classrooms."[111]

(4) Some university professors, who have embraced ID, have tested the limits to which academic freedom will be extended at their open and tolerant institutions that celebrate diversity. Design theorist and Baylor University mathematician and philosopher Dembski, whose academic credentials and publications are of the highest quality,[112] "was stripped of his directorship of a new campus institute on intelligent design after holding a controversial conference on the issue,"[113] which included among its participants M.I.T. physicist Alan Guth, Berkeley philosopher John

Searle, and University of Texas physicist Steven Weinberg, a Nobel Prize winner.[114] The university alleges that Dembski was demoted because of his lack of collegiality.[115]

In another case, Dean Kenyon, a senior biology professor at San Francisco State University and coauthor of the well-known text on the origin of life, *Biochemical Predestination,*[116] "was removed from teaching biology by his department chairman in 1992 after criticizing Darwin's theories, but was reinstated by a vote of the Academic Senate."[117] According to an article in the *Los Angeles Times,* "other scientists report receiving correspondence from colleagues who confess doubts about Darwin's theories but are afraid to go public for fear of career setbacks."[118]

I documented in my analysis of *LeVake* in chapter 2 (section B, part 4) that the Supreme Court has affirmed that a teacher engages in *protected speech* under the rubric of academic freedom (and thus the First Amendment) when she brings into the classroom relevant material that is supplementary to the curriculum (and not a violation of any other legal duties) and she has adequately fulfilled all of her curricular obligations. Given that, it seems to me that any government body that passed legislation to protect the academic freedom of teachers and students to discuss in the classroom scientific alternatives to evolution, including design theory, would simply be affirming by statute or written policy what is already a fixed point in constitutional law.

Religious motivation and the statute's means-end relationship. Since an ID statute likely would have citizen and legislative supporters whose public comments would sound like they are motivated exclusively by a desire to advance their own religious beliefs, this must be addressed in any proposed statute.

First, the statute can appeal to the secular reasons found elsewhere in the statute's text, such as the ones suggested above. As we have seen, the presence of a religious motivation or purpose is not fatal; but the absence of a secular purpose is.

Second, the statute's drafters may want to address the question of motivation head on by making both a philosophical and case law argument against the use of it in evaluating a statute's purpose. Both Justice Black's concurring opinion in *Epperson* as well as Justice Scalia's dissent in *Edwards*[119] are places in which one can find the case law and the jurisprudential arguments.[120] As far as a philosophical argument, I provided an example of a brief one in my exegesis of Justice Scalia's dissent.[121]

Third, a legislature would have to be circumspect in its articulation and crafting of an ID statute so its means-end relationship is clear. For example, in *Edwards* the Louisiana legislature made the mistake of appealing to academic freedom when in fact the statute *limited* the freedom of teachers. A legislature can avoid such mistakes by carefully evaluating its proposed statute in light of criticisms of the statutes struck down in *Epperson, McLean,* and *Edwards*.

3. One Final Objection

There is one final objection that one may raise against the teaching of ID in public schools:[122] Because some ID theorists describe the designer in language that is explicitly theological,[123] and others describe it in language that is implicitly theological,[124] and because the courts have said that the concept of God is inherently religious,[125] therefore, even if ID is scientifically sound,[126] the Establishment Clause forbids the teaching of it in public schools.

There are at least three problems with this argument. First, one could agree that the courts have consistently held that the concept of God is inherently religious, but that they are simply mistaken. For the courts ignore the case made by some scholars that "God" need not always be a religious concept, for "God" can be employed as a theoretical postulate without being an object of worship.[127] Since the Supreme Court has shifted and expanded its view of religion over the past 150 years due to America's increasing religious diversity and new insights about the nature of religion,[128] there is no reason why it could not change again. If the Supreme Court in Equal Protection cases can discard opinions on gender because they are anachronistic,[129] it certainly can do the same with outdated definitions of religion.

Second, even if one were to concede that the concept of God is inherently religious, and that the designer in ID is explicitly or implicitly theistic, it does not follow that ID cannot be taught in public schools. As we have seen, ID could be taught for any or all of the secular reasons listed above, for a religious belief is constitutionally barred from the classroom only if the teaching of it has *no* secular purpose.[130]

Third, it seems reasonable to argue that ID is a research program whose inferences *support,* and are consistent with, some belief in a higher intelligence or deity; it is *not* a creed that contains belief in a specific deity as one of its tenets. As I noted above, Dembski claims that the inference to a disembodied intelligence that can account for specified complexity in nature "is compatible with" an array of metaphysical points of view such as "pantheism, panentheism, Stoicism, Neoplatonism, deism, and theism. It is incompatible with naturalism."[131] To use an analogy, naturalistic evolution is a research program whose inferences *support,* and are consistent with, atheism; it is not a creed that includes unbelief in God as one of its tenets. So, if a scientific research program is "religious" because it supports and is consistent with a belief in a higher intelligence or deity, it would follow that a research program is "irreligious" because it supports and is consistent with the nonexistence of such a being.

In sum, if the concept of God is *not* inherently religious, then ID cannot be barred from public school classrooms for establishment reasons merely because the designer is God; if the concept of God *is* inherently religious, and the designer in ID is implicitly or explicitly theistic, then ID may still be taught in public schools, based on the secular reasons listed above; and if ID is theistic and hence religious because it supports and is consistent with God's existence, then naturalistic evolution is "irreligious" because it supports and is consistent with God's nonexistence, but that would mean that the courts should treat naturalistic evolution like ID.

C. SUMMARY OF CHAPTER FOUR

In this chapter I sought to answer the question of whether ID, if required or permitted to be taught in public schools, would violate the Establishment Clause. In order to answer this question, I first answered the question, "What is religion?" concluding that the courts have provided no clear definition, but rather a few general guidelines. I then answered the question, "Is ID religion?" by applying those general guidelines and then assessing ID by the standard set down by the Supreme Court in *Edwards.* I ended chapter 4 by replying to one final objection. In light of this analysis, it seems to me that a government body that required or permitted the teaching of ID in public schools would not violate the Establishment Clause, if the policy or statute is carefully crafted so that it does not run afoul of the Court's standard in *Edwards.*

The debate over origins—from *Scopes* to *Edwards* to the present day—is one that touches on some deep and important philosophical and scientific questions about the nature of the universe, knowledge, religion, and liberty. In a society of contrary and contradictory religious and philosophical points of view, the law must address, with fairness and consistency, how public schools ought to deal with the question of origins without violating both the deliverances of science and the rights of the nation's citizens.

The infusion of Intelligent Design into this debate has changed the legal landscape significantly. Unlike the creation science repudiated by the Supreme Court in *Epperson* and *Edwards,* ID cannot be dismissed as a transparent attempt on the part of religious people to force their views on the public schools. Instead, ID advocates, if their case reaches our highest courts, will force, even our most cerebral jurists, to carefully and conscientiously assess a jurisprudence that up until now could be—without fear of serious inspection—papered over with the caricature of William Jennings Bryan trying to figure out where Cain found his wife. This quasi-official, "Inherit the Wind" caricature has outlived its usefulness. It has, to enlist a bad pun, not evolved. ID is not your Daddy's fundamentalism.

NOTES

1. *See* chapter 2 of this book; *see* chapter 1, section B, part 3 of this book; and *see* chapter 3 of this book.

2. *LeVake v. Independent School District,* 625 N.W.2d 502 (2001).

3. *See,* for example, Arlin M. Adams and Charles J. Emmerich, *A Nation Dedicated to Religious Liberty: The Constitutional Heritage of the Religion Clauses* (Philadelphia: University of Pennsylvania Press, 1990), 90–91; Thomas Berg, *The State and Religion in a Nutshell* (St. Paul, MN: West Group, 1998), 262–276; Jesse Choper, "Defining 'Religion' in the First Amendment," *University of Illinois Law Review* (1982); "Toward a Constitutional Definition of Religion," Student Note, *Harvard Law Review,* 91 (1978); George C. Freeman, "The Misguided Search for the Constitutional Definition of 'Religion,'" *Georgetown Law Journal,* 71 (1983); William W. Van Alstyne, "Constitutional Separation of Church and State: The Quest for a Coherent Position," *American Political Science Review,* 57 (1963), 873–875; Eduardo Penalver, "The Concept of Religion," *Yale Law Journal,* 107 (1997); Steven D. Smith, "Symbols, Perceptions, and Doctrinal Illusions: Establishment Neutrality and the 'No Endorsement Test,'" *Michigan Law Review,* 86 (November 1987), 295–301; Richard O. Frame, "Belief in a Nonmaterial Reality—A Proposed First Amendment Definition of Religion," *University of Illinois Law Review* (1992); Dmitry N. Feofanov, "Defining Religion: An Immodest Proposal," *Hofstra Law Review,* 23 (1994); Steven D. Collier, "Beyond Seeger/Welsh: Defining Religion under the Constitution," *Emory Law Journal,* 31 (Fall 1982); H. Wayne House, "A Tale of Two Kingdoms: Can There Be a Peaceful Coexistence of Religion with the Secular State?" *BYU Journal of Public Law,* 13, 2 (1999), 251–259; and Michael W. McConnell, John H. Garvey, and Thomas C. Berg, *Religion and the Constitution* (New York: Aspen Publishers, 2002), 869–905.

4. Penalver, "The Concept of Religion," 795 (notes omitted). For a brief overview of the areas in which the Supreme Court has addressed this issue, *see* Erwin Chemerinsky, *Constitutional Law: Principles and Policies* (New York: Aspen, 1997), 972–977. Chemerinsky argues that the Court has dealt with the issue in three contexts: conscientious objector exemption, whether a court may inquire into the sincerity of one's beliefs, and whether sincere personal beliefs are protected even if they are unconnected to an established dogma or group.

5. Joel Incorvaia, "Teaching Transcendental Meditation in Public Schools: Defining Religion for Establishment Purposes," *San Diego Law Review,* 16 (1978–79), 336–337.

6. *Davis v. Beason,* 133 U.S. 342 (1890). Incorvaia points out that *"Davis* involved the criminal prosecution of a member of the Mormon church under an Idaho statute disenfranchising persons from voting or holding elected office if they belonged to any organization practicing or advocating bigamy or polygamy. The Court upheld the statute's constitutionality against a free exercise challenge. It refused to recognize that belief in bigamy or polygamy could be a tenet of a bona fide religious faith, saying: 'To call their advocacy a tenet of religion is to offend the common sense of mankind'" (Incorvaia, "Teaching Transcendental Meditation," 337 n. 51, quoting *Davis,* 133 U.S., 341–342).

7. *United States v. Kauten,* 133 F.2d 703 (2d Cir. 1943).

8. *Kauten,* 133 F.2d, 708.

9. *Kauten,* 133 F.2d, 708.

10. *Torcaso v. Watkins,* 367 U.S. 488, 495 n. 11 (1961).

11. *United States v. Seeger,* 380 U.S. 163, 176 (1965).

12. *Seeger,* 380 U.S., 180, 187, citing Paul Tillich, *Systematic Theology,* 2 vols. (1957), vol. 2, 12; and Paul Tillich, *Shaking of the Foundations* (1948), 57.

13. Paul Tillich, *Ultimate Concern,* ed. D. Mackenzie Brown (New York: Harper & Row, 1965), 106. Similarly, philosopher John Dewey, who considered his own espousal of humanism "religious," defined religion in the following way: "Any activity pursued in behalf of an ideal end against obstacles and in spite of threats of personal loss because of convictions of its general and enduring value is religious in quality" (John Dewey, *A Common Faith* [New Haven, CT: Yale University Press, 1934], 27).

14. *Seeger,* 380 U.S., 176.

15. *School District of Abington Township v. Schempp,* 374 U.S. 203, 225 (1963), quoting *Zorach v. Clauson,* 343 U.S. 306, 314 (1952). For a provocative commentary and collection of documents on the subject of humanism and religion, see David A. Noebel, J. F. Baldwin, and Kevin Bywater, *Clergy in the Classroom: The Religion of Secular Humanism,* 2nd ed. (Manitou Springs, CO: Summit Ministries, 2000).

16. For an explanation and illustration of the "parallel position test," see Penalver, "The Concept of Religion," 799–800.

17. *See,* for example, *Peloza v. Capistrano Unified School District,* 782 Supp. 1412 (C.D. Cal. 1992) (*Peloza I*), *aff'd in part, Peloza v. Capistrano Unified School District,* 37 F.3d 517 (9th Cir. 1994) (*Peloza II*) (maintaining that a public school does not violate the Establishment Clause if it requires teachers to teach evolution, for it is not a "religious belief" because it is not defined as such in the dictionary or in Establishment Clause case law, and it does not explicitly deny the existence of a Creator); and *Alvarado v. City of San Jose,* 94 F. 3d 1223 (9th Cir. 1996) (concluding that the city of San Jose does not violate the Establishment Clause when it installs a sculpture of Quetzalcoatl, an Aztec god, for it is not religious in nature according to a three-part test for religion: it does not address ultimate questions, it is not comprehensive in nature, and its presence is not recognized by certain external and formal signs).

18. *Malnak v. Yogi,* 440 F. Supp. 1284 (NJ 1977) (*"Malnak I"*), *aff'd per curium,* 592 F. 2d 197 (CA 1979) (*"Malnak II"*).

19. Concerning *Peloza II,* 37 F.3d, see chapter 2, section B, part 2 of this book. Concerning *Alvarado,* 94 F. 3d, it is likely that if the city of San Jose had installed a sculpture of Jesus of Nazareth rather than the Aztec god Quetzalcoatl, the city might have run afoul of the Establishment Clause, for belief in Jesus does address ultimate questions, it is comprehensive in nature, and its presence is recognized by certain external and formal signs. *See,* for example, *County of Allegheny v. ACLU* (492 U.S. 573 [1989]), in which the Supreme Court ruled that a nativity display on city property, not surrounded by secular symbols, is unconstitutional because it sends the message that the county promotes and supports Christianity.

20. *See,* for example, Laurence Tribe's comments in which he argues that all "that is 'arguably religious' should not be considered religious in a free exercise analysis [and] anything 'arguably non-religious' should not be considered religious in applying the establishment clause" (Laurence Tribe, *American Constitutional Law,* 1st ed. [Mineola, NY: Foundation Press, 1978], § 14-6). Tribe, however, has since retreated from this position, arguing that having two definitions of religion "presents a number of problems, most importantly the first amendment's text" (Laurence Tribe, *American Constitutional Law,* 2nd ed. [Mineola, NY: Foundation Press, 1988], § 14-6).

21. Chemerinsky, *Constitutional Law,* 973.

22. *Everson v. Board of Education,* 330 U.S. 1, 32 (1947) (Rutledge, J., dissenting).

23. *See,* for example, *Torcaso,* 367 U.S., 495 n. 11, in which the Court writes, "Among religions in this country which do not teach what would generally be considered a belief in God are Buddhism, Taoism, Ethical Culture, Secular Humanism and others."

24. Alan Gomes, *Unitarianism/Universalism* (Grand Rapids, MI: Zondervan, 1998).

25. Among these questions are the following. What is the nature of ultimate reality? What is the nature of humanity? Are there moral norms that I must follow and what are their source? How do I come to know these things (i.e., revelation, natural reason, or both)? *See,* for example, Curtis W. Reese, ed., *Humanist Sermons* (Chicago: Open Court, 1927); Curtis W. Reese, *Humanism* (Chicago: Open Court, 1926); Charles Francis Potter, *Humanism: A New Religion* (New York: Simon & Schuster, 1930); and Curtis W. Reese, *Humanist Religion* (New York: Macmillan, 1931).

26. *See* note 23; and *Seeger,* 380 U.S., 176.

27. "[T]he State may not establish a 'religion of secularism' . . . thus preferring those who believe in no religion over those who do believe" (*School District of Abington Township,* 374 U.S., 225, quoting *Zorach,* 343 U.S., 314).

28. For example, J. P. Moreland (*Scaling the Secular City* [Grand Rapids, MI: Baker Book House, 1987], 209–211) argues that the concept "God," for Aristotle and Isaac Newton, served the same function as "quark" and "continental plate" serve in contemporary science: an explanatory entity and not an object of worship.

29. "The argument advanced by defendants' witness, Dr. Norman Geisler, that teaching the existence of God is not religious unless the teaching seeks a commitment, is contrary to common understanding and contradicts settled case law" (*McLean v. Arkansas Board of Education,* 529 F. Supp. 1255, 1266 [1982] citing

Stone v. Graham, 449 U.S. 39 [1980], *School District of Abington Township*, 374 U.S.).

30. Professor Geisler's account of his own testimony reveals a much more sophisticated argumentation than Judge Overton lets on. Geisler and his coauthors write:

> Geisler said that you cannot reject the Creator just because He is an object of religious worship for some. He illustrated this in two ways: (1) Jesus is an object of religious worship. It is historically verifiable that He lived. Do we reject His historicity just because He is an object of religious worship? (2) Some people have made rocks the object of their religious worship. Do we reject the existence of rocks because they are an object of religious worship? Then he said you cannot reject a creator just because some have made him the object of religious worship. (Norman L. Geisler, A. F. Brooke II, and Mark J. Keough, *Creator in the Courtroom: Scopes II* [Milford, MI: Mott Media, 1982], 116)

31. *Edwards v. Aguillard*, 482 U.S. 578, 605 (1987) (Powell, J., concurring), quoting *Harris v. McRae*, 448 U.S. 297, 319 (1980), quoting *McGowan v. Maryland*, 366 U.S. 420, 442 (1961).

32. See David K. DeWolf, "Academic Freedom after *Edwards*," *Regent University Law Review*, 13, 2 (2000–2001), 480–481.

33. William A. Dembski, *No Free Lunch: Why Specified Complexity Cannot Be Purchased without Intelligence* (Lanham, MD: Rowman & Littlefield, 2002), 334.

34. See chapter 1, section A, part 2 of this book.

35. "[T]he State may not establish a 'religion of secularism' . . . thus preferring those who believe in no religion over those who do believe" (*School District of Abington Township*, 374 U.S, 225, quoting *Zorach*, 343 U.S., 314). In *Torcaso* (367 U.S., 495 n. 11), the Court writes: "Among religions in this country which do not teach what would generally be considered a belief in God are Buddhism, Taoism, Ethical Culture, Secular Humanism and others."

36. *See*, for example, the essays on The Secular Web, at http://infidels.org/ (May 22, 2002); Atheism Awareness, at http://atheismawareness.home.att.net/ (May 22, 2002); and the special ID issue of *Skeptic*, 8, 4 (2001).

37. *See*, for example, *Rosenberger v. The University of Virginia*, 515 U.S. 819 (1995) (ruling that it was a denial of students' free speech rights, as well as a risk of nurturing hostility toward religion, to prohibit the students at a state university from using student funds for a religiously oriented publication); *Widmer v. Vincent*, 454 U.S. 263 (1981) (finding that a religious student group's free speech and association rights were violated when it was prohibited by a state university from meeting on campus); and *Lamb's Chapel v. Center Moriches Union Free School District*, 508 U.S. 384 (1993) (ruling that it does not violate the establishment clause for a public school district to permit a church to show, after school hours and on school property, a religiously oriented film on family life).

38. *See* chapter 3, section C of this book. According to the Court, the "government . . . must be neutral in matters of religious theory, doctrine, and practice. It may not be hostile to any religion or to the advocacy of nonreligion; and it may not aid, foster, or promote one religion or religious theory against another or even against the militant opposite. The First Amendment mandates governmental neutrality between

religion and religion, and between religion and nonreligion" (*Epperson v. Arkansas,* 393 U.S. 97, 103–04 [1968]). In the footnote following this quote, the Court cites a series of prior cases that are well known for their call for government neutrality on matters of religion: *Everson,* 330 U.S.; *People of State of Ill. ex rel McCollum v. Board of Education,* 333 U.S. 203 (1948); *Zorach,* 343 U.S.; *Fowler v. State of Rhode Island,* 345 U.S. 67 (1953); and *Torcaso,* 367 U.S.

39. The Court writes in *Epperson* (93 U.S., 105): "[T]his Court said in *Keyishian v. Board of Regents* [385 U.S. 589, 603 (1967)], the First Amendment 'does not tolerate laws that cast a pall of orthodoxy over the classroom.'"

40. Jay D. Wexler, "Of Pandas, People, and the First Amendment: The Constitutionality of Teaching Intelligent Design in the Public Schools," *Stanford Law Review* (1997), 462 n. 212.

41. Wexler, "Of Pandas, People, and the First Amendment," 462 n. 212, citing Monroe W. Strickberger, *Evolution,* 2nd ed. (Sudbury, MA: Jones & Bartlett, 1996), 598, and citing Douglas J. Futuyama, *Science on Trial: The Case for Evolution* (New York: Pantheon Books, 1983), 10–14.

42. *See* quotes, accompanying notes, and citations of Strickberger and Futuyama in chapter 1, section A, part 2.

43. Strickberger, *Evolution,* 2nd ed., 71–72, 67.

44. Futuyama, *Science on Trial,* 95, quoting from Charles Darwin, *The Origin of Species,* A Facsimile of the 1st ed. (1859), intro. Ernst Mayr (Cambridge, MA: Harvard University Press, 1964), 484; *Science on Trial,* 95 (emphasis added); *Science on Trial,* 37 (emphasis added); and *Science on Trial,* 114 (emphasis added).

45. *See* chapter 1, section A, part 2.

46. In *McLean* (529 F. Supp., 1266 n. 23), for example, the Court writes: "The idea that belief in a creator and acceptance of the scientific theory of evolution are mutually exclusive is a false premise and offensive to the religious views of many. . . . Dr. Francisco Ayala, a geneticist of considerable renown and a former Catholic priest who has the equivalent of a Ph.D. in theology, pointed out that many working scientists who subscribed to the theory of evolution are devoutly religious." Also, in *Peloza* (37 F.3d, 521), the Court asserts that evolution "has nothing to do with whether or not there is a divine Creator (who did or did not create the universe or did or did not plan evolution as part of a divine scheme)."

47. Wexler, "Of Pandas, People, and the First Amendment," 462 n. 212.

48. *See* chapter 1, section A, part 2 and accompanying notes.

49. *See* chapter 1, section B, part 4.

50. *See,* for example, Phillip Kitcher's particularly condescending assessment of ID, "Born-Again Creationism," in *Intelligent Design Creationism.*

51. For example, Stephen Jay Gould suggests what he calls the NOMA principle, "non-overlapping magisteria": "Each subject [science and religion] has a legitimate magesterium, or domain of teaching authority—and these magesteria do not overlap. . . . The net of science covers the empirical universe; what it is made of (fact) and why does it work this way (theory). The net of religion extends over questions of moral meaning and value" (Stephen Jay Gould, "Nonoverlapping Magisteria," *Natural History,* 106 [March 1997], 16). But to what magisterium does NOMA belong? It seems

to be a philosophical principle by which Gould assesses the nature of science and religion, and thus Gould is implying that *philosophy* is *logically prior* to science and
thus the appropriate discipline by which to assess questions of the nature of science.
If that's what he is implying, then it is not clear on what grounds he could object to
or not seriously consider ID arguments against methodological naturalism, for they
are typically philosophical challenges to the prevailing view of the nature of science.

52. "Belief in religion" is so vague it may include everything from Unitarian/Uni-
versalism (some branches of which are indistinguishable from full-blooded atheistic
materialism) to Animism. Since Wexler does not define precisely what he means by
"belief in religion" I take it to mean something that includes belief in the existence of
an immaterial ultimate reality, God, which may be a pantheistic, monotheistic, Platonic, Aristotelian, or panentheistic God, a being whose existence would be a defeater
to materialism as a worldview.

53. *See,* for example, Wexler, "Of Pandas, People, and the First Amendment."

54. *See Peloza,* 37 F.3d at 520; *Africa v. Pennsylvania,* 662 F. 2d 1025, 1031 (3rd
Cir. 1981), *cert. denied,* 456 U.S. 908 (1982) (prisoner denied Free Exercise benefits
on the grounds that the group affiliation to which he appealed, MOVE, was not a religion); and *Malnak II,* 592 F.2d , 200–215 (Adams, J., concurring).

55. *Alvarado,* 94 F. 3d, 1229, quoting *Africa,* 662 F. 2d, 1032.

56. *Alvarado* 94 F. 3d, 1229, quoting *Africa,* 662 F. 2d, 1032.

57. *Edwards,* 482 U.S., 605 (Powell, J., concurring), quoting *Harris,* 448 U.S.,
319, quoting *McGowan,* 366 U.S., 442.

58. *Edwards,* 482 U.S., 605 (Powell, J., concurring) (emphasis added).

59. *Alvarado* 94 F. 3d, 1129, quoting *Africa,* 662 F. 2d, 1032; *Alvarado* 94 F. 3d,
1229, quoting *Africa,* 662 F. 2d, 1032.

60. *Alvarado* 94 F. 3d, 1129, quoting *Africa,* 662 F. 2d, 1032, 1035–36 (internal
quotations omitted).

61. David K. DeWolf, Stephen C. Meyer, and Mark Edward DeForrest, "Teaching
the Origins Controversy: Science, or Religion, or Speech?" *Utah Law Review* (2000),
86–87 (note omitted).

62. *See* chapter 2, section C.

63. *Edwards,* 482 U.S., 587.

64. *See* introduction, section A of this book.

65. H. Wayne House, for instance, points out that "various contributors to the sem-
inal volume, *Mere Creation,* represent diverse theological beliefs, e.g., John Mark
Reynolds (Eastern Orthodox), Jonathan Wells (the Unification Church), David
Berlinski (Judaism), and Michael Behe (Roman Catholic)" (H. Wayne House, "Dar-
winism and the Law: Can Non-Naturalistic Scientific Theories Survive Constitutional
Challenge?" *Regent University Law Review,* 13, 2 [2000–2001], 403).

66. Wexler, "Of Pandas, People, and the First Amendment," 465.

67. The genetic fallacy occurs when the origin of a viewpoint or argument, rather
than its merits, is employed to dismiss it out of hand. Although the origin of an idea
may play a part in assessing its merits, the genetic fallacy is committed when the idea
is dismissed based on its origin even though the origin of the idea is not a necessary
condition for the soundness of the arguments for it.

172 Chapter Four

68. *See* chapter 2, section A, parts 2 and 3 of this book.

69. Remember that the *Edwards* Court rejected the Louisiana Act, not because it had a religious purpose, but because it was entirely devoid of a secular one. *See* chapter 2, section A, part 2 of this book. In *Edwards,* Justice Powell concedes that even if the Louisiana Balanced-Treatment Act has a religious purpose, that "alone is not enough to invalidate" it. "The religious purpose must predominate" (*Edwards,* 482 U.S., 599 [Powell, J., concurring] [citations omitted]). The Court in *Lemon* asserts that "the statute must have *a* secular legislative purpose" (*Lemon v. Kurtzman,* 403 U.S. 602, 612 [1971]), implying that it may have a religious purpose as well.

70. *See* chapter 1, section B, part 3 of this book.

71. *See,* e.g., *Widmer,* 454 U.S. (finding that a religious student group's free speech and association rights were violated when it was prohibited by a state university from meeting on campus); *Lamb's Chapel,* 508 U.S. (ruling that it does not violate the establishment clause for a public school district to permit a church to show, after school hours and on school property, a religiously oriented film on family life); *Zobrest v. Catalina,* 113 U.S. 2462 (1993) (ruling that a school district may not refuse to supply a sign-language interpreter to a student at a religious high school when such government benefits are neutrally dispensed to students without regard to the public-nonpublic or sectarian-nonsectarian nature of the school); *Capitol Square Review Board v. Pinette,* 515 U.S. 753 (1995) (finding that it was content-based discrimination for the government to prohibit a controversial organization from sponsoring a religious display in a public park); *Rosenberger,* 515 U.S (ruling that it was a denial of students' free speech rights, as well as a risk of nurturing hostility toward religion, to prohibit the students at a state university from using student funds for a religiously oriented publication); *Mitchell v. Helms,* 530 U.S. 793 (2000) (finding that direct funding to private schools including religious schools does not violate establishment clause, since the distribution is evenhanded and the use of the money to indoctrinate in religious schools cannot reasonably be attributed to government); and *Mitchell,* 530 U.S. 836 (O'Connor, J., concurring) (finding that direct funding to private schools including religious schools does not violate establishment clause, since the distribution is evenhanded *and* there is no evidence that funds given to religious schools were used to indoctrinate).

72. *Lynch v. Donnelly,* 465 U.S. 668, 688 (1984) (O'Connor, J., concurring).

73. *See* chapter 1, section B, part 3 of this book.

74. *See Everson,* 330 U.S.; *McCollum,* 333 U.S.; *Zorach,* 343 U.S., *Fowler,* 345 U.S.; and *Torcaso,* 367 U.S.

75. *Epperson,* 393 U.S., 103–104 (note omitted).

76. The Court has argued that the Constitution "'forbids alike the preference of a religious doctrine or the prohibition of a theory which is deemed antagonistic to a particular dogma'" (*Edwards,* 482 U.S., 593, quoting *Epperson,* 393 U.S., 106–107). The Court has also said that "the state has no legitimate interest in protecting any or all religions from views distasteful to them" (*Epperson,* 393 U.S., 107, quoting *John Burstyn , Inc. v. Wilson,* 343 U.S. 495, 505 [1952]).

77. *Seeger,* 380 U.S., 176.

78. *Epperson,* 393 U.S., 113 (Black, J., concurring).

79. Michael W. McConnell, "Equal Treatment and Religious Discrimination," in *Equal Treatment in a Pluralistic Society,* ed. Stephen V. Monsma and J. Christopher Soper (Grand Rapids, MI: Eerdmans, 1998), 33.

80. *Planned Parenthood v. Casey,* 112 Sup. Ct. 2791, 2807 (1992).

81. The Court writes in *Epperson* (393 U.S., 105): "[T]his Court said in *Keyishian v. Board of Regents* [385 U.S. 589, 603 (1967)], the First Amendment 'does not tolerate laws that cast a pall of orthodoxy over the classroom.'" The Court asserts in *School District of Abington Township,* 274 U.S., 222:

> The wholesome "neutrality" of which this Court's cases speak thus stems from a recognition of the teachings of history that powerful sects or groups might bring about a fusion of governmental and religious functions or a concert of dependency of one upon the other to the end that official support of the State or Federal Government would be placed behind the tenets of one or all orthodoxies.

82. However, I actually don't believe that substantive neutrality is really possible. *See* Francis J. Beckwith and John F. Peppin, "Physician Value Neutrality: A Critique," *Journal of Law, Medicine & Ethics,* 28, 1 (Spring 2000); Francis J. Beckwith, "Is Statecraft Soulcraft?: Faith, Politics and Legal Neutrality," in *Bioengagement,* ed. Nigel M. De S. Cameron, Scott E. Daniels, and Barbara J. White (Grand Rapids, MI: Eerdmans, 2000); Francis J. Beckwith, "Law, Religion, and the Metaphysics of Abortion: A Reply to Simmons," *Journal of Church & State,* 43, 1 (Winter 2001); Francis J. Beckwith, "Cloning and Reproductive Liberty," *Nevada Law Journal,* 3, 1 (Fall 2002).

83. *Lee v. Weisman,* 505 U.S. 577 (1992).

84. *Lee,* 505 U.S, 578, citing *Engel v. Vitale* 370 U.S. 421 (1962); and *School District of Abington Township,* 374 U.S.

85. *Lee,* 505 U.S., 595.

86. *Lee,* 505 U.S., 592.

87. According to this interpretation, an activity sponsored by a public school violates the First Amendment when "(1) the government directs (2) a formal religious exercise (3) in such a way as to oblige the participation of the objectors" (*Jones v. Clear Creek Independent School District,* 277 F.2d 963, 970 [5th Cir. 1992] [citation omitted]).

88. For example, the Court writes in *Edwards* (482 U.S., 583–584):

> The Court has been particularly vigilant in monitoring compliance with the Establishment Clause in elementary and secondary schools. Families entrust public schools with the education of their children, but condition their trust on the understanding that the classroom will not purposely be used to advance religious views that may conflict with the private beliefs of the student and his or her family. . . . Therefore, in employing the three-pronged Lemon test, we must do so mindful of the particular concerns that arise in the context of public elementary and secondary schools.

89. *See* chapter 3, section C of this book.

90. *Meyer v. Nebraska,* 262 U.S. 390, 400 (1923) (arguing that the Fourteenth Amendment's due process clause guarantees parents' right to perform their duty to educate their children: "Corresponding to the right of control, it is the natural duty of the parent to give his children education suitable to their station in life"); *Griswold v. Connecticut,* 381 U.S. 479, 482 (arguing that the right to educate one's children is not literally in the Bill of Rights, but rather is a fundamental prepolitical liberty protected by the First Amendment); *Pierce v. Society of Sisters,* 268 U.S. 510, 535 (1925) ("The child is not the mere creature of the State; those who nurture him and direct his destiny have the right, coupled with the high duty, to recognize and prepare him for additional obligations"); and *Casey,* 112 Sup. Ct. at 2807 ("Our law affords constitutional protection to personal decisions relating to marriage, procreation, family relationships, child rearing, and education. . . . These matters, involving the most intimate and personal choices a person may make in a lifetime, choices central to personal dignity and autonomy, are central to the liberty protected by the Fourteenth Amendment").

91. In *Engel* (370 U.S., 429, 432 [note omitted]), the Court points out that the First Amendment Framers sought to avoid "the anguish, hardship and bitter strife that could come when zealous religious groups struggled with one another to obtain the Government's stamp of approval. . . . Another purpose of the Establishment Clause rested upon the awareness of the historical fact that governmentally established religions and religious persecutions go hand in hand." *See also* what the Court asserts in *School District of Abington Township* (274 U.S., 222) quoted in note 81.

92. *Edwards,* 482 U.S., 593, 594.

93. According to the Court, Louisiana's Balanced-Treatment Act did not give teachers any more academic freedom than what they already had in supplanting "the present science curriculum with the presentation of theories, besides evolution, about the origin of life" (*Edwards,* 482 U.S., 587). Because "[t]he Act provides Louisiana school teachers with no new authority[,] . . . the stated purpose is not furthered by it" (*Edwards,* 482 U.S., 587). As noted in chapter 2, section A, the Court of Appeals made a similar observation. *See Aguillard v. Edwards,* 765 F.2d 1251, 1257 (5th Cir. 1985) (*Aguillard III*).

94. Justice Scalia, in his *Edwards* dissent, makes this argument in reference to Creationists. *See Edwards* 482 U.S., 630–636 (Scalia, J., dissenting)

95. Ronald L. Numbers, *Darwinism Comes to America* (Cambridge, MA: Harvard University Press, 1998), 20, quoting from David K. Webb, Letter to the Editor, *Origins & Design,* 5 (Spring 1996), 17.

96. Numbers, *Darwinism Comes to America,* 20, quoting from Daniel Dennett and Karl F. Wessel in "Denying Darwin: David Berlinski and Critics," *Commentary* (September 1996), 6, 11.

97. For an analysis sympathetic to the school board's revisions, *see* Phillip E. Johnson, *The Wedge of Truth: Splitting the Foundations of Naturalism* (Downers Grove, IL: InterVarsity Press, 2000), 63–83. For an analysis more critical and less polemical than Johnson's, *see* Marjorie George, "And Then God Created Kansas?: The Evolution/Creationism Debate in America's Public Schools," *University of Pennsylvania Law Review,* 149 (January 2001).

98. Kansas State Board of Education, *Kansas Curricular Standards for Science Education* (adopted December 7, 1999), 38 (*Kansas I*).

99. *Kansas I,* 71. This suggestion was intended to teach the lesson that science is fundamentally about arguments and evidence and not about excluding non-naturalistic points of view a priori. In other words, the board intended to exclude methodological naturalism as a necessary precondition of science and ontological materialism as an entailment. *See* John H. Calvert and Wiliam S. Harris, *Teaching Origins Science in Public Schools* (Shawnee Mission, KS: Intelligent Design Network, 2001), *available at* http://www.intelligentdesign network.org/legalopinion.htm (May 11, 2002).

100. *Kansas I,* 37, 69. *Macroevolution* and *microevolution* are defined in chapter 1, section A, part 2 as well as in note 59 of introduction, section B of this book.

101. Lisa D. Kirkpatrick, "Forgetting the Lessons of History: The Evolution of Creationism and Current Trends to Restrict the Teaching of Evolution in Public Schools," *Drake Law Review,* 49 (2000), 126.

102. The Kansas school board's controversial revisions were removed in February 2001 as a result of a new election in which voters replaced members of the board that had supported the revisions. *See* Kansas State Board of Education, *Kansas Science Education Standards* (adopted February 14, 2001), *available at* http://www.ksde.org/ outcomes/science_stds2001.pdf (April 24, 2002)(*Kansas II*).

103. John Rennie, "A Total Eclipse of Reason," *Scientific American* (October 1999), *available at* http://www.sciam.com/1999/1099issue/1099commentary.html (May 25, 2002).

104. Gene Weingarten, "And So God Says to Charles Darwin: Let There Be Light in Kansas," *Journal & Courier* (August 17, 1999), A5, *available at* http://www.geocities. com/Paris/Cathedral/6070/evolve.html (March 31, 2001).

105. A. N. Wilson, "Land of the Born Again Bone Heads," *Evening Standard* (August 13, 1999), *available at* 1999 Westlaw 23722898.

106. Johnson, *The Wedge,* 75.

107. Teresa Watanabe, "Enlisting Science to Find the Fingerprints of a Creator," *Los Angeles Times* (March 25, 2001), *available at* 2001 Westlaw 2474375. For a less sympathetic narrative of Mr. DeHart's predicament, *see* John Gibeaut, "Evolution of a Controversy," *ABA Journal* (November 1999), *available at* http://www.abanet.org/journal/ nov99/11FEVOLV.html (October 25, 2001).

108. Watanabe, "Enlisting Science."

109. Watanabe, "Enlisting Science."

110. *Kansas II,* 97; *Kansas I,* 71.

111. "'Kansas Decision on Evolution Is Censorship,' Says Discovery Institute, an Intelligent Design Think Tank," *U. S. Newswire* (February 15, 2001), *available at* 2001 Westlaw 4140006.

112. *See* introduction, section A and accompanying notes in this book.

113. Watanabe, "Enlisting Science." *See also* Tony Carnes, "Design Interference: William Dembski Fired from Baylor's Intelligent Design Center," *Christianity Today* (December 4, 2000), *available at* 2000 Westlaw 11062939.

114. Nancy Pearcey, "We're Not in Kansas Anymore," *Christianity Today* (May 22, 2000), *available at* 2000 Westlaw 11062678.

115. "The university says Dembski was removed because of uncollegial behavior, not the content of his work; Dembski continues his design research at Baylor as an associate research professor" (Watanabe, "Enlisting Science").

116. Dean Kenyon and Gary Steinman, *Biochemical Predestination* (New York: McGraw-Hill, 1969). Kenyon has since repudiated the materialism he presupposed in this text. *See* Percival Davis and Dean Kenyon, *Of Pandas and People: The Central Question of Biological Origins,* 2nd ed. (Dallas: Haughton, 1993).

117. Watanabe, "Enlisting Science."

118. Watanabe, "Enlisting Science."

119. *Epperson,* 393 U.S., 274–275 (Black, J., concurring); *Edwards,* 482 U.S., 634–640 (Scalia, J., dissenting).

120. See also DeWolf's outstanding analysis on this matter: DeWolf, "Academic Freedom after *Edwards,*" 461–462.

121. *See* chapter 2, section A, part 4 of this book.

122. *See,* for example, Wexler, "Of Pandas, People, and the First Amendment," 457–468. According to *Aguillard III* (765 F.2d, 1254), the District Court below "reasoned that the doctrine of creation-science necessarily entailed teaching the existence of a divine creator and the concept of a creator was an inherently religious tenet. The court thus held that the purpose of the Act was to promote religion and the implementation of the Act would have the effect of establishing religion." In *Edwards* (482 U.S., 592), the Court writes: "[T]he term 'creation science,' as contemplated by the [Louisiana] legislature that adopted this Act, embodies the religious belief that a supernatural creator was responsible for the creation of humankind."

123. For example, J. P. Moreland speaks of ID as "theistic science." See J. P. Moreland, "Theistic Science and Methodological Naturalism," *The Creation Hypothesis: Scientific Evidence for an Intelligent Designer,* ed. J. P. Moreland (Downers Grove, IL: InterVarsity Press, 1994). Hugh Ross believes his design argument is an adequate proof for God's existence. See Hugh Ross, "Astronomical Evidences for a Personal Transcendent God," in *The Creation Hypothesis.* William Lane Craig maintains that his kalam/cosmological argument establishes the existence of a nonmaterial, personal, all-powerful creator of the world. See William Lane Craig, "Naturalism and Cosmology," in *Naturalism: A Critical Analysis,* ed. William Lane Craig and J. P. Moreland (New York: Routledge, 2000). Phillip E. Johnson talks of "theistic realism" as an alternative to materialist science. See Phillip E. Johnson, *Reason in the Balance: The Case against Naturalism in Science, Law, and Education* (Downers Grove, IL: InterVarsity Press, 1996), 89–110.

124. Davis and Kenyon (in *Of Pandas and People*) maintain that they are not arguing for a "supreme being," but rather for an "agent" "cause," or "designer" who "devised" the blueprint for "creating" life. DeWolf, Meyer, and DeForrest assert that "[d]esign theory, unlike neo-Darwinism, attributes this appearance to a designing intelligence, but it does not address the characteristics or identity of the designing intelligence" (DeWolf, Meyer, and DeForrest, "Teaching the Origins Controversy," 85).

125. "The argument advanced by defendants' witness, Dr. Norman Geisler, that teaching the existence of God is not religious unless the teaching seeks a commitment, is contrary to common understanding and contradicts settled case law"

(*McLean,* 529 F. Supp., 1266, citing *Stone,* 449 U.S. and *School District of Abington Township,* 374 U.S.).

126. "The First Amendment forbids the government from establishing religion; it does not require it to teach science. . . . [A]s a constitutional matter, the question of whether . . . [ID] is science ultimately turns out not to be a very important question at all" (Wexler, "Of Pandas, People, and the First Amendment," 468).

127. *See* notes 28–30 of this chapter. Justice Scalia, in his dissent in *Edwards,* correctly points out that the notion of a designer or prime mover, as found in ancient Greek thought, was not religious. See *Edwards,* 482 U.S., 629–30 (Scalia, J., dissenting). *See also* my analysis of Justice Powell's use of *Malnak I*'s definition of religion in his concurring opinion in *Edwards* (chapter 2, section A, part 3 of this book). Wexler cites Justice Powell's use of *Malnak I* in "Of Pandas, People, and the First Amendment," 462 n. 213.

128. *See* section A of this present chapter.

129. For example, in *Goesaert v. Cleary* (335 U.S. 464 [1948]) the Court affirmed the constitutionality of a Michigan statute that did not permit female bartenders unless they were the male owner's wife or daughter. However, in *Craig v. Boren,* 429 U.S. 190 (1976) the Court held that an Oklahoma statute that had different minimal drinking ages for males and females violates equal protection. The Court writes in *Craig* (429 U.S., 210 n. 23) that "[i]nsofar as" *Goesaert* [335 U.S.] "may be inconsistent, that decision is disapproved. Undoubtedly reflecting the view that Goesaert's equal protection analysis no longer obtains, the District Court made no reference to that decision in upholding Oklahoma's statute. Similarly, the opinions of the federal and state courts cited earlier in the text invalidating gender lines with respect to alcohol regulation uniformly disparaged the contemporary vitality of Goesaert."

130. *See* note 69 of this present chapter.

131. Dembski, *No Free Lunch,* 334.

Index

About the Author

Francis J. Beckwith, a 2002–2003 Madison Research Fellow in Constitutional Studies & Political Thought at Princeton University, is a Fellow at the Center for the Renewal of Science and Culture, the Discovery Institute (Seattle) as well as a Research Fellow at the Newport Institute for Ethics, Law, and Public Policy (Newport Beach, California). He has held full-time faculty appointments at the University of Nevada, Las Vegas, Whittier College, and Trinity International University. A graduate of Fordham University (Ph.D., M.A., philosophy) and the Washington University School of Law, St. Louis (M.J.S.), his books include *Do the Right Thing: Readings in Applied Ethics and Social Philosophy*, 2nd ed. (Wadsworth, 2002), *Relativism: Feet Firmly Planted in Mid-Air* (Baker, 1998), *The Abortion Controversy 25 Years After Roe v. Wade: A Reader*, 2nd ed. (Wadsworth, 1998), *Affirmative Action: Social Justice or Reverse Discrimination?* (Prometheus, 1997), *Are You Politically Correct?: Debating America's Cultural Standards* (Prometheus, 1993), and *David Hume's Argument Against Miracles: A Critical Analysis* (University Press of America, 1989). His articles and reviews have been published in numerous journals across a diversity of disciplines including *Harvard Journal of Law & Public Policy*, *San Diego Law Review*, *Nevada Law Journal*, *Journal of Law, Medicine & Ethics*, *Journal of Church & State*, *Scientific Evidence Review*, *Notre Dame Journal of Law, Ethics & Public Policy*, *Public Affairs Quarterly*, *Journal of Social Philosophy*, *International Philosophical Quarterly*, *Journal of Law & Religion*, *Faith & Philosophy*, *Philosophia Christi*, *Social Theory & Practice*, and *Ethics & Medicine: An International Journal of Bioethics*.